CW01371859

*Ground,
Path
& Fruition*

Ground,
Path
& Fruition

by

THE 12TH KHENTING TAI SITUPA

*Zhyisil Chokyi Ghatsal Charitable Trust
Publications*

Acknowledgment

We would like to express our sincere thanks and appreciation to His Eminence, the 12th Kenting Tai Situ Rinpoche for his great compassion and wisdom in bestowing these precious teachings.

We would also like to thank the many persons who helped make these teaching available. We wish to thank Sherab Ling Monastery and Rinpoche's local and international students who organised these teachings. Noeleen Lam for transcribing the teachings and especially Ruth Gamble who has worked very hard editing the teachings and clarifying certain points with Rinpoche.

May this supreme, peerless teaching,
The precious treasure of the Victorious Ones,
Spread and extend throughout the world
Like the sun shining in the sky.

Copyright © 2005
His Eminence Tai Situ Rinpoche &
Zhyisil Chokyi Ghatsal Charitable Trust

This book is copyright. Apart from any fair dealing for the purpose of private study, research, criticism or review as permitted under the Copyright Act 1968, no part of this book may be stored or reproduced by any process without prior written permission. Enquiries should be made to the publisher.

Zhyisil Chokyi Ghatsal Charitable Trust Publications
PO Box 6259 Wellesley Street, Auckland, New Zealand
Email: inquiries@greatliberation.org
Website: www.greatliberation.org

National Library of New Zealand Cataloguing-in-Publication Data

Pema Donyo Nyinche, Tai Situpa XII, 1954-
Ground, path & fruition / by the 12th Khenting Tai Situpa.
Includes index.
ISBN 1-877294-35-37
1. Dharma (Buddhism) 2. Mahamudra (Tantric rite)
3. Buddhism—History. I. Title.
294.3420425—dc 22

The calligraphies on the inside covers are by Tai Situ Rinpoche, the front cover calligraphy means "one who has kindness in the heart has all happiness and joy." The back cover calligraphy means "path of peace."

TABLE OF CONTENTS

Foreword by Venerable Choje Lama Shedrup   9
Biography of Kenting Tai Situ Rinpoche   11

Chapter 1
INTRODUCTION   15
Understanding the Dharma   16
Devotion   26

Chapter 2
THE HISTORY OF INDIAN BUDDHISM   39
How Buddhism Was Brought to Tibet   52

Chapter 3
BUDDHIST PHILOSOPHY   67
Prajnaparamita   67
Rangtong and Shentong   80
Madhyamaka   90
Pramana   98

Chapter 4
BUDDHIST PRACTICE   115
Refuge   115
Precepts   120
Avalokiteshvara (Chenrezig) Practice   123

Chapter 5
    THE SEVEN POINTS OF MIND TRAINING   145

Chapter 6
    MEDITATION   195
    Shamatha   201

Chapter 7
    THE FIVE SKANDHAS   213

Chapter 8
    THE FOUR NOBLE TRUTHS   231

Chapter 9
    VIPASHYANA (INSIGHT) MEDITATION   245

Chapter 10
    MAHAMUDRA   263

    Conclusion   277
    Dedication   278

APPENDIX
The Buddhist Schools   283
The Six Realms of Samsara   284
The Five Paths   285
The Bodhisattva Levels   286
Transforming Consciousness into Wisdom   287
The Fifty-one Mental Factors   288

Notes   293
Glossary of Terms   309
Index   337

VENERABLE CHOJE LAMA KARMA SHEDRUP CHO GYI SENGE KARTUNG

Foreword

IN EARLIER TIMES DILIGENT dharma practitioners would collect, study and memorise large numbers of dharma texts. However these days our lives are often quite busy, so finding time and the opportunity to study many texts, let alone all the vast teachings of the Buddha, can be difficult. For this reason, what is valued the most, and considered the easiest to study, are commentaries that explain the essence and meaning of the Buddha's teachings. As the title of this book suggests, what is contained herein is such a commentary: the basis or foundation of practice (the ground), the realization of that ground (the fruition), and the means to accomplish this (the path).

For such teachings to be complete and effective, and in order to practice and realize the meaning of dharma, it is necessary to connect with and receive such teachings and transmissions from a qualified teacher of an unbroken lineage. His Eminence Tai Situ Rinpoche is such a teacher. Tai Situ Rinpoche, an emanation of the future Buddha Maitreya, is one of the supreme teachers of our time and holder of the Mahamudra/Kagyu lineage. Rinpoche has realized the meaning of the Buddha's teachings and also has the ability to explain the essential points of the Buddhadharma and to clarify its profound aspects.

So it is with great joy that we make this book of Rinpoche's teachings available and pray that all who receive and read these teachings generate faith and sincerity towards the Buddhadharma thus receive the blessings of the lineage and awaken to complete enlightenment for the benefit of all beings.

Choje Lama Shedrup
Auckland
February 2005

Biography of Tai Situ Rinpoche

Tᴀɪ Sɪᴛᴜ Rɪɴᴘᴏᴄʜᴇ ɪs ᴛʜᴇ twelfth in an unbroken line of incarnations which began in the 11th century. A spiritual master of unsurpassed significance in the history of Tibetan Buddhism, he was trained by the 16th Gyalwa Karmapa and is the current holder of the main Kagyu Lineage. The title Kenting Tai Situ means "far reaching, unshakable, great master, holder of the command."

The origin of the Tai Situpas can be traced to one of the senior followers of Shakyamuni Buddha, the bodhisattva Maitreya, who has been prophesied as the next Buddha, the fifth of the 1,000 Buddhas to appear in this fortunate aeon.

An early and important incarnation in Tibet was that of Marpa Lotsawa, the great teacher of Milarepa. Marpa helped revive Buddhism in Tibet undergoing many hardships on journeys to India to acquire Buddha's teachings, which he later translated and form the core instructions of the Kagyu School of Buddhism.

The great Indian mahasiddha, Padmasambhava clearly foretold all the names of the Situpa incarnations in a treasure text known as *The Command Seal of Prophecies* (Tib. *Lungten Kagyama*), which was later discovered by the great terton Sangye Lingpa. The Situpa incarnations have been very closely connected to the Karmapas; alternating as teacher and disciple from one lifetime to the next. The first to carry the title Situpa was Chokyi Gyaltsen (1377-1448), however the specific lineage began with Drogon Raychen (1088-1158) who was a close disciple of the 1st Karmapa.

The 12th Tai Situ Rinpoche was born in 1954 in Palyul District of the Derge Kingdom, east Tibet into an agricultural family. He was identified according to traditional methods and at the age of eighteen months was enthroned at Palpung Monastery, the main seat of the Tai Situpas in eastern Tibet. When he was six years old political circumstances forced him to leave Tibet with a few attendants, journeying first to Bhutan and then to Sikkim where he was united with the 16th Karmapa. This time of adversity, struggling to survive as a refugee was exacerbated by illness. During his convalescence he went to live at the newly built monastery at Rumtek in Sikkim, the new seat of the 16th Karmapa. At the age of twenty-one he assumed his own traditional responsibilities and established a monastery called Sherab Ling at the request of some of his Tibetan followers who have settled in northern India.

In 1980 he made his first European tour at the request of Buddhist organizations and since then has traveled widely in North America, Europe, South-East Asia and New Zealand lecturing on Buddhist philosophy and meditation. He visited Tibet in 1984 for the first time since leaving and again in 1991, journeying to his historical seat Palpung Monastery. During this visit he ordained more than 2000 men and women and presented a plan of suggestions to the Chinese authorities for the rebuilding, preservation and propagation of the Tibetan Buddhist culture.

A renowned artist and calligrapher, Tai Situ Rinpoche speaks fluent English and is the author of several books in which he illuminates Buddhist teachings in commonsense terms using down-to-earth examples. He is currently involved in the advancement of inter-faith and inter-cultural humanitarian efforts and was the inspiration and motivator for the 1989 Pilgrimage for Active Peace. In addition Rinpoche is the founder and Spiritual Head of the extensively enlarged Sherab Ling Monastery. Rinpoche was also involved with the recognition of His Holiness 17th Gyalwa Karmapa Ogyen Trinley Dorje and is able to offer him the complete transmission of the Mahamudra lineage.

GROUND, PATH & FRUITION
by
His Eminence Tai Situ Rinpoche

The essence of the Lord Buddha's teachings is a secret,
When heard through the compounded ears of the stained ones.
Compositions themselves make stains possible,
Therefore the ultimate teaching is the non-dualistic dharmakaya.

The Lord Buddha's teaching evolved into two, three, seven, nine and so on.
And again from each of these numerous teachings developed,
After a few more millennia,
The teachings will be as abundant as the most profound cloud of offerings.

Through pure devotion, intention, diligence and faith,
We listen, contemplate, meditate, teach, debate and compose properly,
Becoming learned, morally disciplined and compassionate.
Finally, their essential meaning comes down to the same thing.

Whether you know the many terms and philosophies of relative truth or not,
If you practice the path of your lineage (samaya), which is the root of the three vehicles,
With your body, speech and mind,
I have no doubt the primordial wisdom, the essence of everyone, will manifest from within.

Relaxed, newly exposed to the sacred dharma,
We become confused by the complexities of
The view, meditation, action and fruition of the great central
 texts.
[Confounded] I saw our heads turn like the spinning peacock-
 feather umbrellas meant for the noble ones.

Therefore the ground, path and fruition, are simplified and
 made short.
I have done this for my own notes, so I don't forget,
and maybe they will also benefit some beginners.

The ultimate is beyond description,
 But we use relative ideas to describe it,
 Therefore the descriptions are not completely accurate
 And our view needs to continually evolve.

As you climb the stairs of this house
You reach towards liberation.
With each step your view, meditation and action progress,
As this happens your realizations will also progress.

Chapter 1

INTRODUCTION

AT THE REQUEST OF DEVOTEES from many different parts of the world I will spend the next six days, two sessions a day, teaching dharma. My hope is that these teachings will make your knowledge of the dharma fuller, more complete, and perhaps you may even develop some wisdom, but this remains to be seen. Developing your wisdom is our ultimate aim but I cannot really convey wisdom to you – you have to realize it yourselves. The source of wisdom, the primordial wisdom, is inside each and every one of you but you have to realize it is there yourselves. I can't take off my wisdom hat and put it on your head. If I could, I would have bought lots of hats with me, one for each of you and spare ones to take home for your friends! At least though, you will definitely get some more information and this may bring a few missing pieces of the puzzle together for you.

Unfortunately, even Lord Buddha Shakyamuni couldn't give away his wisdom, so how could I who am only his follower. I can only hope to be like him, even if it takes me a couple of million lifetimes. As long as each lifetime improves by one millionth that is good enough for me. Not that this life has been that bad, everything has been wonderful. I have had all kinds of experiences to learn from and I appreciate them; they have all been fuel for the flame. Other people might have thought they were problems, nuisances or difficulties but I feel they have done me good. I honestly appreciate them. I have learnt a lot about myself, about other people, and the things that can happen in a human life. It has been very interesting. This doesn't mean you should all go around creating problems for me though!

Now, to make these sessions as comprehensive as possible, I am going to share with you some of the notes I have made over the years. Some of these notes are in books and others are on loose pages. I have hundreds and hundreds and hundreds of pages of them and I want to share them with you. Through them I hope to convey to you, as much as possible, the things I have learned from my great masters, the lineage transmission I have received from them. If I teach for six days, doing two sessions a day, with each session lasting two hours, that is quite a long time. Still, if we were to go through one of the great texts we would not even get a quarter of the way through it. You would all have to come back here again and again, three or more times, until it was complete, and this would be very inconvenient for you. So I think sharing my notes with you is the best way to utilize our time.

Understanding the Dharma

I would like to start with some particular notes that I completed in 1980, when I was twenty-seven years old. I am now half a century old! I will not go through all the notes because some sections are very philosophical and complicated but I think you may find other parts useful. First of all I would like to focus on these four lines:

The essence of the Lord Buddha's teachings is a secret,
When heard through the compounded ears of the stained ones.
Compositions themselves make stains possible,
Therefore the ultimate teaching is the non-dualistic dharmakaya.

The essence of the Lord Buddha's teaching is a secret to us, but not to him. Having realized his own and everyone else's ultimate essence, he was able to manifest or reveal the dharma. This essence is something we have but don't know we have. It is a secret, our secret. By "our secret" I don't mean something we have done that is so unbecoming we don't dare mention it to anybody else. I mean something that remains a secret even to us – our real, limitation-free essence. This secret was revealed to the Buddha when he overcame the dualism between how he manifested and what he always was, when he developed stainless wisdom. Then he overcame that dualism too; he stopped seeing himself as "me the Buddha." We call him Buddha Shakyamuni, but he doesn't say to himself, "I am the Buddha Shakyamuni." He did not have to work hard, make notes, and then teach into a microphone in broken English as I do either. He manifested the dharma. This manifestation was the outcome of his stainless, primordial wisdom. It is the secret of the Lord Buddha's teaching, the Lord Buddha's speech.

The second line says, "When heard through the compounded ears of the stained ones."

At first the Buddha only had five disciples. Seven weeks after his enlightenment, when he first taught the dharma in Varanasi, there were only five disciples who received his teaching on the Four Noble Truths. These five people bowed down to the Buddha, then sat there on their knees listening to him teach. The Buddha glowed magnificently – there was two meters of light around him that everybody could see – so for these disciples there was no question that he was a Buddha. Even the unfortunate people who did not appreciate the Buddha during his lifetime at least had to acknowledge his presence. Even if they said, "I haven't seen anything great about you," they would have to add, "except of course for the two meters of light surrounding you."

These first five disciples listened to him speak the Four Noble Truths with the ears of dualism. They were stained ones, just like us. Not entirely like us because they were fortunate enough to hear these words directly from the Buddha, whereas we are trying to understand them 2500 years later, but like us in that we also hear through stained, dualistic ears. We are not equal to these five people, but we are like them. We also retain his teachings in dualistic minds, thinking, "I heard that the Buddha said that." I am sure these five people talked to each other about the Buddha's teaching on the Four Noble Truths. I am sure they asked each other, "Did he really say that?" They must have discussed it among themselves before finally coming to a conclusion about it. They heard it through dualistic ears, and they remembered it in a dualistic mind.

The third line says, "Compositions themselves make stains possible."

This sentence says that even the way we hear means compositional stains are possible. All sorts of things are compositions; patterns are compositions, molecules are compositions. Our ears, for example, are composites of many different things, even things that look like snails. Our eyes are balls of water, our hearts are pumping muscles and our brains are very complicated, neatly wired jello. Therefore, it is highly likely that the understanding of these first five disciples was also stained by composition – *duche* in Tibetan – the composition of subject/object, and that they did not hear exactly what the Buddha manifested. If they had understood exactly, there would have been no need for further teachings after the Four Noble Truths. No need for the other Sutras, the Abhidharma, or the Tantras. This was not the case though: instead as the disciples evolved the Buddha's teachings manifested according to their capacities. If there were no evolution Buddha would have manifested Tantra first, without all of the other teachings. As things were his teachings manifested in stages, step by step: after the Four Noble Truths, he manifested the second turning of the wheel, the Mahayana, then the third turning of the wheel and Tantra, which can manifest at any time[1].

The last line says, "Therefore the ultimate teaching is the non-dualistic dharmakaya." The ultimate meaning has to be the non-dualistic dharmakaya.

This is to say that we only hear the ultimate teaching of the Buddha when we become Buddhas ourselves. Until we have completed this transformation we will hear something, practice it and achieve it. Then we will hear something else, practice and realize it, then yet another thing and another realization as we progress. Even if we say a simple prayer like, "May all sentient beings be free from suffering," it will mean different things to each of us. For you it will mean one thing and for him it will mean something slightly different. Also today's prayer, "May all sentient beings be free from suffering," will have a different meaning to next years' prayer, "May all sentient beings be free from suffering," because we will have evolved. In five, or ten years from now, it will mean something different again. It will evolve. If we are progressing its meaning will become deeper and more profound. If we are not progressing, if we are going backwards, it will have a shallower, less profound meaning. Eventually though, the ultimate dharma, the ultimate teaching, the ultimate essence of Lord Buddha's teaching is the dharmakaya itself. This is the meaning of these four sentences.

I wrote this a long time ago and I cannot say I have evolved very much since then. I was very skeptical and pragmatic then and I still am today, but perhaps a little less so. This last verse may be confusing; I don't regret I wrote it but it may leave you a little confused. To resolve this confusion let us look at the next verse.

The Lord Buddha's teaching evolved into two, three, seven, nine and so on.
And again from each of these numerous teachings developed,
After a few more millennia,
The teachings will be as abundant as the most profound cloud of offerings.

This first line refers to the Buddha's Theravada and Mahayana teachings, which then became the Theravada, Mahayana and Vajrayana teachings, before expanding further into the Theravada, Mahayana, Kriya, Charya, Yoga and Anuttarayoga teachings. Eventually the Buddha's teaching expanded into the Theravada, Mahayana, Kriya, Charya, Yoga, Mahayoga, Anuttarayoga and Atiyogas. Then the next sentence says, "And again from each of these numerous teachings developed."

This refers to, for example, the Vajrayana Buddhism of Tibet, which has eight main lineages and many sub-lineages. It also refers to the Mahayana itself, which has developed into different entities; the Mahayana of India, the Mahayana of Burma, the Mahayana of Cambodia, of Korea, Japan, China and so on. Then even within these broad groups there are different types of Mahayana. Among others there are the Mahayana that follows the Lotus Sutra, the Mahayana that follows Amitabha and the Mahayana that follows Chenrezig. It is like a big jungle now – many trees with many branches. I know where I belong because I was born into this tradition, but those of you who become followers of the Buddha have a job finding out which tree you belong to. It is quite complicated actually. Is it a maple tree? Or is it a pine tree? A banyan tree? Or a cypress tree? Depending on your final decision you will become part of one of these trees, but you should, of course, respect all trees.

Then the third line says, "After a few more millennia."

The Lord Buddha taught dharma a little more than 2500 years ago. Since then so many branches have already grown that in another couple of thousand years, as the last line says, "The teachings will be as abundant as the most profound cloud of offerings."

It will become like the great offering visualization we call the *kunzang chötrin,* the most profound cloud of offerings. In this visualization you generate five offerings from each of your five fingers, and then from each of these offerings you also generate five. This process goes on forever filling the sky with offerings. This line suggests that after a few thousand years the Buddha's teachings may also become like this. I am not saying this is wrong; this is just how complicated it has become.

I will skip the next four sentences that continue on from this, but after them I wrote:

Through pure devotion, intention, diligence and faith,
We listen, contemplate, meditate, teach, debate and compose
  properly,
Becoming learned, morally disciplined and compassionate.[2]
Finally, their essential meaning comes down to the same thing.

These four lines try to bring this incomprehensible growth to a conclusion. Based on pure devotion, pure intention, pure diligence and faith, we listen, contemplate, meditate, teach, debate and compose correctly. At the end of this process we realize that all the different branches, all the different ideas that sometimes seemed to contradict each other, have the same meaning. If we sincerely study and debate them, in the end we find they have the same essence but we need lots of faith, patience and diligence to come to this conclusion. If we don't have these qualities we may get halfway through the process and become stuck, seeing only the differences. We need enough patience to go further until we see the similarity and the sameness – until we see it all comes down to the same essence.

Now we come to the next four sentences. These sentences describe a process of surrendering. When I wrote these verses my study of Buddhist philosophy and practice of yogas were quite fresh in my mind. I had been practicing and doing retreats quite seriously and had became a bit like a balloon that has been blown up too large – I was about to burst. When you are twenty-something, have learned a lot and to be honest have developed a little bit of an ego this can happen. The more you learn, the more you can see what you don't know. We can find ourselves thinking, "I am better than so many, I know a lot, but yet I don't know anything." This is a little hard for the ego to swallow. I am sure it is happening to those of you who are that age right now. If I had gone on like this I would have been quite stressed, so I had to do some surrendering. That is what was happening when I wrote the next four sentences.

> *Whether you know the many terms and philosophies of relative truth or not,*
> *If you practice the path of your lineage (samaya), which is the root of the three vehicles,*
> *With your body, speech and mind,*
> *I have no doubt the primordial wisdom, the essence of everyone, will manifest from within.*

Whether you know relative terms – the details of endless things – or not, if your lineage is pure and you follow the morals, ethics and methods of that lineage sincerely with your body, speech and mind, the ultimate primordial wisdom – the essence of everyone – will manifest from within. I have no doubt about this. I am sure of it.

It does not matter whether I know a lot or not. It does not matter how much more there is to know, or whether I don't know all the things it is difficult for me to admit I don't know yet. If I am following an unbroken lineage of the Lord Buddha's teaching with faith and devotion, practicing sincerely in accordance with the morals and ethics of each of the practices, then whatever the ultimate essence is, it will definitely unfold from within. Even if it is very, very hard to explain and very hard to put my finger on it, I have no doubt that it will happen. Whether I know about it or not really doesn't matter very much. If I wrote a hundred, or two hundred books on the subject, it wouldn't matter. If I read three hundred books and received teachings on fifty philosophical sacred texts, it wouldn't matter. If I am practicing any one of them sincerely, the wisdom, the essence of all of these, the thing we are trying to say that cannot be said, will manifest.

At the end of our teaching here you will know that the ultimate essence cannot be explained. That it is impossible to express because there are no words for it. It is like asking a Buddha, "What does it feel like to be a Buddha?" If the Buddha answered, "I feel this or that way," they would be expressing dualism, not Buddha. If they experimented by saying, "I feel this way – no, no, not always – in that situation I also felt that way," they would be just like one of us – not enlightened.

"Buddha" means to reach beyond dualism. It does not mean Buddha doesn't have feelings; it means Buddha is above feeling and not feeling, above knowing and not knowing. We have to reach beyond dualism, cross over it, so we are speaking the unspeakable. It is ineffable. It is unspeakable. It is unexplainable. This means I have to talk about it here for six days, four hours a day. How many hours is that? Twenty-four. I will talk for twenty-four hours so you can discover we cannot say anything about it!

The next verse is about how we human beings think we are so clever because we have language, culture and all kinds of sophisticated things. We think we are really smart, but actually we are more stupid than cockroaches. Cockroaches survive everything. They develop immunity and crawl everywhere. Human beings try their best to exterminate them but cannot. Cockroaches even show up in the best places because they are so good at adapting. We are not as smart as we think. This is the reason I then wrote in my notes:

Relaxed, [Nyom le] newly exposed to the sacred dharma,
  [Sar-bu-wa]
We become confused by the complexities of
The view, meditation, action and fruition of the great central
  texts. [Zhung]
[Confounded] I saw our heads turn like the spinning peacock-
  feather umbrellas meant for the noble ones.

Sar-bu-wa means the new, fresh ones, those who have been newly exposed to the dharma. *Nyom le* means "a little bit lazy." *Zhung* means central and refers to the great texts. They are called "central" because there are many commentaries and thoughts derived from them. For those, including me at that time, who are newly exposed to the dharma and a little bit lazy, the great, central texts – their view, meditation, action and fruition – are so holy, sacred, deep and vast we become confused by them and our "heads turn."

In this verse I say our "heads turn like the spinning peacock-feather umbrellas meant for the noble ones." This refers to the peacock-feather umbrellas kings and great masters used in the old days when they traveled. They had people carrying between three and thirteen umbrellas for them; only the highest rank could use thirteen. They had only one head to cover, but needed thirteen umbrellas. The people carrying these umbrellas would turn them clockwise as they went. This is what this verse refers to – it means we get confused and our head spins. In Hindi there is a very good expression for this, "Chaka ah hai," or "Chaka ah raha hai." It means,

"My head is turning like a wheel." When I wrote these lines I saw myself doing this.

The conclusion of this section I actually wrote before I made the other notes; it says:

Therefore the ground, path and fruition, are simplified and made short. I have done this for my own notes, so I don't forget, and maybe they will also benefit some beginners.

I wanted to share these notes with you so you would know what dharma is and what gaining knowledge of the dharma is. By knowing this you will understand that we are not gaining knowledge of the dharma in order to finish this process, because finishing our dharma studies is impossible. We could learn about the dharma for 10,000 lifetimes, and there would still be more to learn. We could earn 200 PhDs and there would still be more to learn. It is impossible to complete our knowledge of this subject. Impossible. Learning about the dharma is just like learning about anything else. If I wanted to learn about this glass of water, if I wanted to know everything about it, how many lifetimes would it take? I cannot know everything about this glass of water until I know everything about the whole universe – all sentient beings, the entirety of space, everything. Until I know everything I will not know everything about this glass of water.

Even then it would only be one perspective. I would have only learnt about this glass of water as a human being of planet Earth with a human mind, human eyes, ears and tools my human hands can use. What if I was a dog? I would have a dog's hands, eyes, ears and the tools any civilized dog would use. That would be another way for me to understand this glass of water. Still, knowing all a dog could know would also take forever. What if I was a spirit? Spirits do not have this body; they have another kind of body and other kinds of eyes. For them to learn about this glass of water would again take forever. And as a god, we would have a god's eyes, ears, body and perception but it would still take forever to learn about this glass of water.

The human beings of planet Earth, and the human beings of other universes, are also totally different. Other humans may not have eyes, they may see through sound. They may not eat food like ours. So even the different kinds of human beings are countless; planet Earth's humans are just one kind. Among us there are also white people, yellow people, black people, brown people, red people – so many different kinds – but these are hair-splitting differences, not real differences. Everybody on Earth has one nose with two holes, one mouth filled with bones and teeth, two eyes, two ears, two sides and hair on top. This is all the same whether you are black, white, red, yellow or whatever, there is not much difference. Human beings of other universes, however, have to be different. Our evolution followed a certain pattern, and if other evolutionary patterns were even slightly different the beings that evolved from them would look totally different.

They would have a totally different composition, even if their environments were the same as ours. We might be able to see them though, shake their hands, tail or whatever they have, maybe their ears! Perhaps they don't have hands but very long ears with which they write and do things. Perhaps we could shake their ears. Yet other human beings of yet other universes may have such a totally different environment that we would not even see them and they might not even see us. Still, if their realm is the human realm, they are human. We have animals like dogs, snakes, worms and fish that are all in the animal realm but look totally different. The human realm is similar, it is a realm because of its level, but in different environments humans will evolve differently.

When I or anyone else knows everything about this glass of water, we are a Buddha. A scientist who wants to know everything about anything, has to become enlightened, otherwise it is impossible. They may discover some truths, write the findings of their research, even in 200 books, but they will still die with an unfinished job. Then others may be their critic or their fan and continue on, writing another 200 books before they die. Then yet another person could do the same thing, until they also died. They may even win a Noble Prize for science, or become very respected, have statues of themselves placed in front of science institutes and their portraits hung in galleries. All of this can happen but, without realization, they would still not know everything. It is impossible. We shouldn't get discouraged or encouraged by simple facts we have to know.

I have shared these things I wrote with you because they are very important. They do not come from me: they came from the great wisdom of my masters, which they received from their masters, transmitted to me with compassion and received with devotion. This has been my transmission and blessing. I put them on paper to keep my own notes. In those days I knew a lot, but since then I have been working like a coolie to serve the Buddha and the lineage: teaching, building, traveling the world and doing all kinds of things. For the past ten years I have also been handling things I have had no exposure to or training for. This has also been very interesting.

I have been working like a coolie to serve the dharma and I am grateful for this, it is a great honor, but during this time I have had very little opportunity to learn new texts. I cannot work and study at the same time. I cannot teach and study at the same time, so my knowledge of Buddhist philosophy and texts has pretty much stayed at the same level. Although, through teaching, talking to people and other events, I have a little more experience.

Devotion

I would now like to discuss one of the most important teachings and practices, the fundamental, basic practice of the Vajrayana – devotion. In the Vajrayana devotion is the most important thing, but it is a little difficult to express because it is not that politically correct. Compassion is more politically correct. I can talk about compassion to anybody, but when I talk about devotion, I have to be very clear and quite sure about who I am talking to. I consider all of you to be very serious about the dharma, however, not just experimenting, so I must talk to you about devotion.

The foundation of devotion is confidence in your essence. If you don't have confidence in your essence, you cannot have true devotion; it becomes more like fear than devotion. In the Mahayana Buddha taught bodhichitta. Bodhichitta is your essence. The thought, "I wish to become a Buddha to show all sentient beings how to become Buddhas," is bodhichitta. On the way we may also wish to alleviate other beings' suffering and so on, but the ultimate goal is for them to become Buddhas. We need a lot of confidence in ourselves to enable us to say this. Each one of us, no matter what kind of façade we put on, has thousands of problems and shortcomings. We know we do. We don't have to exhibit them to others, it is not necessary, but we have to know about them ourselves. We need to know we have attachment, anger, jealousy, pride, ignorance – all of them – and that each one of us has more than enough of these defilements.

Not only do we have these defilements but the amount of karma each of us has committed because of these defilements is enormous. Each one of us has lived countless lifetimes trying to fulfill our big or little dreams. In order to achieve them we have done so many things. Sometimes we have experienced a little tweak of conscience over what we have done and become more careful, but at other times with no conscience we have been ruthless and caused a lot of harm to others. I am sure each one of us has behaved like this countless times. We can see the results now. If we want to do good things now we have to work very hard at it. If we are not careful, without even realizing it we do not-so-good things.

For example, if a mosquito lands here and bites me, I could very easily swat it. It is very easy – even automatic. What we have done, we do. All this mosquito did was to try to take a little blood from me. It may have even been good for me. In fact, it would definitely have been good for me because I have high blood pressure. I have too much blood. A hundred simultaneous mosquito bites would be good for me. Unless of course they had malaria, then it would be good for my doctors. By going to the doctors I would give them work, they could go to their clinic and sell some medicine. I would get well and they would make money.

Fortunately, or unfortunately, my doctor refuses to take money from me. I buy medicine from pharmacists, but my doctor will not take money from me. If I get sick it does not really benefit me, but it will benefit him because he then has the opportunity to be generous. He considers me a follower of the Buddha, as someone special, so he treats me for free. This is a good habit for him but a little difficult for me to digest. I need a good stomach to digest my doctor's generosity. My stomach has to be pure, strong, healthy and genuine, otherwise digesting other people's service and donations is not easy. If you don't have the stomach for it, it could short-circuit your merit.

In the Mahayana, Lord Buddha taught about motivation; specifically the motivation "to attain Buddhahood for the benefit of all sentient beings." For this motivation you need full confidence in yourself. You need to believe you can become a Buddha. You can develop this kind of confidence in yourself by knowing what a Buddha is. If you do not know this your motivation will become egotistic, an ambition. The motivation "I wish to become a Buddha" is not egotistic or ambitious. It is a truth and a destination. My essence and the essence of the Crown Prince Siddhartha, before he became a Buddha, are the same. Buddha called this essence the Buddha-nature, the *Dewa shegpa nyingpo* in Tibetan, the *Tathagata-garbha* in Sanskrit and the *Fau-shing* in Chinese. It is the Buddha-essence that is in everyone. It is our essence and knowing this, having faith in this, is the basis of devotion.

If you don't have faith in this truth, and still try to be devoted, this devotion may become fearful. We describe some types of devotion in this way: "law-abiding," "God-fearing." When people say this I don't really know what they mean. I am not saying it is wrong, I just don't recognize it. In Buddhism we do not fear the Buddha. If we do something bad we may go to hell, or somewhere else not so good, but the Buddha does not send us there. It is not the Buddha punishing us. Buddhas do not have torture chambers or implements of torture – they are embodiments of compassion and wisdom.

This doesn't mean we can hide anything from the Buddha though. If we do something that nobody knows about, we may think the Buddhas do not know about it either, but they are in front of us all the time. Some people make little shrines in their houses and when they are in front of them they behave very, very well. They change their clothes before they come into the shrine room, they walk on their knees and try not to think of anything unbecoming. Doing all of this is wonderful, it is an excellent gesture, we should do it and it is meritorious, but if we do these things thinking the Buddha is only present in the shrine room and not everywhere else then we don't understand the Buddha. The Buddha is everywhere. We should have a shrine, keep it clean and not engage in worldly activities before it – we shouldn't keep our business desk in that area, our kitchen or our fridge – but we do these things because of ourselves, because *we* are dualistic, because we are doing our best in our own dualistic way to respect the Buddha.

It is like taking your shoes off, but not your socks. In India we take our shoes off outside every respected place – our parents' home, religious places, and our teachers' room. We take our shoes off outside the door, but we don't take our socks off. Sometimes it may even be better to go in with your shoes on! If you go shopping, then to lunch, then for a nice walk in the very nice park near here called Loti Gardens, and then came back here I would prefer you did not take off your shoes. That would be more polite and meritorious!

Anyway we do our best, so that is fine. We take off our shoes, we behave very nicely, we are super-duper good in front of our shrine and that is wonderful, but it does not mean the Buddha is only there. The Buddha is in the park, in the restaurant, in your office, in your street, in your car. The Buddha is everywhere. In the same way that wherever you go so does your shadow, the Buddha is everywhere. The Buddha is omniscient – you can't hide anything from the Buddha. We need to know this as well. If we know this and still keep a nice clean shrine that is good.

Without knowing this we may develop strange ideas about the Buddha and become afraid. If we fear the Buddha we will lose our confidence. Someone like Hercules may be happy that a lion has gotten loose but without this confidence the rest of us will hide under the table. Whether hiding will help I don't know, but we will anyway, leaving Hercules to stand up and manhandle the lion. Without confidence we have fear. Bodhichitta is confidence and with this confidence comes devotion.

When I say "devotion" I mean that which we direct towards our dharma masters. I have respect for my music teacher but not devotion. Not that I am learning piano, but if I was a teacher would come to my house every week, once or twice, and I would pay them a fee. I would learn from this teacher and respect him or her because he or she would be teaching me something I don't know. I would not be devoted to him or her, however, because although I want to learn piano I don't want to become like him or her. My ultimate devotion is to the Buddha because I want to become like Buddha and I have devotion for my dharma masters because in the process of becoming like the Buddha, I want to become like them. This is the difference between respect and devotion.

I don't know how worldly people outside the dharma community think about devotion and respect, but in a dharma context devotion is based on your potential. I have the potential to become a Buddha and as Prince Siddhartha already achieved this I want to become like him, hence my ultimate devotion is to the Buddha. This devotion also continues down through his lineage. I am devoted to my guru, because my guru transmitted the blessing of the Buddha's lineage to me. For me he is the Buddha's substitute. He may have the body of the sangha, but his teaching is the Buddha's teaching. His mind is a treasury of the Buddha's teaching because he or she – it doesn't matter which – received it from their master with devotion. In this way devotion is very important.

There are two devotional prayers I would like to explain to you.

I think the first was written by the first Jamgon Kongtrul, Lodro Thaye of Palpung Monastery. I cannot say for sure, perhaps he only emphasized this prayer, but I think he wrote it.

SÖL WA DEB SO LAMA RINPOCHE
I pray to you, precious Lama.
DUNG WÄ BÖ DO DRIN CHEN CHO KYI JE
Kind Lord of Dharma, I call out to you with longing.

KÄL MEN DAG LA RE SA CHE LEY ME
For me, the unworthy one, you are the only hope.
THUG YI YER ME DRE PAR JIN GYI LOB
Bless me that your mind blends with me.

This four-sentence prayer is very common in our lineage. With devotion, we pray and supplicate the precious master, the precious guru. We call with sincere, genuine devotion and feeling to this most kind Lord of Dharma. As up until now we have not had the fortunate karma to attain Buddhahood we are not yet enlightened, so we turn to the precious master and ask for our minds to become one with theirs. We request that our wisdom and their wisdom become one. Our guru's wisdom is the unbroken lineage of the Buddha's dharmakaya; becoming one with the guru means becoming one with all the lineage gurus back to the Buddha himself.

In our lineage tree, which is like a family tree, the Buddha is at the top, the guru is in the middle and all the lineage masters are in between. The Buddha is in the form of Vajradhara, which is the dharmakaya, sambhogakaya, and nirmanakaya all in one. The guru is also in the form of Vajradhara. This represents the unbroken transmission lineage of Buddha's enlightenment.[3] Therefore, requesting to become one with the guru is requesting that our mind and Buddha's mind become one. If we have un-forced, un-fabricated true devotion this will happen. It might take many lifetimes, but at least we can learn about it and cultivate it in the meantime.

The next prayer elaborates on this:

LA MA RIN PO CHE LA SOL WA DEB
Precious Lama, I pray to you.
DAG DZIN LO YI TONG WAR JIN GYI LOB
Bless me that my mind gives up ego-grasping.
GÖ ME GYU LA KYE WAR JIN GYI LOB
Bless me that contentment arises in the stream of my mind.
CHO MIN NAM TOG GAG PAR JIN GYI LOB
Bless me that non-dharmic thoughts may cease.

RANG SEM KYE ME TOG PAR JIN GYI LOB
Bless me that my mind be realized as unborn.
TRUL PA RANG SAR ZHI WAR JIN GYI LOB
Bless me that confusion may subside in its own place.
NANG SI CHO KUR TOG PAR JIN GYI LOB
Bless me that all phenomenal existence be realized as dharmakaya.

This prayer is very specific. The first line says: "I pray to, and supplicate with devotion the precious guru, the precious master." Then we enumerate the kind of blessings we want. The first blessing we ask for is to be able to renounce our ego. When we pray we should not be pragmatic, we should be limitless. Of course we cannot renounce our ego. I have not totally renounced my ego. I have a very big ego. If you could see it you would be surprised, you just cannot see it. Everybody has an ego. Don't tell me you don't have an ego; I will not believe you. Our ego can be bad, our ego can be good and it can be mixed. A good ego is confidence, a bad ego is ruthlessness. I think a bad ego is what we have most of the time. "May I be able to renounce my ego," is the first prayer. When sitting in front of a judge we pray. We say, "I want this, this and this." In a similar way, in front of the Buddhas we ask for their blessings.

The second prayer is, "May I realize the meaninglessness of worldly activities and worldly things." We request that understanding of how meaningless worldly activities are is born within us. This understanding should not just be intellectual but a true understanding. "Worldly activity" means activities that serve our ego, our attachment, jealousy, fear and greed. We are slaves of our greed. We are slaves of our hatred. We are slaves of our jealousy. We do everything to fulfill our attachment, anger, jealousy, pride and so on, and these are meaningless activities because they can never be fulfilled. Our greed can never be fulfilled. If you become the king or queen of planet Earth today and all five thousand million humans respected you like a god, within a week – maybe it wouldn't even take a week – you would have complaints. There would be so many things that you wanted. You would find out that you did not have so many things.

Even the most comfortable thing would feel uncomfortable within a week. I guarantee it. Desire is impossible to satisfy. This prayer doesn't mean you should stop your business, your work. It does not mean that you should stop everything right now. It means you have to know these things have no end, that there is nothing in them. No matter how many clothes we have we can only wear a certain amount at any one time, otherwise we get too hot. No matter how much we have we can only eat a certain amount, otherwise our stomachs will burst. This goes for all the otherworldly things we enjoy also.

Take me for example. I have always had what I needed. I wanted to build my monasteries, so very devoted people gave me money from here and there and I was able to. I needed the land and the land became available, somebody made it available. Whatever I needed somehow came to me. I appreciate this very much. I think this happened because of the great deeds of my predecessors; it is the result of their karma. I have very few extras however, which I also appreciate. I am not saying you shouldn't have extras, you should. Otherwise how are you going to live if you retire? Your living standards shouldn't go down after you retire, so you need extras. I don't have that much extra though and I never have had, which has been nice for me. For example, if I had ten elephants but no circus what would I do with them? Feeding and cleaning them would be an awful lot of work. If I had a whole circus it would not be a problem. There would be lots of performers and all kinds of people necessary to the circus who could take care of the elephants. If the circus just had ten tigers and ten elephants though, it would kill me. I would be their slave!

So I am grateful for the blessing of not having extras. For the duties I needed to perform I have had whatever I needed – devoted and generous people have realized what needed to be done – and I have had no extras that would have been a burden for me. The Buddha has blessed me with not having a surplus. I don't have to worry about those things.

The third prayer is, "Please bless me that all thoughts except the dharma cease to exist in my mind." As I said, we aspire to the maximum, we shouldn't be pragmatic and practical. We should aim for the ultimate – to make our mind totally occupied by thoughts of the dharma. This means thoughts of compassion, thoughts of devotion, thoughts that are positive for developing wisdom, thoughts that are beneficial to us and others. We pray, "May my mind be totally occupied by these thoughts."

The fourth prayer is, "Please bless me to recognize and realize the immortal, primordial essence of my mind." My mind that was never born and never dies is incorruptible and limitless. Each of our minds' tathagatagarbha, Buddha-nature, is incorruptible, limitless, has never died and has never been born. It is ever-present, always pure, and always perfect. It has never been stained by anything. It is like the best diamond in the worst coal mine: whatever happens there, however black it is, however dirty it is, the best diamond is never stained. When it is discovered it still shines. It is pure.

The essence of what we call "I" is our Buddha-nature or Buddha-essence. Every one of us calls ourselves "I" first, and then says our name, "I, Mr, or Mrs so-and-so." This is the essence of that "I." Some of you think that you are just made up of molecules, so there is nothing to you, but then who thinks this? Who says this? The "I." Some of you say, "Maybe there is something." Who says this? There are others who say, "My essence is Buddha as is the essence of all these other people." Whether they believe in their essence or not it is ever-present – it is the dharmakaya. To know it is our next prayer, the fourth prayer.

The fifth prayer is to realize that all of the things happening to us right now, in our past lives, and in all our future lives until we become Buddhas, are perceptual illusions. They are the result of our karma, derived from and generated by our ego. We can see this quite clearly in this room. Some of you like to keep your hair short, others like to have long hair. Some of you have gray hair, others dye your hair red or black. Some of you like to wear certain kinds of clothes, others like to wear another kind. Each one of you perceives the world in a certain way. Some of you like your tea very sweet, others like their tea salty. Some of you even like your tea bitter – it is called coffee. Each one of you has different tastes and a different manifestation.

Something that you may think is beautiful and wonderful others may not. Something others may think is beautiful and wonderful you may not. Each person's definition of pleasant, nice, beautiful and tasty is different. Some of you like lots of chili, others hate chili. Some like to add honey, some of you even like your food fried. Some of you like to eat with your hands, some of you like to eat with sticks and others like to eat with a spoon. We are all different, we all have different ways; our karma manifests differently.

When I was growing up I always ate with my hands. My Lamas did not think this was very polite. They put a separate spoon out for me and I put it aside and ate with my hands. I would say to them, "My mother will be happier if I eat with my hands because she gave them to me." The real reason was that it was tastier if I ate with my hands. When I used the spoon I tasted the spoon, when I used chopsticks I tasted them, but when I ate with my hands I only tasted the food. This may have been because I was so familiar with the taste of my hands that there were no other tastes involved. These days, when I travel the world I use a knife and fork or chopsticks in order to be polite. When I am in India, however, I like to eat with my hands. It really does taste different.

These examples show that everything is an illusion, and we pray that, "all this illusion comes to rest by itself." That it will be exposed by itself. How is our illusion exposed? Let's look at a simple example. The world's biggest illusion is the importance of pieces of paper with numbers on them, usually ending in zeros. This illusion dominates every so-called civilized human. We call it money. Money is the world's biggest illusion. Still we need money to have a home. If we have no money we have to walk, we cannot travel by car. With no money getting food to eat or clothes to wear would be difficult. We could still have everything without money, but it would be very difficult. With no money to buy clothes or material to make clothes we would have to plant a cotton seed, wait for it to grow, collect the cotton, save it somewhere then plant another cotton seed. When we had enough cotton, we would then have to work very hard spinning and making a sweater before we could wear it. It might take three or four years before we had clothes.

The illusion of money has become so established that it is now a bit too late to live without money. Anyone who wanted to live without money would have to work very, very hard. We would rather have money and use that to live. We have spent the last maybe 20,000 or 30,000 years creating this difficult situation for ourselves but this illusion we created has succeeded and now dominates us. We are totally controlled by pieces of paper with one number at the beginning and many following zeros. This is a simple example of our illusions. We created money, it didn't just appear, we worked very hard to create it. The history of the evolution of money is very interesting. It shows us how it is an illusion.

We can still make money knowing this, but our perception of and attachment to it will not be the same. We will see it as a tool, not a god. We will earn our money according to our needs, instead of the limitless, objectless, crazy pursuit of it. We will make a certain amount of money because we want to do this or that. Our purpose will be very clear. If we know money is an illusion, a tool, we can approach it like this. Most people do not think this way though – they will do anything to get money. They will kill, cheat, commit fraud and all kinds of things to make money. Do they really need all this money? Maybe yes, maybe no. In any case it is very good to have a clear understanding that everything is an illusion.

Another example is our health. To be healthy is very good, but if the illusion of being healthy becomes an obsession, we can kill ourselves by wanting to be healthy. By refusing to touch this or that we may eventually become so fragile that without any resistance we die from a virus because we do not have the strength to handle it. Our body may be so defenseless that one little thing can kill it. Staying healthy by behaving like this is another illusion we have created. We should be healthy, but we should also know that being healthy is an illusion – nobody can live for 10,000 years. We may say to someone, "You are so great, you should live for 10,000 years." That someone may even stand up, smile and say, "Yes, I am going to live for 10,000 years," and nobody would call them a hypocrite because the idea is so far-fetched. No one can live for 10,000 years or would want to. We all enjoy life, but at a certain point we have had enough of it. At a certain point we would not mind a new beginning, a new start. We would not mind going to kindergarten again – it may even be interesting.

It is all an illusion. Out of necessity we have to participate in it, but we have to know it is an illusion. Knowing it is an illusion we can still do our best to keep healthy and make money. Otherwise, we may get lost and when we are lost, it is very difficult to find ourselves. And when we can't find ourselves nobody else can find us either. This is very, very, very important so we pray, "May all illusions be exposed by themselves."

That was the first, second, third, fourth and fifth prayers. Now we reach the last prayer, "May I realize that everything is the dharmakaya." The word used here, *nang si* – translated as "everything," actually means "everything that is visible or invisible:" this makes our prayer very clear. It is extremely important, the essence of the Vajrayana teachings. Here we pray to realize the ultimate essence of everything as the dharmakaya. In the Vajrayana, the Lord Buddha's teachings on Tantra, the highest teachings of Lord Buddha, he manifested that the essence of everything is perfect. If you were to hold the worst, most disgusting thing in your left hand and the most precious, sacred thing in your right hand, their essences are the same. They cannot have two different essences. The highest being – the Buddha – and the lowest being – whoever that is – have the same essence. The essence of everything is perfect, but their characteristics like good or bad, clean or dirty, right or wrong are in between. Relatively there is wrong and right, but nothing is ultimately wrong, ultimately everything is right.

This is the last line of Jamgon Kongtrul Lodro Thaye's prayer. Right now the best thing we can do in relation to this last prayer is respect everyone and everything; to do good things, not bad things; to associate with good people and if you can help them bad people also. If you have the strength and ability to help bad people become good, associate with them. If you don't have the strength and ability to do this, keep away from them physically and pray for them. Dedicate your merit to them. Pray for them, but if your lack of strength means they can make you bad don't associate with them.

Bad company is bad company if you are weak, bad company is good company if you are strong, because you can make them good. Sometimes it can be a lot of work to make bad things good, but you should also remember that ultimately the essence of bad people and things is also good. There is no such thing as ultimate badness, ultimate evil, or ultimate dirtiness – ultimately everything is perfect.

Chapter 2

THE HISTORY OF INDIAN BUDDHISM

AFTER TRYING TO DESCRIBE THE basis of dharma for you, from my notes, I would now like to go into the history of Buddhism. As you know Buddha Shakyamuni is our Buddha. He became enlightened more than 2500 years ago. Along with other Buddhist traditions, we are going to celebrate the 2550th anniversary of Buddha's birth in 2006. This was not that long ago; in terms of the universe 2500 years is nothing, Buddha attained enlightenment very recently.

The history of Buddhism has been clearly recorded since the time of the Buddha. In Tibetan there are volumes specifically dedicated to the history of Buddhism in India and Tibet. There are also volumes dedicated to the history of Buddhism at large: in India, Tibet, Mongolia, China, Japan, Thailand, Burma and the rest. Of course, the histories written in the Tibetan language are more focused on India and Tibet, but there are also sizable sections on Buddhism in China. There is very little written about Buddhism in Thailand, Burma and Japan, but these countries are mentioned.

As we briefly look at this history you will see how the different lineages developed slightly differently from one another. For example, Lord Buddha's first teaching was at Varanasi, a holy place visited by Buddhists from all traditions. This is where he taught the Four Noble Truths: the truth of suffering, the truth of the cause of suffering, the truth of the path to become free from suffering; and the truth of peace – the state free from suffering. These are the Four Noble Truths.

The second major turning of the wheel of dharma was in Rajgir, also a very holy place. There Lord Buddha manifested the Prajnaparamita teachings on bodhichitta and emptiness. This is an enormous teaching; in it he manifested the true potential of everyone and everything as well as the shortcomings that hinder our recognition and full development of this potential. These teachings are all about Prajnaparamita, emptiness. Here emptiness does not mean nothingness. If there were nothing then why would we bother? We could relax, do nothing or whatever we liked. But it doesn't mean this.

This emptiness means that everything is only relatively true. Ultimately everything is nothing more, and nothing less, than an interdependent manifestation of everything else. For example, light makes us see color. If there were no light there would be no color. Our eyes would also be useless without light and therefore nobody would have eyes, they would not exist. It is the same with sound. Sound comes from movement; if a thing doesn't move it doesn't make noise. Everything that makes noise does so through the production of energy, through movement. When people move, for example, they make lots of noise. When an individual makes noise they can do so through moving their hands, moving their vocal chords or breathing in a certain way. Even this table here can make a noise when it is moved, but if nothing is moved there will be no sound. This shows how everything is interrelated, how everything is nothing more, or less, than an interdependent manifestation of everything else. The Buddha manifested this teaching of emptiness at Rajgir.

The Buddha's last set of teachings was manifested in several places. These teachings were not limited to one topic, like the Four Noble Truths or emptiness, but covered all aspects of the dharma. The

Buddha's disciples compiled these teachings, which came to be called "the third turning of the wheel," after his paranirvana. On several different occasions there were earlier and later councils of his disciples and they made compilations of his teachings. What finally emerged from these meetings was the classification of Lord Buddha's words into four parts: Vinaya, Abhidharma, Sutra and Tantra. This is interesting. Many times when somebody is reading even this text I have here somebody will say, "He is reading a Sutra." But it is not a Sutra. And it is not an Abhidharma text. It is "Ground, Path and Fruition" written by me.

The compiled texts that make up the Tibetan Buddhist canon are in over 100 volumes and were translated from Sanskrit into Tibetan more than a thousand years ago. Not all of this canon is composed of Sutras though; only one section is. If somebody is reading from this canon it may be difficult to know what he or she is reading; maybe they are reading Abhidharma, maybe Vinaya, maybe Sutra or maybe even Tantra. These days, however, any Buddhist book is called a Sutra. It is like calling all magazines *National Geographic*, when there are also other magazines like *Time*, *Newsweek* and *Vogue* for example. This phenomenon is very interesting. For me it is a clear indication that even though many people are very devoted their real knowledge of Buddhism is limited. They are like somebody who has come from the mountains and has never seen a magazine before. If the first magazine they see is a *National Geographic* and someone says to them, "That is a *National Geographic*," they will assume all magazines are *National Geographic*.

There is also another aspect to this. As this word has entered into our household language even very knowledgeable people, even professors in Buddhism, will habitually say, "He is reading a Sutra." Or, "This is a Sutra printing press." It may actually print Sutra, Abhidharma, Vinaya, Tantra and other texts, but they will call it a "Sutra printing press." There is a very famous printing press in the kingdom I come from, a very comprehensive wood block printing press.[4] It is actually the biggest Buddhist, Tibetan language printing press in the world and many books have been printed there, yet they all call it a "Sutra printing press." They do print Sutra texts there but they also print texts that do not contain the words of the Buddha, including the words of Buddhist masters, and even history texts.

The Tibetan Buddhist canon is a compilation of the Vinaya, Abhidharma, Sutra and Tantra. The Vinaya describes oral and physical morals and ethics. It is about discipline. It describes what to say and what not to say, what to do and what not to do. Actually there is more about what not to do and what not to say; do not kill, do not steal, do not lie, etc. It contains all the basic morals and ethics. The Abhidharma is about psychology – mental activities and mental facets – and the physical sciences – atoms, the smallest objects, the shortest time, cosmology and mathematics. All of these teachings are in the Abhidharma; it is a very big part of the Lord Buddha's teaching. The other aspect of the canon is the Sutras. The Sutras deal mainly with mental discipline. They emphasize bodhichitta, compassion, loving-kindness and the six paramitas. All of these are mentioned in one teaching or another, but their focus is different. There are a large number of Sutras, such as the Lotus Sutra, the Lankavatara Sutra, and the Diamond Sutra – so many Sutras – and they are the third aspect of the Buddha's teachings.

The fourth aspect is Tantra. This is also a large part of the Lord Buddha's teachings. The way Tantra was received is very different from the way the Sutras, the Abhidharma and the Vinaya were received. Very highly evolved individuals received the Tantras. When the Buddha manifested the Tantras he manifested as the main deity of the Tantra, with a retinue of deities, and the surroundings manifested as the mandala of the deity. The translation of "mandala" into Tibetan, *kyil khor*, actually means "central and surrounding": *kyil* means middle and *khor* means surroundings. The deity is in the middle and the surroundings are the deity's surroundings.

This is how Buddha manifested Tantra. This manifestation is called the sambhogakaya. When Buddha manifested the Vinaya, Abhidharma and Sutra he was in the nirmanakaya form, the Prince Siddhartha who became Buddha Shakyamuni. Prince Siddhartha himself had a perfect human form, but after his enlightenment his physical appearance was so glorious that two meters of light could be seen around him. When he spoke, when he manifested teachings, everybody heard him in their own language. He did not need interpreters; everybody heard and understood him.

The Buddha also had thirty-two major and eighty minor physical marks, but these were based on the already existing physical manifestation of Prince Siddhartha. If a photographer had taken a picture of Prince Siddhartha before he became a Buddha, and then again after he became a Buddha, they would look pretty much the same, except the Buddha would appear more glorious. If it was you, for example, who became a Buddha, you would still look like you but more glorious and you would have two meters of light around you. This is the nirmanakaya form of the Buddha. If we had two meters of light around us it would be wonderful, but if we had to hide somewhere it would be very difficult wouldn't it? Even if you hid in a box the light would shine out from it; there would be a box with two meters of light around it. I don't really mean to make a joke of this though, it is just my layman's understanding.

The sambhogakaya form of the Buddha is the deity. I think you are probably very familiar with tantric deities. I think, however, that I should explain Tantra a little because people tend to have a lot of misgivings about it – Tantra seems to be having a public relations crisis. I don't know who is responsible for it, but it has an image problem so I have to do some PR for Tantra. What Tantra really refers to is the practice of the most evolved beings: the practice for those for whom the only obstacle left is the final aspect of dualism. Except for this everything else has been done; attachment, anger, jealousy and pride have all been purified. Each one of them had their fair share of these, then through purification they got rid of them. They still have the final, most subtle dualism though. They still have dualistic notions of good and bad, positive and negative, subject and object. When this is the only obstacle left, Tantra manifests.

As a result of the manifestation of Tantra and its practice, the final dualism is transformed and purified. This is Tantra. Tantric practice works to bring this final purification about. Tantric practice engages in overcoming the most subtle and final aspects of dualism – the dualism that is the base of samsara. Through calling myself "me," all of you become "you." In the whole universe, if I search, I will find only one "me" but limitless others. This makes me feel small, insignificant and limited. I want to be bigger, richer and more powerful than "me," but this "me" is so insignificant that as long as it is there greed, jealousy and the like will come about.

If you really look into this "me," if you really scrutinize it, it is not even there. Where is this "me"? Where is this "you"? Is it in your head? Your chest? Your pocket? Where is it? We call ourselves "I," "Mr," "Mrs" or "Doctor," but where are we? If we look we cannot find anything, but it is there, we are here. We may not be able to find it, but the one looking for it is there. Somebody is looking for it; somebody is trying to find it. The "I," the ego, is based on this basic dualism.

This dualism, samsara, starts in every moment; it did not start at any particular point and as long as we create it, as long as we generate it, it will continue. It does not have a beginning, but it can have an end. It ends when we reach Buddhahood. There is no beginning of samsara because when we reach Buddhahood we realize nothing ever happened, that time is relative. When we reach Buddhahood, we will realize that the countless lifetimes we have had, including the hundreds of millions of lifetimes in which we followed the path, did not last more than a second. They will not appear to have lasted more than a second and not less than countless lifetimes. There will be no difference between the two because time is relative.

Even my own common sense tells me time is relative. For example, when I see ants working they have such tiny bodies, such tiny legs, but from my point of view they move so fast. From their perspective they have to move each limb, each digit otherwise something will break. They move very carefully and comfortably and do not get tired. If we moved like that, in twenty minutes we would be dead from a heart attack but for them it is normal, it is like walking comfortably for us. Ants' time and human beings' time are relative in this way, as are elephants' time and the biggest dinosaurs' time.

Our time and somebody else's time are also relative. For example, right now we feel very comfortable and firmly on the ground, we feel very secure, but you know we are actually in the sky not on the ground. Our little world is moving in a circle every twenty-four hours at the speed of 20,000 miles per second – it is not on the ground. We have the illusion that we are on the ground. We dig the earth and make foundations in it. We build a house, we build a Gurumoha room, and we sit in this room comfortably. A Gurumoha is a very beautiful tree with yellow flowers. This room has the same name as these flowers, and there is also a park in Delhi called Gurumoha Park. The appearance of this room is an illusion though and time is an illusion, everything is an illusion. And we have to overcome even the final illusion, the subtlest dualism, to become a Buddha. For this the Buddha manifested Tantra.

I met a very good Mahayana monk in Malaysia; he was very nice and we became quite close. One day he very honestly asked, if Vajradhara's face was the Buddha's face and the Buddha was a *bhikshu*, why was he painted naked with a consort? The Buddha is a monk, a bhikshu, he said, "If you portray the Buddha with a consort and expose him totally, isn't that very bad karma?" He was very sincere and honest in asking me this, and I am glad he did.

I told him that this image was not actually Buddha with a consort because the consort was also the Buddha – both the deity and the consort are the Buddha. The wisdom aspect of the Buddha manifests as the consort and the method or skillful aspect of the Buddha manifests as the male form. They are one, there are not two people up there, there is only one true manifestation of the Buddha in union, and it is a symbol of non-dualism. After that I met him again, and I asked him, "Now what do you think?" He very honestly replied, "I still feel very uncomfortable about it." I respect this. He did not receive the transmission lineage or teachings of Tantra, so he doesn't know about it. He is very serious about the Vinaya and the Sutras, so he sees things from their perspective.

Another way we work on removing this subtlest dualism when we do tantric prayers and practices is to offer everything there is to the Buddha – not only the clean, beautiful flowers, but everything. We visualize an ocean of all good and bad things. We don't have to make this physically – don't worry – we visualize it all. Then we melt it into ourselves, we become the ocean of everything. This we bless by saying, OM AH HUNG: OM represents the body, AH represents the speech, HUNG represents the mind. When doing this we reverse the normal way we visualize these syllables. Normally the OM is at the forehead, the AH is at the throat and the HUNG is at the heart. When we bless this ocean of offerings, however, the OM is at the heart, the AH is at the throat, and the HUNG is at the forehead.

First the OM blesses the physical aspect and transforms it into its essence. The body is blessed and transformed first because it is the roughest of these three. We can see our bodies, touch them, and become sick. The AH blesses our speech after this. Speech is more profound, less tangible than physical form. Your body can become ill, but your speech cannot. You may be too ill to speak, but your speech is not ill. Finally the HUNG blesses the mind. The mind never gets sick; you can have a terrible body with a very strong mind. You can die, your body can lie there, but this does not mean your mind is dead. Your mind can never die. Through this process then, the body, speech, and mind are blessed. After this blessing, this ocean of everything becomes nectar – *amrit* in Hindi, *dutsi* in Tibetan and I think *kan-lul* in Chinese.

As Vajrayana Buddhists, we have not necessarily reached the level of the most evolved beings whose only obstacle left is the final aspect of dualism. As followers of the Vajrayana we practice Tantra for many purposes, including the goals of the Vinaya, Abhidharma, Sutras and Tantra. How do we do this? For example, I am a monk, so I follow the Vinaya vows. I also take bodhisattva vows, which means I try to keep bodhichitta, the wish to attain Buddhahood for the benefit of all sentient beings.

The statement "all sentient beings," includes the worst person who did the worst things to me in any of my past lives or this life, or the person who will do the worst things to me in my future lives. I am sure there is somebody like this for all of us, someone that we are allergic to. Or perhaps somebody has an allergy to us. We may call them our enemy, but perhaps they are so allergic to us that they must do things to us otherwise they can't stand it. It is as if we are something that has gotten up their nose and they have to sneeze. Perhaps we are like powder in their nose that makes them sneeze involuntarily, just because of their karma.

Wishing to attain Buddhahood to benefit all sentient beings includes even those who have done the worst things to us. We can't exclude anybody. I might shout at them if they try to strangle me, I might try to hit them back so they lose their strength, knock them out so they are unconscious until the police arrive, but if I had the opportunity to make them a Buddha right now, I should do it without hesitation. I can never say someone has been so bad to me that I don't want them to attain enlightenment. This is the basic vow of the bodhisattva.

As Vajrayana practitioners we take the vows of the Vinaya and the bodhisattva, but our practices, meditation, ritual and chanting are Tantra. We visualize ourself as the Buddha, in both male and female manifestations. These are the positive aspects of each one of us. A lady practicing Chakrasamvara, a male deity, will visualize herself as Chakrasamvara and Vajravarahi, his consort. Both are aspects of the same Buddha. They are both you, not two different people. When I, a man, practice Vajrayogini or Vajravarahi, the main idem[5] of our tradition, even though I am not a lady I visualize myself in feminine form. If Vajravarahi is your main deity, this is how you visualize yourself. This is how tantric practice is performed by Vajrayana Buddhists.

There are also tantric Vajrayana practitioners who are not monks or nuns. Even though they do not have to follow the vows of the Vinaya, they can still practice Vajrayana Tantra. They may even be married couples. As married couples they do not have to follow the Vinaya's celibacy vow, but they have to keep all the other vows. If you are a layperson practicing the Vajrayana seriously, upasaka vows are taken. An upasaka is a layperson who does not kill, steal, lie, engage in sexual misconduct, or take anything intoxicating. As an upasaka you must follow these vows.

Speaking of intoxication, in our practice of the great Tantras we have ganachakras. In ganachakra ceremonies we drink a small portion of wine or whiskey. We take a small spoonful or three or four drops in our hand as a blessing and drink it. There is no way you can get drunk from this small amount of alcohol, but nowadays people have become so politically correct that they use orange juice instead. I find this very funny, why do we have to be so paranoid? The Tantras say to have a drop of whiskey or wine blessed by the Buddha so why are they so worried? In some monasteries they use milk and in others they use orange juice mixed with lots of water. I think this is a little paranoid, or perhaps a little egotistic. Maybe I am wrong though. Maybe it is good. But can you get drunk from one drop of whiskey?

If you are a couple, and have a very good teacher instructing you exactly, you don't have to waste your time spent as a couple in a worldly manner either. You can practice the tantric sacred union as part of your family life. These activities do not have to be all samsaric, you can use them as a practice. People like me cannot teach you this sort of thing though. I can only teach you how to practice using visualizations; for instruction on sacred union you have to find a married yogi who has this kind of practice, receive instructions from them and even then you can only do this practice with a moral, ethical partner. This is also part of the upasaka vow. The upasaka vows are of two types: one type of upasaka is celibate, the others are not celibate, not full upasakas. They are almost full upasakas.

People somehow misunderstand all of this and make up all kinds of stories about Tantra. When they see Buddha images of male and female union, they look at them in a samsaric way, as if these are true people, and this gives Tantra bad PR. In all honesty though, and with due respect to everybody, it is actually our fault. During the time of Tilopa, Naropa, Marpa and Mila, ordinary people would never have seen these images – practitioners were not allowed to show these images publicly. Now we have books and calendars of them. There are calendars which have a different mandala for every month; January is the Guhyasamaja mandala, February is the Kalachakra mandala, March is the Mahamaya mandala, April is the Vajravarahi mandala, and so on. During the time of Tilopa and Naropa, gurus would only expose these images to their disciples and the disciples would keep these images and their practice to themselves. They were never viewed in public. So no one else is to blame for this bad PR; these images were not supposed to be shown in public.

I think the practice of showing these images in public started about eighty, ninety or a hundred years ago when public initiations were first given. I wouldn't say it is a bad thing, it is breaking the lineage, but out of compassion. Now thousands and thousands of people can participate in tantric empowerments and I can talk about it to all of you. This evolved by itself, slowly, over many years. It wasn't just one master who said, "Okay there is some interest in these, so let's make them public." It is not as if a newspaper wrote a sensational article about it: it happened over the centuries in Tibet, slowly, slowly. I don't think it is wrong, but I think all of Tantra's bad PR came about as a result of it. If this change hadn't happened most people wouldn't know of Tantra. Is that good, or is that bad? In my opinion this bad press, this bad PR is good. It means we all get to participate in Tantra and we all get to receive teachings on it. It is good, even if there is some negative fallout.

There will always be people who misuse what they know, and they might use Tantra to show their power, attract or use people. These people are human and every human has weaknesses. In the past people like this may have used Tantra to justify their personal weaknesses and this may have caused some of these basic misinterpretations. I hope now, however, I have made it clear to you what Tantra actually is.

Each Tantra is also an enormous text. Some of the Tantras, like the Hevajra Tantra, have many volumes; it is a complete teaching and philosophy on its own. The Tantras are actually in four categories: Kriya, Charya, Yoga and Anuttarayoga. Anuttarayoga can also be divided into Maha, Anu and Ati. Ati is the highest of the Tantras; Kriya is the lowest of the Tantras.[6] If you are a practitioner of Kriya you cannot eat meat – you have to be vegetarian – you have to be very clean, you cannot have long nails, you have to keep everything absolutely clean. When you practice the higher Tantras, these kinds of things become irrelevant. You reach above whatever makes them relevant.

As a practitioner it is very hard for me to know whether you are at a Kriya, Charya, Yoga or Anuttarayoga level. I don't know, therefore I have to give initiations according to different situations, needs and requests. In doing so I emphasize to the initiates that they have to follow a strict, Vinaya-based ethic and base their practice on bodhichitta. I have to teach in this way because I am not omniscient and don't know which level people are on. If I were omniscient I would know whether you were at the Kriya level, the Charya level, the Maha level, the Anu level or the Ati level and would instruct you according to this, but I can't do that. Therefore, even if I am giving a very high empowerment – such as Hevajra, Guhyasamaja or Kalachakra – I still emphasize that my students should take their bodhichitta and Vinaya vows very seriously.

There is nothing wrong with practicing the very basic practices anyway, even if you are very highly developed. If on the other hand you are not highly developed and still don't think morals and ethics are relevant to you that is a very big problem. It is very wrong. It is safer to practice in accordance with ethics, so that is how we practice. His Holiness the Dalai Lama, for example, gives Kalachakra empowerments all over the world – in Europe, America and different parts of India – everywhere. At the same time he teaches people basic morality, and compassion. He doesn't say, "Kalachakra is the highest of all the Tantras, it is an Ati level Tantra of Anuttarayoga and now you have to live your life at that level." In fact he teaches very basically. My guru, my supreme guru, His Holiness the 16th Karmapa, was also like this. He gave us many different empowerments but he was very, very strict – super-duper strict – about morals and ethics. So that is how we practice.

I hope any misunderstandings of Tantra you may have had have been cleared through this discussion. I don't mean to brainwash you. I am just doing some PR for our precious lineage. You also need to understand this as followers of the Vajrayana.

Tantra, along with Vinaya, Abhidharma and Sutra make up the Buddha's basic teachings. There are over 100 volumes of them in Tibetan. Several of these volumes, including the Vajrakalpa Sutra, have also been translated into English by Tharthang Rinpoche and published by Dharma Publishing in California. He has only translated some of the canon into English and I think these translations already make up four very condensed, big volumes. If we were to translate all 100 Tibetan volumes into English it would run to at least 200 volumes, maybe 300 or 400. These are the words of the Buddha that were absorbed by his direct disciples and later put down on paper.

After the compilation of the Buddha's teachings, a great many masters also composed texts. Especially the eight great masters of India: Nagarjuna, Aryadeva, Asanga, Vasubhandu, Dignaga, Dharmakirti, Gunaprabha and Shakyaprabha. We describe them as the world's six ornaments and two great beautifiers, the *Dzamling Dzä-bä-che-bä Gyen trug tang Chog nyi*. *Dzamling* means the world, *Dzä-be-che-bä* means beautifier – that which makes the world beautiful, *Gyen* means ornament, *trug* means six, and *Chog nyi* means "supreme two." Apart from these eight there were also many other masters of course: the eighty-four taras for example, and over thirty enlightened women mahasiddhas.

The Buddha's teachings are translated and collected into the *Kanjur* in Tibetan: *Ka* meaning command, the Buddha's command, and *jur* meaning translation. This collection is over 100 volumes long. All of the teachings and writings of the great masters that followed the Buddha, having been translated into Tibetan, were collected into what is called the *Tenjur*. The Tenjur does not contain the Buddha's words but those written by the enlightened masters. *Ten* is short for *tenchö* meaning *shastra*, or commentary, and *jur* once again means translation.

Any text in the Tenjur must have two qualities: practicing in accordance with its teachings must firstly purify defilements and secondly liberate beings from the lower realms and samsara. Any text that has these qualities and was based on the teachings of Buddha was included within the Tenjur.

The five teachings the Lord Maitreya taught to Asanga, for example, are included within the Tenjur. In the last of these five teachings, the *Mahayana Uttaratantra*, Lord Maitreya actually describes his own teaching as tenchö (shastra), and therefore belonging in the Tenjur. In this text he says, "If all of the tenchö that I have taught were condensed into their essence, it would consist of these seven essential chapters." Here he was referring to the *Mahayana Uttaratantra*, which has seven chapters.[7] From this we can see that these teachings of Lord Maitreya are "tenchö" not "ka" – that is they are not commands from the Buddha himself.

The Tenjur comprises over 220 volumes of Tibetan texts. If all these were to be translated into English, there would be two, three or four times as many volumes as this. These two, the Kanjur and Tenjur, are like our old and new testaments; the Kanjur is like the Old Testament, and the Tenjur is like the New Testament, its commentary. I don't know if there is exactly the same relationship between the old and new testaments, but by calling them "old" and "new" it sounds like one is a commentary on the other.

How Buddhism Was Brought to Tibet

These developments form the basic history of the dharma in Indian Buddhism. The next thing to look at is how Buddhism was bought to Tibet. This happened in two ways. Some Tibetans went to India, found masters, spent many years receiving transmissions from them and practicing dharma, then translated texts into Tibetan before bringing them back to Tibet. There were also quite a few Indian masters who went to Tibet, such as Guru Rinpoche. These teachers gave direct teachings in Tibet.

As is usually the case in the history of religions, Tibetan Buddhism came into being through the patronage of kings. In Tibet it was particularly through the work of our great King Trisong Detsen that Buddhism arrived in Tibet. Trisong Detsen, along with Guru Rinpoche and the Abbot Bodhisattva Shantarakshita, bought about the translation of many texts from Sanskrit into Tibetan in a very short time. These three great masters worked together on this project. The King, as the patron, had young Tibetans sent to India to train in Sanskrit, and then had them translate texts. Some of the texts were translated early on and others were translated later, but most of them were translated within one, two or three generations – a great achievement.

The history of the different lineages that developed in Tibetan Buddhism after this are purely technical; a master would come to Tibet, or a disciple would go to India, they would end up somewhere in Tibet, build a temple and that would become their seat. From there the teachings would be transmitted to their followers and that would become a lineage. There are eight major lineages in Tibetan Buddhism. The Nyingma is one of these and another is the Kadam lineage. The Kadam lineage was brought to Tibet by Atisha Dipamkara, and later, after Tsongkhapa built Ganden monastery, it became known as the Gelug, or Ganden lineage. The third main lineage was originally called the Lamdre lineage but later became known as the Sakya. This was because its main seat, in the Tsang region of Tibet, was in a very gray place – there were no trees or greenery there and the earth there was pale. *Sa* means earth and *kya* means gray or pale. This description of the land surrounding its main monastery became the name of this lineage.

As well as these three lineages the Marpa Kagyu also developed. A Tibetan whose family name was Marpa founded this lineage. Traveling to India three times Marpa Lotsawa received transmissions from many enlightened masters, especially Naropa. Marpa spent twenty-one years in India, exactly sixteen years and seven months of this with his masters, and received all their transmissions. He bought back fourteen main Tantras to Tibet and his lineage is called the Marpa Kagyu.

At about the same time, a great master from an area in Tibet called Shang-Shung, Shedra Trungpo Naljor, went to India and received teachings from the female mahasiddhas Niguma and Sukkasiddhi. The teachings he bought back to Tibet from these two enlightened women are called the Shangpa Kagyu.

Then there is the lineage of the great man, Padampa Sangye, and the great lady Machig Lachi Drolma. Their lineage is a practice of Prajnaparamita we call *Chö*. Its original name was *Zhije*; *Zhi* means peace, *Zhije* means pacifier – the pacifier of all defilements. Chö means to cut through. The practice they developed is a shunyata, Prajnaparamita practice.

There was also another great master called Jonangpa. The main transmission he received was based on the Kalachakra Tantra. It is known as the *Jor-truk*: *Jor* means union and *truk* means six. Sometimes this lineage is called the *Jor-truk* lineage, and at other times the Jonangpa lineage.

The eighth lineage is that of the great master Druptub Ogyenpa. This lineage focuses mainly on breathing and physical exercises that we call *tsa-lung*. The main deity of these practices is the bodhisattva Vajrapani and its lineage is called the *Orgyen Nyen-drup*, or the *Dorje-sum Nyen-drup*. *Dorje-sum* means "the three vajras": the body vajra, the speech vajra and the mind vajra. *Nyen-drup* means "Approach and Accomplishment." These then are the eight lineages and this is how, through history and geography, they came to be.

Today there are only four or five fully functioning lineages. The Nyingma is fully functioning, the Marpa Kagyu is fully functioning, the Sakya is fully functioning and the Gelug is fully functioning. The Shangpa Kagyu almost disappeared, but during the time of the ninth Tai Situ it was resurrected. The eighth Tai Situ built Palpung monastery and the ninth Tai Situ recognized the potential of a child incarnation who would grow to become Jamgon Kongtrul Lodro Thaye. At Palpung Monastery, Jamgon Kongtrul Lodro Thaye helped to revive the Shangpa Kagyu, which had almost died out. It spread through the monastery, then throughout Tibet, and nowadays it has spread all over the world. The Shangpa Kagyu and the Karma Kagyu[8] have become like the same family.

The Tai Situpa is supposed to be an incarnation of Marpa and Drogon Raychen, a disciple of the first Karmapa. There were quite a few generations between Marpa and Drogon Raychen though, so Marpa has to have lived at least one life in between these two incarnations. Marpa's disciple was Milarepa, Milarepa's disciple was Gampopa and Gampopa had quite a few disciples, one of which was the first Karmapa, Dusum Khyenpa. The first Karmapa had a main or lineage disciple called Drogon Raychen. Quite a few incarnations after Drogon Raychen came the first Tai Situ. I am supposed to be the twelfth, a great honor, but I tell you I don't feel like Marpa.

Perhaps if I felt like Marpa then some of you would feel like Milarepa! But I don't know if you would like this very much either.

Marpa told Milarepa that if he wanted dharma teachings from him he had to build a house for his son – not for himself but for his son. He told him to build a triangular house. Milarepa couldn't understand why he had to build a triangular house. Nowadays it would be considered "new age," a pyramid or something, but in those days it did not make very much sense to Milarepa. So Marpa went and marked out the land in all the directions and told him how to build a triangular house. He also told Milarepa that nobody was to help him, he had to do it himself. Milarepa carried earth and stone on his back and built a triangular house. He had completed quite a lot of it when one day Marpa walked past and asked him what he was doing. Milarepa replied, "I am building a house for your son."

Marpa look at him and said, "Who told you to do that?"

Milarepa answered, "You did."

Marpa got very angry and beat Milarepa. Later Marpa said, "I was drunk, you really should build a house for my son a round one. Take every stone back to where you got it from, every piece of earth, and then start to build a round house."

Milarepa built the round house, then a half-moon shaped house before finally Marpa told him to build a square house, a normal house. So he built a nine-story building, out of stone and wood, which is still standing even today. He built it totally by himself for Marpa's son – not for Marpa but for Marpa's son. After undertaking many hardships like this Milarepa finally received transmissions from Marpa and through their practice became enlightened. For us, he is a great example.

This is how Marpa was but I don't feel like him. I would never dare tell anyone to build me a triangular house. Besides, if I did, as I don't have a son, I would have to live in it myself. I wouldn't know how to live in a triangular house! It is very bad Feng Shui. And these days if I told you to break down a house you had just built because I was drunk, there would be a court case against me. I don't feel like

Marpa, but I am a believer, so it is okay. Maybe I am an incarnation of Marpa's left sandal, if he wore any.

The Tai Situpa is supposed to be an incarnation of Marpa and from Drogon Raychen onwards he was always in the Karma Kagyu lineage. The Shangpa Kagyu lineage, which was revived in Palpung monastery, came about at the same time as the Marpa Kagyu. The Karma Kagyu came much later, but through history the Karma and Shangpa Kagyu lineages have became like brother and sister lineages. It is very interesting.

So that was the history of Tibetan, Vajrayana Buddhism made simple. I will stop here and spend some time answering your questions.

Questions

Question: There is a Chinese practitioner called C.C. Chang who translated some of Gampopa's work into Chinese. In his work he mentions that there are lots of similarities between Mahamudra, Chan Buddhism in the Chinese tradition and Zen Buddhism in the Japanese tradition.

Rinpoche: C.C. Chang, yes, I knew him. He passed away a long time ago. He came to my monastery, Palpung, during the time of the eleventh Tai Situ. I met him in America and in Malaysia. He wrote many books and was, I think, an upasaka.

I have heard that Chan and Zen are the meditation practices that were called "dhyana" in Sanskrit and when they where transmitted to China the pronunciation changed a little to became "Chan." From there it went to Japan and the pronunciation changed again so it became "Zen." It makes sense, but I am not sure how true it is. This is what some professors told me who did research into these things. I don't know that much about Zen Buddhism though, so I can't really make objective remarks on it. I know a little because the first English book I read from cover to cover was *Zen Mind, Beginner's Mind*, by Suzuki Roshi. There is one page in this book that is totally empty apart from a fly. It is as if somebody has closed the page and caught a fly. It is there in the middle of the page. That is very Zen, right?

I found this book very profound. It sounds simple but yet it is very difficult – the simplest things are the most difficult. I will give you an example. Try touching a fingertip on one hand to the fingertip of the next finger on the same hand. They are very close to each other, they are right there but to touch the two fingertips is very difficult. You could use a mirror to do it, or a camera, but with just your fingers it is very difficult. It is like trying to see my eye with my eye, very difficult. I can see my eyes in a mirror, but by themselves it is so close, so simple, but very difficult. In this book Zen is a little bit like this.

Mahamudra, by definition, is that everything is a gesture or manifestation of the essence, the dharmakaya. That is Mahamudra: *Maha* means great, *mudra* means manifestation, gesture or seal. It is like a trademark, a seal. The seal of the ultimate is on everything, the cleanest things, the dirtiest things, the holiest things, and the most unholy things – it is on everything. If I knew how to drink this quarter of a glass of water ultimately and perfectly, I would be a Buddha. I drink so many glasses of water a day, but because I don't know how to drink them ultimately and perfectly I don't become a Buddha. From the Mahamudra point of view, if you are able to understand and realize the ultimate essence of anything, you will understand and realize the ultimate essence of everything. To do this we try and recognize the ultimate, natural essence of our mind, which is within us. Doing this is also like trying to touch a fingertip from one hand with the next fingertip from the same hand because we need to realize who is trying to recognize the nature of whom. Trying to recognize the essence of the nature of our mind is very simple, yet very difficult.

From this point of view maybe there is some similarity. It is like the Zen koans of one hand clapping and so on, the examples used in Zen. These examples make sense from this point of view but from any other point of view one hand clapping doesn't make any sense. It would be like somebody trying to say something but not really having anything to say. From the Mahamudra point of view, however, it makes sense. I think that maybe what Suzuki Roshi wrote in *Zen Mind, Beginner's Mind* could be more easily understood by Mahamudra practitioners than by non-Mahamudra practitioners, and this is maybe why Lama Chang said this. He was a wonderful, nice person. Did you meet him?

Student: No.

Rinpoche: Oh, I see. He was a wonderful, very humble, very simple, very good person. I met him twice and my teacher met him many times, they spent many years together in my monastery when he was young. This was before we lost our country. Well we didn't really lose our country, it is still there. Lots of things happened there but every inch of it is still there.

Question: You mentioned one can virtually walk into an Ati yoga initiation and have an Ati yoga teaching today. So what do you think is a safe course to take? Would it be safer to start with Kriya yoga practices?

Rinpoche: Not necessarily.

Student: So then one should be instructed by a teacher?

Rinpoche: Yes. I will tell you how we go about it in my lineage. Other teachers, other lineages have their own way, but this is how we go about it. No matter who you are, first you must take refuge in the Buddha, dharma and sangha. Then you may do some basic practices like Chenrezig. At some point, however, you have to take the bodhisattva vows. Whether you take full upasaka vows or become a monk or nun is up to you, but you have to take basic precepts. After this you will receive teachings on the foundation practices. We have twelve foundations or preliminaries, and out of these we practice eight, in order.[9] Firstly, the four contemplations: the precious human life, death and impermanence, karma, and the causes of suffering in samsara. You have heard of these many times. I will elaborate on these when I explain the Seven Points of Mind Training.

Then those who are not going into long-term retreat begin by practicing another four foundations for purification and accumulation, part of what is commonly known as Ngondro practice. The first is prostrations, which focus on physical purification. Then we do recitations of the Vajrasattva mantra, which focuses on mental and oral purification. After this we do mandala offerings to accumulate merit and then guru yoga for the accumulation of wisdom and abhisheka or blessing transmissions like those we receive in initiations. How many times an individual does these practices depends on them; some people do them many times, other people do them twice, but most people do them at least once. Then we do practices like Nyungne, a fasting practice. People can do this practice as many times as they like, but a good number is one hundred and eight, we call this the *Nyungne cha gya*.[10]

After this, we usually receive an initiation into our main yidam. The main yidam of our lineage is Vajravarahi. It is our main yidam because the female aspect of the sambhogakaya represents wisdom, while the male aspect represents method. As method actually refers to the method for developing wisdom, we consider that which represents wisdom to be superior to that which represents method. This is why Vajravarahi is our main deity rather than Chakrasamvara.

Having received the Vajravarahi empowerment we do three stages of practice; outer, inner and secret – three practices, three stages. Initiates do a certain number of recitations, fire ritual and visualizations at each stage. Once we have completed these practices we receive the abhisheka of Chakrasamvara. Chakrasamvara also has a complete practice. After completing the practice of Chakrasamvara, practitioners will receive the initiation and do the practices of the Six Yogas.[11] Finally, after performing these they may be ready for the transmission of the nature of mind.[12]

Somewhere in among all of this the protector Mahakala's practice is also performed; this involves visualizing Mahakala, reciting the mantra and so on – the entire practice of Mahakala. Mahakala and Mahakali are always visualized together, they are just like

Chakrasamvara and Vajravarahi, and we consider them to be not only protectors but also deities. Other protectors are just protectors and not deities, but Mahakala and Mahakali are considered deities as well as protectors; they are a deity manifesting as a protector.[13]

This is one example of the way things can work. Common people, who don't do all of this, normally recite the mantra OM MANI PEME HUNG. They go to initiations and receive teachings but only say OM MANI PEME HUNG and do fasting practices from time to time. Their aim is to complete one hundred million recitations of OM MANI PEME HUNG. They repeat it again and again. Some very old people complete five, six, seven, eight, or ten hundred million recitations of OM MANI PEME HUNG. We call a hundred thousand recitations a "*tung*." This literally means a conch shell. They also use prayer wheels. Prayer wheels are spun clockwise, a conch shell is used underneath the prayers in the wheel and there is bamboo in between the two. Eventually the conch shell breaks the bamboo and that is supposed to equal one hundred million OM MANI PEME HUNG recitations. I know people who can complete a conch shell in a week in this way. Normally it takes six months, but if you are a really good practitioner and use it all the time you can do it in a week. Of course they are not using iron, they are using bamboo. If they were to use iron they would finish a conch shell in two hours, but not with bamboo. Some of these people then collect the finished conch shells to use as a mala. Malas like this show they have finished off all these conch shells. This is how they practice, very simply. If you want to do a more systematic practice, however, you could follow the path I described earlier.

Another way to practice is to prepare for and then do a three-year, three-month retreat. Everything is included within this retreat: preliminary practices, two protector practices, two deity practices and all the physical yogas including breathing. It is a solitary retreat, only fellow retreatants can speak to each other and some people even take vows of silence during this time. This way you can do these practices quickly. Three years and three months is nothing. If you are thirty-three years old, you have lived through three years and three months more than ten times.

Through all these processes there is not much distinction made between Kriya, Charya, Yoga and Anuttarayoga practices.

Question: Are Dzogchen and Mahamudra the same?

Rinpoche: Yes, of course. Mahamudra and Dzogchen are pretty much the same thing with different names, different lineages – Dzogchen is part of the Nyingma lineage – and slight differences in their methods. In Dzogchen particular methods such as *Treg chö*, Cutting Through practice, and *Tögal*, Direct Crossing, are emphasized. In our lineage, we say *Tse chig*, the stage of one-pointedness, *Trö drel*, the stage of non-conceptuality, *Röl chig*, the stage of one taste and *Gom me*, the stage of non-meditation. In the Dzogchen tradition they use different names for these stages of development.[14] They use different terminology, but I would say their essence is the same. I have received Dzogchen teachings and transmissions but I am not a Dzogchen practitioner, so I cannot say too much about it. These teachings are definitely talking about the same thing though.

Question: Most of us do not know Tibetan so when we attend prayer sessions we do the prayers through the English translation. Is that effective?

Rinpoche: This depends on the transmission. If the prayer is translated, the translator must have the lineage of that prayer, and the prayer should be read to you by somebody who holds the prayer's lineage. If all these things happen you receive the complete lineage of the prayer. Generally if you only read a translation from a book this will be less effective. This, of course, depends on the individual's devotion and many other things though, so you can't really generalize. If it is transmitted to you in English, or Hindi, you will have the lineage of that prayer in that language, so when you say it, it will be more meaningful.

Student: At least if we say it in English I understand it. If I say the same prayer in Tibetan I don't understand it.

Rinpoche: I understand what you are saying, but I say mantras in Sanskrit and I don't understand them either. Take for example the hundred syllable mantra of Vajrasattva, OM BENZRA SATO SAMAYA MANU PALAYA, BENZRA SATO TAYNO PATITRA DRIDHO MAY BHAWA, SUTO KAYO MAY BHAWA, SUPO KAYA MAY BHAWA, ANU RAKTO MAY BHAWA, SARWA SIDDHI MAY TRAYATSA, SARWA KARMA SU TSA MAY TSITAM SHRIYA KURU HUNG HA HA HA HA HO BHAGAWAN SARWA TATHAGATA BENZRA MA MAY MUNTSA BENZRI BHAWA MAHA SAMAYA SATO AY. I said this one hundred and ten thousand times when I was eighteen or nineteen years old. I didn't know exactly what it meant. I knew the general meaning, but not each of the words' meanings. Now I know it is not even correct Sanskrit, it should be, OM VAJRA SATWA SAMAYA MANU PALAYA, or something like that, but we don't say this because we received the transmission as OM BENZRA SATO SAMAYA. We say it as we received it, we don't correct it.

Question: How exactly did saying the Vajrasattva mantra affect you?

Rinpoche: It is the purification mantra, the mantra of the deity Vajrasattva. Vajrasattva is considered the crowning deity of all five Buddha families and each of these families represents the transformation of a defilement from amongst the five poisons – attachment, anger, ignorance, jealousy, and pride In Tibetan Vajrasattva is called *Rig Tamche kyi chab dag Dorje Sempa,* "the king of all five Buddha families," and we practice Vajrasattva to purify the defilements whose transformation is represented by the five Buddha families.[15]

Student: For the negative karma that we have done?

Rinpoche: It is the same thing, yes.

Student: Can you say it for somebody else?

Rinpoche: Yes of course, but how much it will affect them depends on certain factors. If they know you are saying it for them, are appreciative and believe it will help them it will benefit them more. If they don't know but would appreciate it if they knew, it will benefit them a little less, but if they don't know and don't appreciate it the blessings cannot be forced. It depends on these things.

Question: Which is more powerful, the thirty-five Buddha chant or this practice?

Rinpoche: There is no such thing as a "more powerful practice." The most powerful practice is the one done totally. When your body, speech, mind, motivation, intention – everything – is concentrated one hundred percent with faith, devotion and compassion, that is the most powerful practice. There is a Tibetan folk song, from my part of Tibet, which says, "Singing a nice song with a good heart is better then saying OM MANI PEME HUNG with a bad heart." OM MANI PEME HUNG is sacred but if you have a selfish, cruel, jealous mind and say OM MANI PEME HUNG it may be a lot better than not saying it, but not as good as singing a nice song with a very good heart, happiness and joy. This is a folk saying but there is a lot of wisdom in it.

Question: When you talked about practice, you mentioned studying Sutras as part of practice, real Sutras. Often times we read books on Buddhism and do practices, but at what point do we study Sutras?

Rinpoche: We study in order to be able to practice. We study because we want to know. If you know already, you don't have to study, unless you want to teach. If you don't study, even if you know the meaning's essence you will not know the details needed in order to teach others. In order to attain enlightenment you don't have to know everything. If you believe, that is good enough. If you know your practice, have faith in everything else and aim for Buddhahood, that is good enough. This is like Milarepa. He was not a scholar, he even said as much in his own songs, but he attained enlightenment. We study because we want to know, if we know already we should practice what we know.

Dharma study is a transmission in itself, but this can be very interesting. The other day I was talking with a professor from Delhi

University, a wonderful person, and he told me he was teaching Hevajra. He qualified this by saying it is not like "a teaching" but just part of his college's curriculum. The students pay a fee, he gets a salary, and he teaches Hevajra. This way of studying is okay but it is not a lineage transmission. If this professor had the lineage of transmission, if he had received these teachings, his students would become his disciples, not his students. On the other hand, if he doesn't have the transmission and has only researched the topic and put a book together making his own comments on it, then it really doesn't mean anything. It is just like what we do with a lost lineage. If we no longer have the lineage of a teaching, then we have to interpret it our own way.

When we study from the lineage, when we study a Sutra from a master who has the lineage of that Sutra, then that itself is a practice. The master will teach us so that we will be able to practice it more efficiently. Sutras talk about compassion, Sutras teach on loving-kindness, on emptiness, on the Buddha's lives, on morals and ethics. By learning these we can practice them, apply them in our day-to-day lives.

There are also certain Sutras, like the Diamond Sutra, that we can chant every day. In this way chanting is a practice in itself. In Sanskrit proper this Sutra is chanted, "Namo Ratna Trayaya, Nama Arya Avalokiteshvaraya." In Tibetan, however, we say a variation of this "Namo Ratna Tayayaya Namo Aya Awolokiteshwaraya." In Chinese I think you say, "Nama Hala Tala Tolaya." It is a different sound, it has changed, but you use the changed sound because that is the lineage you received. For example, I know now that the correct pronunciation of Chenrezig's mantra is OM MANI PADME HUM, but I continue to say OM MANI PEME HUNG, because that is how I received the transmission and I can't re-receive it. In order for me to say OM MANI PADME HUM I would have to receive the transmission from a Sanskrit speaking master. Having received this lineage reciting it in this way would then be effective.

There is a story, about a mahasiddha of the Nyingma lineage, I think. He was a mahasiddha of the Vajrakilaya practice – you know, *Dorje Phurba*, "The Vajra Knife One." You may know about phurbas because there are even movies made about them. In "The Golden Child" with Eddie Murphy they have something like a phurba. I think they copied it from Vajrakilaya. Anyway, this man was a master of Vajrakilaya, he was able to perform all kinds of miracles with his phurba. When he received the practice of Vajra-kili-kilaya he was told the deities name was Vajrachilichilaya. Later somebody told him that he was saying it wrong, that the deity's name was Vajra-kili-kilaya, but when he said Vajra-kili-kilaya no miracles happened. Then he said it like he had before, the way he had received the transmission – Vajrachilichilaya – and the miracles started happening again.

In order to get the true value of the practice I think the transmission is very important. Without the transmission it is just your own thing. It is like trying to create fire by rubbing two pieces of wood together; it takes a long, long time. If you have a ready-made match, on the other hand, it is very, very quick. The lineage is there, the living blessing is there and with it everything happens more efficiently.

Question: How should we see tantric Hinduism?

Rinpoche: I don't know. I do not know a lot about it. Buddha Shakyamuni, the fourth Buddha of this eon, was born into a Hindu family, and due to their shared location Hinduism and Buddhism have some similarities. This has been especially true since the time of Nagarjuna and the Hindu Archarya Adi Shankara. The holy places are the same, the names are similar; we have Vajravarahi and Chakrasamvara, the Hindus have Sri Chakra. There are a lot of similarities and it is very hard to see the differences. Without practicing Hindu Tantra, I wouldn't know what the differences are. I think this question would be better put to a Hindu master after you have listened to him or her teach. You have listened to me teach and are now asking questions, but if you were to base your questions to a Hindu priest on what I have said that would not make any sense. You will have to listen to what they have to say before you can ask them questions properly. If you are going to ask him what the differences between Vajrayana Buddhist Tantra and Hindu Tantra are though, I think he will say the same thing to you. He will tell you to come and ask me, or somebody like me.

Chapter 3

BUDDHIST PHILOSOPHY

I HAVE BEEN THROUGH A FEW aspects of Buddhist history and certain particulars I thought would help you establish a good foundation for Buddhist practice, or remind you of your good foundation.

PRAJNAPARAMITA

Now I would like to go through some of the teachings that relate to emptiness, the Prajnaparamita. Within the teachings of Lord Buddha the Prajnaparamita Sutras belong to the Sutra section. There are six main Sutras in this group, known as the six mothers, and eleven other Sutras, known as – let's say – the Daughter Sutras. In Tibetan these seventeen texts are called the *Yumse*: *yum* means mother, *se* means child. This *se* could be short for *se-pa* and therefore mean sons or *se-ma* and refer to daughters – it doesn't say which it is. This means the six main texts are described as "mothers" and the eleven smaller texts are described as "children," either daughters or sons.

These six main texts are all the Lord Buddha's words. The first of these has 100,000 *shlokas*. A *shloka* is a verse of four sentences; this means the first of these main texts has 400,000 sentences and is the largest Prajnaparamita Sutra. The second and second largest text has 20,000[16] shlokas, the third 18,000, the fourth 10,000, and the fifth 8,000. The sixth is known as the *Do-du-wa,* the condensed text. The *Do-du-wa* is quite a short text compared to the others. If you were to read the *Do-du-wa* quite quickly but not very quickly it would probably take you between half an hour and an hour. It is a text suitable to be read as a daily practice. The 100,000 shloka text, on the other hand, runs to twelve huge volumes and is certainly not able to be read as a daily practice.

Out of the Rinpoches around today in our lineage, one of the best readers is Sangye Nyenpa Rinpoche. If he reads from dawn to dusk, he can finish three volumes – two volumes comfortably – where it might take me one and a half to two days to finish one volume. It is an enormous task to read this many of these very thick volumes. According to the standard Western way of counting pages, where both sides of a page are counted, each of these volumes would have 800 to 1,000 large pages. [Tibetan texts have many different page sizes.] The pages of these volumes are called "arrow size;" they are the size of an arrow in length, in other words quite large texts.

The texts known as the "Eleven Daughters," include the 700, 500, 300, 150, 50 and 25 shloka Prajnaparamita Sutras. They also include the Prajnaparamita Sutras requested by the disciples Rabtsel Namnön (Suvikranta Vikrami) and Koishika, the one word Prajnaparamita Sutra and the Prajnaparamita Sutra of a few sentences. Finally there is the Prajnaparamita Sutra known as the *Heart Sutra*.

The reason some of these texts are called "mothers" and others are called "daughters" is not necessarily because of their size. It depends on whether or not the individual text includes the eight aspects of the Prajnaparamita; any text that has all eight aspects is known as a "mother" text and any text that does not have all eight aspects is known as a "daughter" text. These eight aspects were clearly enumerated by Lord Maitreya in his text called the *Abhisamayalankara,* or the *Sherab kyi par rol tu chin ba men ngag gi ten chö ngon bä tog bä jen* in Tibetan. In English it is called, *The Ornament of Clear Realization: An instructional shastra of the Prajnaparamita*.[17] This text was the first of the five teachings Lord Maitreya taught to his disciple Asanga in the Tushita heaven. It is a Prajnaparamita text taught in these eight aspects. Each of the eight aspects or characteristics is to be found in a separate chapter so they can be easily understood.

When we try and find these eight characteristics in a big text like the 100,000 shloka Prajnaparamita, which is usually in twelve huge volumes, it is difficult. These eight characteristics are not lined up in order so trying to find them is like trying to separate out the ingredients of a fruit shake. It is like trying to separate the mango out from the kiwi fruit and the orange when they have all been blended together.

These eight characteristics are an important part of Mahayana Prajnaparamita practice and as many of you read the *Heart Sutra* I think it will be helpful to go through them, even if some of you already know them. I will go through them according to Lord Maitreya's clear description in the *Abhisamayalankara*.

One interesting thing about this text is that it begins and ends in the same place. It begins with the motivation and ends with the fulfillment of that motivation. The first chapter of the book is omniscience, the Buddha-essence or Buddha-nature, the *namchen*. The second chapter describes the knowledge of the path, *lam sheba*. This knowledge of the path fulfills the essence's aspiration. The third deals with the knowledge of the foundation, *zhi sheba*. This foundation is the essence, the omniscience. It is a mystery. It is out there. We may think the Buddhas are great and wonderful. We may think the bodhisattvas are great and wonderful. We may think that we want to be like the Buddhas and bodhisattvas but we can only achieve this if we have the Buddha-essence. It is the basis for this achievement. Only because we have Buddha-nature can we become Buddhas.

It is also only because of the Buddha-nature that we can purify the karma we have created. It is impossible to accumulate good or bad karma ultimately because the creation of karma is dualistic and it is only because karma cannot be created ultimately that it can be purified. All the karma we have accumulated for countless lifetimes can be purified because ultimately it never happened, it only happened relatively. As long as we are dualistic it is still relevant, but as soon as we are free from dualism it has been purified. Through this foundation, the Buddha-essence, we can say, "I wish to become a Buddha in order to lead all sentient beings to Buddhahood." Without this base it would just be blah, blah, blah.

If you are not a Buddhist you may use other words to describe this process. You can say everyone has limitless potential. You can say everyone's essence is perfect, limitless, sacred and holy. You can use whichever words you like to describe the non-dualistic primordial essence. Whatever you call it this is the third of the eight characteristics.

These three characteristics refer to the existence and knowledge of omniscience, the path and the base. The next few characteristics describe the implementation of this knowledge. The first of these and the fourth chapter of the *Abhisamayalankara* describes the complete implementation, the *namchen jorwa*. In this text this topic is described by 173 stages of meditation and contemplation. This covers all 173 aspects of the Prajnaparamita practice in a step-by-step way.

The fifth characteristic, and the second implementation, is a description of the *tsemor jorwa*. This means the implementation that reaches towards the top. The word *tsemo* means the peak or tip of something. Practicing this implementation means you are climbing towards the top. Beings implementing the aspects of meditation in this way still practice every aspect, though. They progress in every aspect of meditation. In the same way that saying, "I take refuge in the Buddha" today will not have the same depth and profundity as saying it after ten years of practicing refuge would, they increase their understanding of these aspects through the implementation of their knowledge. They may be using the same words, saying the same things, but the meaning becomes deeper and more profound.

The sixth characteristic, and third implementation, describes implementing all these 173 aspects of the Prajnaparamita in one session. That is being able to comprehend each of them, from step one to step 173, one after another without a break in one meditation session. It is called the *thar ji bä jorwa*, the gradual implementation.

The seventh characteristic, and fourth implementation, is a description of how these 173 aspects become non-dual. It is called the *kechigmä jorwa*, the momentary application. All the aspects are implemented in a snap of the fingers. The other ways of implementing these practices were to go through them one by one, but here they are all implemented at once. Not one by one. Not one each month, or one each minute. They are all implemented in a single second. The only way this can possibly happen is when the aspects are observed non-dualistically. Otherwise they could not be comprehended in an instant. How could your mind comprehend 173 points in a moment dualistically? It would be impossible.

The eighth and last characteristic and chapter is a discussion of the final fruition, the dharmakaya, the *chö ku*. Any texts that teach on all eight of these topics is called a "Mother Prajnaparamita Sutra" and those that only focus on seven, six, five or fewer of them are called "Daughter Prajnaparamita Sutras."

Included within the six Mother Sutras is the brief text I mentioned earlier, the *Do-du-wa* that can be read as a daily practice. This text is actually a chapter of the third Mother Sutra that has 18,000 shlokas. There are eighty-seven chapters in this Sutra, and the eighty-fourth chapter is the *Do-du-wa*. It is also called a "Mother" Sutra by itself because all eight aspects of the Prajnaparamita are included within this one chapter. When this chapter is extracted from the 18,000 shloka text, the remaining text still contains these eight aspects. Therefore, both this chapter and the entire text are both considered "Mother" Prajnaparamita Sutras. If they were not enumerated separately like this there would only be five Mother Sutras and eleven Daughter Sutras. As it is there are six Mother Sutras and eleven Daughter Sutras.

There are also other Prajnaparamita texts that are not included within these two groupings; such as the *The Essence of the Sun, The Essence of the Moon, The Prajnaparamita Kuntuzangpa, The Prajnaparamita at the Request of Vajrapani,* and *The Prajnaparamita at the Request of Vajra Jeltsen.* A *Jeltsen* is like a flag, a victory banner. These texts, and many others, are not included within the seventeen texts mentioned earlier but are still considered Prajnaparamita texts.

Now you know where the Prajnaparamita teachings, the teachings on emptiness, come from. It is also important to note the connection between the teachings on emptiness and their meaning, how they are both part of the Prajnaparamita. The Prajnaparamita and emptiness have the same meaning; Prajnaparamita means the wisdom paramita.[18]

I am sure my Sanskrit pronunciation is not very good. I only studied it for two or three weeks. My Guru, His Holiness the Karmapa, invited a Sanskrit professor to Rumtek to teach us but he left after two or three weeks and never came back. I think maybe it was our food or our habits. He was very learned, I think he knew seventeen or eighteen languages, a wonderful person, but somehow he couldn't stand us. In those days I, at least, was a real teenager. I was fifteen or sixteen and he had to teach a handful of teenagers like me. It was too difficult for him I guess so he left after two weeks and never came back! Because of this my Sanskrit is totally zero and I will pronounce these words in the traditional way other Tibetans pronounce them.

I actually have an important historical connection to Sanskrit. The eighth Tai Situpa was supposed to have been one of the greatest Sanskrit scholars since the initial period of the transmission of Buddhism to Tibet. During this initial transmission, the time of Guru Rinpoche and slightly afterwards, there were many Tibetans who mastered Sanskrit. After this time though, there was a gap of about 800 years until the eighth Tai Situpa became a master of Sanskrit. He encountered Sanskrit panditas in Nepal who told him that if he were to visit India he would receive the honor of thirteen peacock umbrellas. I don't know exactly what that means. I believe it is umbrellas with many levels. Not actually thirteen different umbrellas but one umbrella with many levels, they keep adding more and more levels. I think they represent something similar to a general's stars, they would have shown he had enormous respect because of his knowledge of Sanskrit.

When we arranged a program once for His Holiness' teachings in Talkatora, a stadium in Delhi, he only had one umbrella but it was a peacock umbrella, very beautifully embroidered with many glass or gem ornaments on it. It was beautiful.

Anyway, I have a history behind me that should make me very good at Sanskrit but unfortunately I am not. I am not blaming our teacher who left but somehow I haven't been able to learn Sanskrit since then. Now I am not at an age where learning comes easy so I don't think I am going to become a Sanskrit master in this life. My English isn't very good either. I never learned from a teacher, I just picked it up. My English writing is very, very bad. I only know how words are spelt differently, like the difference between "good" and "god" and that if you reverse "god" it becomes "dog." I know this kind of thing, but beyond this my written English is terrible. My spoken English is not as bad as my written English but I am sure a linguist would find grammatical problems in every few sentences. I really cannot afford to care or worry about this though, otherwise I would be so self-conscious I wouldn't dare say anything to all of you.

Now back to the connection between Prajnaparamita and emptiness: prajna means wisdom, paramita means completion, accomplishment, reaching beyond. If you want to reach the far shore of a river, the paramita of river crossing is reaching the other side. Prajnaparamita means to reach beyond wisdom. What is the difference between wisdom and reaching beyond the accomplishment of wisdom? Reaching beyond wisdom is the realization of primordial wisdom. Wisdom itself is derived from primordial wisdom but you can have wisdom without realizing primordial wisdom, there is a difference between the two. For example, if you put an expert businessman, politician and computer technician together for a weekend or three-day session they may come up with a brilliant master plan that has lots of insight and depth. To develop this plan would take wisdom but each one of these individuals may be in a terrible state. They may have lots of problems at home, for example, and as their primordial wisdom has not been realized, they can only derive wisdom from their primordial wisdom as part of a team. In this way, wisdom and primordial wisdom are different.

In Tibetan, the word for wisdom is *sherab*. *She* means knowing, *rab* means best and profound. Primordial wisdom is *yeshe*, primordial knowing. You may have *sherab* but your *yeshe* is primordially within you as your essence. When you have *sherab* you can be very intelligent, very good at certain things, but as long as you also have ego – the ignorance of self[19] – your primordial wisdom will not manifest. If your primordial wisdom has not manifested you will still experience all kinds of limitations to your knowledge: when your primordial wisdom is manifest there are no limitations. Your limitless potential and your primordial wisdom are the same thing; the Prajnaparamita is the realization of this primordial wisdom.

What does that have to do with emptiness? It is very simple. "Emptiness" means that everything is nothing more and nothing less than the interdependent manifestation of everything else. It doesn't mean you are not there, it doesn't mean I am not here. It doesn't mean I am not talking, it doesn't mean you are not hearing. I am talking, you are hearing, you are taking notes. You are there, I am here and each one of us has a history, a family tree, pluses and minuses, but all of these things we have are nothing more and nothing less than the interdependent manifestation of everything else.

Look at the relationships between us in this room. Some of us feel very clear about each other, some of us might be a little bit confused about each other, some of us might be positively allergic to each other and some of us could be negatively allergic to each other. All of these relationships exist because of our countless lifetimes of relationship. To be bold and clear, each one of us has been a father, a mother, a brother, a sister, a husband, a wife, a lunch, a dinner, an enemy, a friend, a neighbor and a stranger to everybody else in this room countless times. Each one of us has been a king, a queen and a god. Each one of us has been to hell and has been all the animals you can think of – dinosaurs, tyrannosaurus, amoebas, earthworms, cockroaches, beautiful peacocks, mighty lions. You name it, each one of us has been it, not once but countless times.

The result of all this is the life we have today. This life is a final fingerprint of all the past lives we have lived. How we look, how we sound, how we feel, and how we perceive are all results of our past lives. This is what we are. This lifetime is the tip of the iceberg, the signature, the reflection, the production, the cream, the butter of all our countless past lives. In this way we are all unique, each one of us is a masterpiece, a piece of art that has taken billions of lifetimes to create. This is what we have managed to create!

This also means time is relative, that perceptions are relative. All aspects of the environment out there and the perceptions experienced inside our heads are relative. "Relative" in that they are not ultimate. My manifestation is here and your manifestation is there this is true, but it is a relative truth. Ultimately I am not this. Ultimately you are not that. Ultimately you and I are the Buddha's equals but because of the relative karma we have been accumulating for countless lifetimes I am not yet a Buddha and neither are you.

I don't mean to be negative but we are like a big piece of coal with a very large diamond at its center. This big piece of coal may be very nice and clean or it may be very dirty and messy. It may have a nice shape or it may have an ugly shape. It may be in a bad place, it may be in a good place, it may be put on an altar, it may be under a pile of garbage, but it has a diamond in it and that diamond is the best and biggest of all diamonds. It is the limitless potential in each one of us, our primordial wisdom, and right now it is covered by relative truth – a relative truth that is our own doing.

The Buddha said, "*Tong pa nyi la zuk me, tsol wa me, du she me, du che nam me.* There is no form, no feeling, no this, no that, no eye, no ear, no nose, no form to look at, no sound to hear." In manifesting his teachings on the Prajnaparamita, the Buddha went into all this detail. In the very short *Heart Sutra*, each of these details is included very clearly. It says, "Form is empty," but it doesn't stop there, it also says, "Emptiness is form." Just saying, "Form is empty" does not complete the equation, so the Buddha also said, "Emptiness is form." Then he said, "Emptiness is not other than form," and "Form is not other than emptiness." After this the Buddha went on and on describing feelings, perceptions, effort, consciousness and so on in this way.

For this reason it is important to know the connection between the Prajnaparamita and emptiness. Otherwise we will have a strange perception of what the Prajnaparamita is and what emptiness is. I have seen this confusion in people. I have seen it in some very devoted, very hardworking practitioners. They have some pieces of the puzzle missing from their practice. They tend to think that emptiness means something like "everything is nothing" and that the Prajnaparamita is something so very complicated and hard to understand that they don't even try to study it. All they do is read a Prajnaparamita Sutra every day. Yet if you connect emptiness and the Prajnaparamita clearly it takes care of this misperception, it becomes very simple.

The Prajnaparamita is about primordial wisdom. Primordial wisdom is the essence of everything, the emptiness that is the ultimate truth. The way everything manifests is relative truth. This is the connection. Emptiness is actually a very simple subject to understand, and by understanding it everything makes sense. Otherwise everything is very hard to explain. Why do you think the way you think? Why do I think the way I think? Why do you look where you look? Why do I look where I look? Why does the world manifest in such a way? Why do things exist in certain ways? Why are some things extinct and other things manifest? Why? How? Without an understanding of emptiness you have no really satisfying, commonsense, true answers.

Without understanding emptiness I would have to draw simple conclusions like, "It is my fate," or, "It is predestined," or "It was a bad accident," or, "It was a good accident," or, "Somebody made me like this because he or she wanted me this way." There are all kinds of easy conclusions like this that will make us feel temporarily okay. There may even be somebody else who agrees with us and says, "Yes, that's true." Then when three, four or five people agree with us we may become comfortable about our belief. We may even accept it as fact. If you really sit down and think clearly though – and the limitless potential we all have enables us to think carefully and clearly – then these kinds of conclusions don't make any sense.

If somebody had the ability to make me, why didn't they make me perfect? If we think on this theory a little more deeply the person who made us becomes responsible for all our problems. If that person made me this way, he, she or whoever it was is responsible for all of my problems. They cannot just take credit for all the good things and blame me for all the bad things. That would be saying, "I made you to do good but you won't listen so you do bad things." They cannot say this, there has to be two-way traffic. If a person has the power to make you, they would have to be able to make you any way they wanted.

Easy conclusions like this are okay for making people feel comfortable from day to day; they are like finding a nice pillow to lie down on, a glass of wine, nice air conditioning, or even nice music to put us to sleep. They can do this, but they cannot really take us any further. We cannot evolve through thinking like this. It does not help us find out exactly what we could be. It is not a bad thing, it does act as a stopgap measure, but the Prajnaparamita breaks through stopgap measures.

I am not talking about a particular religious view here, just reality. As Buddhists, for example, we all know about karma, but if karma is "hard cooked" it becomes fate and we look at it as ultimate truth. If karma was the ultimate truth we would all be finished, we could never become Buddhas. It would take countless lifetimes to purify the karma of drinking a glass of water, or even to purify the karma we accumulate by killing all the germs in the water to make it drinkable. We accumulate all this negative karma before we drink a drop. There must be ten thousand, or maybe scientists would even say ten million, germs killed in order to make one glass of water drinkable. It is not that these germs are so small we can't see them and therefore there is no karma in killing them. This is a false assumption; we take many lives to make one glass of water drinkable.

As we walk, how many little beings do we squash? Walking from over there to here how many dust mites did I kill? I am very heavy, how many of their hearts came out of their mouths when I stood on them? How many of their intestines oozed out? How many of their eyes popped out when I stood on them? To them I would be like

Gulliver in Lilliput. Going from that side of the room to this would be like Gulliver's travels for all these little creatures living there with their families, their little dust-mite babies, their cousins and nephews. Just by walking from there to here I squashed many of them.

This is why in India we have a religious group called the Jains who put white cloth on their mouths to make sure they don't breath in any insects, never walk on carpet, and carry a piece of wood to sit on. They are also very careful not to stand on insects. The real masters of this religion don't even wear clothes and take a long time to eat their meals. They take one handful of food, look at it and inspect it very carefully to ensure it contains no bugs and then eat it, even though these meals are vegetarian. In this religion there are also nuns, I think, who are covered totally by cloth and carry a very soft, cotton broom to sweep away small insects in front of the masters when they walk. These masters themselves wear very special shoes that are soft like cotton and when they walk they make a sound, like ringing a bell, to drive away all the bigger insects. They do their best, but even if we behaved like them, if there was no emptiness, how many lifetimes would it take just to purify the karma of drinking a glass of water?

This is the greatness, the sacredness, and the profoundness of the Lord Buddha's second turning of the wheel, the Prajnaparamita, which he manifested at Rajgir on the top of Vulture's Peak. There he said that, "Everything is nothing more and nothing less than the interdependent manifestation of everything else." This means we have hope. Our hope is based on this truth, the ultimate truth that we are perfect at all times; that ultimately everything is perfect at all times because everything is *shunyata*. I am *shunyata* – emptiness – everything is emptiness, perfect.

Relatively, as long as I have defilements, this shunyata is only something I can understand intellectually and have faith in. As long as I have defilements I cannot experience it directly. I can have confidence that enlightenment is possible, but relatively we have to do lots of hard work to achieve it. Should I say, "hard work" or "honorable work"? I don't know. All honorable work is hard, and all dishonorable work is not. We have a lot of honorable work to do. I will give you a very simple but cruel example of how honorable work is difficult. This example happens all over the world. It takes a lot of time and energy to make a good human being. The father, the mother, the relatives, the family, the school, the college, the teachers, the tutors, the doctors all use everything they have got for about thirty years to bring about a good human being. It takes about thirty years from the time a baby is born until they become a complete person, someone you don't have to worry about going in the wrong direction. Until they are thirty people can be influenced negatively because they lack experience. As they have not been exposed to certain things, they can be overwhelmed when they experience them. Even though today's legal age of adulthood is eighteen, it really isn't the case that we become adults at eighteen. It is very difficult to influence a truly mature thirty year old, but even quite mature twenty-five year olds can be much more easily influenced.

Then of course we may have a mid-life crisis at forty or fifty where a little window opens through which we can be negatively influenced. Somebody may flatter us and say, "You really don't look that old." And we may think, "I don't look that old," go out and buy a new, red Ferrari and go bungee jumping. Even if bungee jumping at that age is very dangerous and we may break our back we may still try it to prove to ourselves that even though we are forty, fifty or sixty, we are not like a forty, fifty or sixty year old. There is this window of time in which we may do these things, but generally it takes about thirty years to really set a person.

Even then, though, all this hard work can be destroyed with no cost in the snap of a finger. To bring up someone well takes so much effort but one careless, cruel – or maybe not even cruel, maybe ignorant person can destroy all this work by, for example, killing this well brought up person just to steal some money from their pocket to buy drugs with. This kind of thing happens all the time. Anything that is good to do is not easy, but anything that is not so good to do is quite easy.

This is the way things are relatively. Although ultimately everything is perfect and emptiness, relatively we need constant effort, awareness and diligence to continue progressing. From this point of view, it is very hard work. It is only just before we reach the first bodhisattva level that we can say, "Okay now I don't need to do anything because everything will happen by itself." We call this state *zopa,* "forbearance," the third level of the second of the five paths, the path of application: the path of application has four levels, warming, summit, forbearance and highest worldly dharma.[20] The five paths are accumulation, application, seeing, meditation and no more learning. When we reach this state of *zopa* everything will happen automatically, but until we reach this state we have to stay totally on our toes; we have to use our ears, eyes, nose and tentacles – everything we have – to detect the negative influences that may overwhelm us. As Buddhists, we always have to be disciplined and follow the guidelines of Lord Buddha. If you are not Buddhists then you have to implement the guidelines of whichever religion you follow.

Rangtong and Shentong[21]

Everything is also relatively empty, as is exemplified by the different emphases placed on the concept of emptiness in the different schools of Buddhism. There are so many of these different schools.[22] Here, however, I am only going to go through three of them from my notes, as examples. The first school is called the *Rangtong Mä-gag*, [Proponents of a Self-Empty, Non-affirming Negation]. *Rang* means "self," *tong* means "emptiness," *mä* means "non-existence" and *gag* means "total cessation." How does this school describe emptiness? They say the essence of everything, including the concept of "everything" itself, does not have any true, solid existence. Emptiness is nothing, from the forms we can see up to enlightenment itself nothing exists in a solid manner. This is the view of the Rangtong Mä-gag School, non-existence by itself.

Then there is the *Rangtong Ma-yin-gag* [Proponents of a Self-Empty, Affirming Negation]. The negation *Mä*, which the previous school asserted, means something doesn't exist at all. The negation *Ma-yin* means "it is not that." There is a difference between these two negations. For example, if somebody is looking for Mr Agawul, and Mr Agawul is not here, his absence is the negation *Mä*; his not being here is *Mä*. If, on the other hand, the person looking for Mr Agawul has mistaken Mr Marter for Mr Agawul and we say, "He is not Mr Agawul, he is Mr Marter," this kind of negation is a *Ma-yin*. The first negation says he is not here, the second says he is not this. A *Mä-gag* means "not there," but a *Ma-yin-gag* means "not that." With a *Ma-yin-gag* we are saying that it is not Mr Agawul, it is Mr Marter.

How then does this particular school or lineage, the Rangtong Ma-yin-gag, describe Buddha-nature? It describes it as lacking a solid, permanent entity and as having a nature that is ineffable, indescribable. That is, it is not there as a dualistic, solid entity because its nature is unexplainable. Buddha-nature, the primordial wisdom itself, does not have any solid existence because it is ineffable, unexplainable – there is no example for it. We do not have to use Buddha-nature as our example of a phenomenon, we can use any phenomena, but if we use Buddha-nature it is easier to understand.

The Rangtong Mä-gag School says there is nothing and the Rangtong Ma-yin-gag school says it is ineffable, unexplainable and unimaginable. The third school is the *Shentong Ma-yin-gag*. The only Shentong School is the *Ma-yin-gag*; there is no Shentong Mä-gag school. Remember, "Mä" means "to not exist." The Shentong Ma-yin-gag School says that Buddha-nature is always there, it is never not there. This presence is one of its qualities. It is there, but it is not dualistic. The non-dualistic, primordial essence is there but it is void of any kind of dualistic existence. It is not there like a table, not there like a thought, not there as a subject, not there as an object. These words refer to "other things," they are dualistic. The Buddha-nature is a non-dualistic, limitless, primordial perfection that is always present.

This is the view of the Shentong Ma-yin-gag School of which I am a follower. Being a follower of this school means I will never say we are nothing; I will say we are everything. I will say our limitless essence is ineffable, indescribable perfection. I will say it is the same as the dharmakaya of the Buddha but it is not there dualistically as a subject or an object. I will say the primordial essence is there but that it is free from dualism. This is the view of the Shentong Ma-yin-gag School.

These three examples describe a little of the various Buddhist philosophical schools, but there are so many others. The differences in views of the schools sometimes even developed further and became schools by themselves. The three I described were the Rangtong Mä-gag, the Rangtong Ma-yin-gag and the Shentong Ma-yin-gag. There is no Shentong Mä-gag but the Rangtong School has both a Mä-gag and a Ma-yin-gag version. The Rangtong Mä-gag says that the Buddha-nature itself is empty, it doesn't exist. The Rangtong Ma-yin-gag says it does not exist because its quality cannot be described. The Shentong Ma-yin-gag says its essence exists but not dualistically. In *Shentong*, *Shen* means other, *tong* again means empty. "Empty of other" means empty of a dualistic entity, but the non-dualistic, perfect essence that has a limitless potential is there in everyone and everything at all times.

There has been so much debate between these three schools that volumes have been written on them. One of the greatest texts written by a Shentong master in our lineage is called, *The Faith of Shentong, the Lion's Roar*. It sounds very nice, "Lion's Roar," these days there is no greater roar than the roar of a lion. Maybe the tyrannosaurus had a greater roar but they are a long time gone. The lion, the king of the animals, the king of the jungle, has the loudest, most majestic roar. This title likens the words of the Shentong Ma-yin-gag to this lion's roar; ultimately everything else can fall into it.

The Shentong followers, for the sake of debate, will say there is no better way to describe the essence of the Buddha than the Shentong Ma-yin-gag. Actually, though, if you learnt the Rangtong Mä-gag view properly, in the end it becomes the same as the Shentong Ma-yin-gag and if you learn the Shentong Ma-yin-gag truly, in the end you will have no problems with the Rangtong Mä-gag, or the Rangtong Ma-yin-gag. In the end there will be no problem between the different approaches, but you really have to study hard to reach this point. Reaching this understanding from the point of view of the Rangtong Mä-gag may be a little harder than reaching it from the point of view of the Rangtong Ma-yin-gag, from which in turn it may be a little harder to reach this point of view than from the Shentong Ma-yin-gag. But of course you are hearing this from a Shentong practitioner and you shouldn't forget that. Anyway in the end it is really the same thing.

The description of emptiness has evolved in very subtle ways into many, many schools. The transmission of teachings on emptiness may be given in various ways, but they truly are the key to the basic definitions of enlightenment, samsara, karma and all the other things that the dharma involves, that life involves. The Lord Buddha's teachings on emptiness are very profound. Of course all of the Lord Buddha's teachings are profound, but when he taught at Rajgir, he manifested much more than when he manifested the Four Noble Truths in Varanasi. The Four Noble Truths are a very important base but by the time he manifested the Prajnaparamita teaching, his disciples had evolved much more. In these teachings he not only describes good and bad, but also the essence of everything that is good and bad. Still later the Tantra aspect of the teachings manifested, but I will stop here, this subject is quite vast so you may have lots of question.

Questions

Question: Could you describe the difference between Rangtong Mä-gag and Rangtong Ma-yin-gag again?

Rinpoche: Rangtong Mä-gag says there is nothing. Rangtong Ma-yin-gag says it is ineffable, indescribable. That is the difference. Rangtong Ma-yin-gag is closer in view to the Shentong Ma-yin-gag.

Question: Can you say something about ignorance, and it being co-emergent with wisdom?

Rinpoche: Actually ignorance could not exist if it were not for wisdom. Ignorance is like wisdom's shadow. You have the capacity to know, you have a limitless potential and because of that when you don't know, there is ignorance. Ignorance, ego, self and I are all the same thing. There are four sentences, written in a prayer by the third Karmapa, that describe this.

> *Self-appearance, which never existed, has confused itself into projections;*
> *Spontaneous intelligence, because of ignorance, has confused itself into a self;*
> *By the power of dualistic fixation one wanders in the realm of existence –*
> *May ignorance and confusion be resolved.*

The object never existed out there; it is my own perception but I have mistaken it as an object. The second sentence says that I constantly encounter my realization – the essence of my self, my awareness – but I mistake it for "I." Due to this everything out there becomes an object and everything in here becomes a subject. Dualism develops out of these two types of ignorance, these two steps of ignorance, and I wander around samsara in circles. Samsara actually means to go around in circles. The final sentence requests that we expose this process. That this is exposed to us and we realize the illusion of ignorance.

My environment, all of this is the nirmanakaya and the sambhogakaya, a pure land, but I don't recognize it. I see a table with lots of things on it and all kinds of people. I know the names of most of these people and the faces of almost everyone. It is quite an interesting room. I am not certain why some things have been done in certain ways in this room, but it is a nicely put together room. I don't perceive it as a mandala though, and I don't perceive myself as a Buddha. I perceive myself as someone who was born somewhere, became something, came here to India and grew up here. I perceive myself as someone to whom many things have happened. I remember what I used to do, what I am doing now, what I know and what I don't know. I perceive myself like this.

Based on this perception I go around in circles. Sometime these circles are so big I don't even realize I am going in circles! Sometimes the circle is so small I not only realize I am going in circles but also pass out, or throw up. When I go around in big circles, I call that success. When you are successful you are going around in circles so big you don't even know you are going around in circles. When you are in trouble the circles are so small it is like you are spinning.

This is the definition of wisdom and ignorance. When you realize something, you understand what you haven't realized. Therefore wisdom and ignorance are two sides of the same hand, they are connected. The transformation of ignorance is wisdom and it happens in many different ways.

Question. So one could say that ignorance is a manifestation of primordial wisdom?

Rinpoche: You can definitely say that, with full confidence to anybody. If this were not the case where does it come from? It is like saying the sharpest shadow is the outcome of the brightest light. Ignorance is the outcome of our limitless potential. The reason we are so greedy, for example, the reason it is so impossible for us to be content if we decide not to be content, is that we have a limitless potential for anything. We have to work quite hard to decide, "Okay, enough. I have this and that, it is enough." We have to keep saying this to ourselves and pull on our own ears, otherwise our greed would have no end. If we just let our attachment, anger, jealousy and pride take over there would be no end to them. Take jealousy for example: if we don't control it we will be jealous of our own brothers and sisters, our own wives and husbands, our own children, our own parents. We may start off being jealous of other people who are not close to us, but if we don't control it, it may develop like this. Greed can also develop like this, and hatred, there is no end to them. There is no way to fulfill the appetite of our ego. Why? Ironically, because our potential's essence has no limit. This is the flip side of our potential; the brighter the light, the sharper the shadow.

We need to know how to take care of this potential. We do not take care of it by doing everything we like, hoping we will become tired of whatever it is we are doing and not want to do it anymore.

There is no such point. Behaving like this we may even end up in jail where we can't have what we want, where you are told what you can and cannot have. Apart from something like imprisonment there will be no end to our behavior.

If we continue to behave like this we may also end up "meeting a mother's son." This is a Tibetan expression, an eastern Tibetan expression. If someone is being very greedy and manipulative, taking advantage of others, we say they have never met "a mother's son." "A mother's son" is a strong man, a strong person who will not take any nonsense from them. So if somebody is being a bully, getting away with everything and taking advantage of everyone, we say they need to meet a mother's son. Their greed will stop if they meet a mother's son, lose a few teeth and have to "Sit in their own chair." This is the way we say, "Be put in your place." This is a rough but clear way to describe this process.

We have an impossible appetite like this because we have a limitless potential. Indulging in everything we have an appetite for is not the way to deal with it though. This only makes it worse. The way to deal with it is first to be content, second to take precepts, and third by practicing meditation so that our limitless potential can manifest. When we have no limitations whatsoever, when we have nothing more to want, we become a Buddha. A Buddha is not greedy because they have no limitations. When our limitless potential is fully developed, we have no limitations and are a Buddha. This is the ultimate goal for every one of us. When our limitless potential is combined with ignorance, however, we develop all the other defilements, like unlimited greed.

For example, a long time ago people had to wait about six months to get a reply from letters they sent across the ocean. They would wait, and when they received their answer they would be very happy. Now we can e-mail these letters directly, we can do a six month or one year job in an instant and even correct the spelling of the person replying to us on our computer, yet we still don't think we have enough time. Now we can also be more certain of delivery. When letters were sent by ship, the ship might have sunk in the middle of the ocean and no one would have received our letters. Still, with all this uncertainly, people got things done and were happy, perhaps even happier than we are now.

Now we have so much; I don't even have to go somewhere to see something. Somebody with a video-camera can go instead of me, shoot a video and I can watch it on my laptop. I can see what is happening right now, somewhere else, or talk to my friends, via my laptop. I may not be able to eat the food on the table that they have cooked for me, but I can talk to them, look at them, hear from them – everything. Yet, still this isn't enough – we want virtual reality. I won't be surprised if before long we will be able to actually eat the food people have put out for us. It may be possible. It may create problems if we try to travel through the computer screen and come back mixed up with other people doing the same thing though; somewhere in between computer screens we may get someone else's head. I may get her head and his head and his legs. I would appear back in front of my computer in a very funny way. Or perhaps a mosquito would get mixed up in it all and I would end up with a mosquito's head, there would always be this danger. There is a Tibetan saying, "If you do all kinds of things, all kinds of things will happen to you." This is true, there is no limit.

Question: Rinpoche, just now you said that the primordial state is the state of pure wisdom, but at the same time you said that ignorance is also from primordial reality. This doesn't appear that clear to me.

Rinpoche: It is true it is not clear. It is not very clear for me also. Without doubt, we have primordial wisdom within us, but without doubt we also have ignorance. In order to understand where this ignorance comes from, we first need to understand what we are ignorant of – we are ignorant of our primordial wisdom. Then we need to understand how we are ignorant. Our ignorance can be based on jealousy, anger, attachment, fear or greed.

I will give you an example. I have a very funny problem that I want to solve and have spoken with many doctors and experts about. It is not serious, it is actually quite funny and stupid but I still experience it. I don't like flying in big airplanes in the aisle seat, even at night when you can't see out the window. The worst is when I am in a 747, it is night and I am in the aisle seat. You can't even see out the window at night, but it makes a 100% difference to me whether I am in the window seat or the aisle seat. I have tried to find out what's wrong with me, but it is just my ignorance.

The father of one of my friends was a TWA pilot for many years. He is now retired. Before working for TWA he was a fighter pilot in Europe. He flew one of those planes with a propeller on the nose whose appearance is quite majestic – they have all kinds of windows, glass like bubbles on top, underneath and behind – a big bomber. He told me how he was flying one of these planes when he wasn't even nineteen. He said he fought in Germany, flew through all the bomb drops with shells exploding here and there all around him and that he would get holes in his airplane's wings, tail, and sometimes even in his fuselage. After flying in the war he flew a TWA passenger plane for many years then retired. Trying to help me get over my fear he pulled out his suitcase. He was one of those really American people, from the East coast, and he had used this suitcase the whole time he was flying. It was very square, solid and black with all kinds of stickers on it from the places he had visited. He said to me "I would never fly a plane if I was not sure it was going to make it to my destination. I have a wife, I have children and I don't want to die. You should remember this, it might help."

Now I know this but it doesn't help, I am still the same! This is how ignorance manifests. I know the danger of crashing in a 747 is low, there is nothing to hit in the sky and the only dangerous time is when you take off or land. Still I have no problem taking off, and when we are landing I am so glad we are landing I am not afraid at all! But in the middle of the air when nothing is going to happen to me I become afraid, not just mentally but physically afraid. I have been studying this phenomenon, it is very interesting. This concern actually occupies a little bit of my time, especially before I fly long distances. I tell my secretary to make sure I get a window seat and if he doesn't get me one I get quite annoyed. Many times I have swapped my first class aisle seat with people who have economy class window seats. I have. I have said to them, "Please take my seat up there, your economy window seat will be more comfortable for me than my first class aisle seat." People normally buy these expensive tickets for me; it's nice, but if I get the wrong seat I would rather have a window seat in economy. This is what ignorance is like.

I am not saying this is the only thing I am ignorant about, there are many other things, but this is the one that really sticks out, the one I can't understand. A helicopter is smaller and much more dangerous than a large airplane, but I enjoy riding in helicopters much more than any other type of vehicle. One time I was in a helicopter in the UK and there was fog so we didn't know where we were going. We could only go exactly over the highway with all its wires and everything. Finally we landed on the lawn of a hotel and called the Dharma center to send a car to pick us up. All this happened and I didn't have a problem with it. I enjoyed it. This fear does not really have anything to do with dying either; cars can be very dangerous and many people become afraid in cars, but I never do. I am never afraid on the train or on ships: just in big airplanes, which are the safest, and in the aisle seats, which are the most comfortable.

To go to sleep on a plane at night would be wonderful! All the lamas with me sleep like babies right next to me, but I am wide-awake all night and all day. This is how I exhibit my ignorance, which has to have something to do with my primordial wisdom. It has to be interconnected. When I don't know what I am supposed to know, that is ignorance and it continues all the time. I have flown so many times, for so many years, for so many hours and it hasn't become any better; actually it has become worse. Each one of you must have something like that in your life.

Question: Rinpoche, you said that everything is nothing more and nothing less than the interdependent manifestation of everything else. What does this "else" mean?

Rinpoche: The "else" is not necessary. Maybe it is...

Student: Everything is alright?

Rinpoche: Yeah, everything is alright. You can take out the "else." You are a lawyer, so you have to get it right don't you? We can skip the else.

Madhyamaka

I would like to go through *Madhyamaka* and *Tsema, Pramana* in Sanskrit. We have already covered these two subjects somewhat but not specifically, so in order to fill out your knowledge I would like to go into them in more detail. Madhyamaka is translated into English as "the Middle-way." Pramana is translated as, "dialectics," "cognitive signs," or "valid cognition." It involves reasoning; in this subject we do not give superstition or simple, blind belief any room. Instead we dig into every aspect of the subject, making sure the truth is revealed, which means "valid cognition" is a good translation.

When we study Buddhist philosophy, we study five subjects: Vinaya, Abhidharma, the Middle-way (Madhyamaka), Prajnaparamita and valid cognition or Tsema/Pramana. These five subjects refer to the *Zhung-chen-po-nga,* the five central texts. All of these teachings are of course the Lord Buddha's but later several great masters elaborated on them in some ways and condensed them in others. This group of masters are called, in Tibetan, *Gyen-drug-chog nyi,* the six ornaments and two beautifiers or excellences. From among these eight great Indian masters four wrote root texts and four wrote commentaries on these root texts. The first of the four to write a root text was Nagarjuna, Lündrup in Tibetan. Then there was Asanga, whose name is Togme in Tibetan and Chog-gi-langpo, Dignaga in Sanskrit. Dignaga's name means "Elephant," or "Great master of all directions:" he wrote a root text on Valid Cognition. The last of these masters to write a root text was Yön-ten-wö, Gunaprabha in Sanskrit; his name means "The Light of Knowledge." The four who wrote commentaries were Aryadeva, Pak-ba-lha in Tibetan, Vasubhandu, Ignyen in Tibetan, Dharmakirti, whose name is Chöji-drakpa in Tibetan, and Shakyaprabha, Shakya ö in Tibetan. Vasubhandu was Togme/Asanga's half brother.

Nagarjuna wrote six main Madhyamaka root texts. Asanga wrote five texts on Abhidharma and then two texts that summarized his previous works, for a total of seven. Dignaga wrote 108 texts on Pramana then collected their essence into the *Tse-ma-kun-du, Pramana Samuccaya, The Compendium of Valid Cognition*. Each one of Dignaga's 109 texts is quite sizeable. Gunaprabha wrote the root text on Vinaya, the *Dulwa-do-tsawa,* Vinayasutra and a commentary on his own text. Actually, many of these masters wrote commentaries on their own works.

Aryadeva, Vasubhandu, Dharmakirti and Shakyaprabha wrote commentaries on the root texts I have just mentioned. There are many Madhyamaka commentaries but the one considered the most comprehensive, the largest, is the *Four Hundred Shloka Madhyamaka*, the *Uma-zhi-je-pa,* (Skt. *Chatuhshataka shastra karika nama*) by Aryadeva. Asanga's brother Vasubandhu wrote a set of Abhidharma commentaries known as "The Prakarana Eight." In Tibetan we approximate Sanskrit and call them the "Drakarana Eight," because we pronounce "p" and "r" together as "dr," but in Sanskrit there is no such thing as a "Drakarana."

The next set of commentaries are the seven Dharmakirti wrote on Pramana. These seven are divided into two sets: the three texts "like a body" are 1) *Tsema Namdrel* (*Pramanavartika, Commentary of Valid Cognition*), 2) *Tsema Nam-nge* (*Pramanavinishcaya, Discernment of Valid Cognition*) and 3) *Tsema Rigtig* (*Nyayavindu, Drop of Reasoning on Valid Cognition*). The four texts "like limbs" are 1) *Tentsig Tigba* (*Hetubindu, Drop of Logical Reasoning*) 2) *Drelwa Tagba* (*Sambandhapariksha, Analysis of Relationship*) 3) *Gyu-zhän Drup-ba* (*Samtanantarasiddi, Establishing Alternative Continuum*) and 4) *Tsö-pä-rig-ba* (*Vadanyaya, The Science of Debate*).

The last of the four commentators, Shakyaprabha, wrote *The Three Hundred Shloka Karika*, a very important Vinaya text. He also wrote quite a few other texts on Vinaya, but this is considered his major work.

I talked about the Vinaya and the Abhidharma a little earlier, but I have not talked about Madhyamaka and Pramana clearly so I will now go into these two in more detail.

"Madhyamaka" is translated into English as "the Middle-way." There are quite a few schools of thought, or lineages, of Madhyamaka. I have already spoken of the Rangtong and Shentong (See appendix page 283). Then, within the Rangtong, the two main schools are known as the Middle-way Autonomous School (Svatantrika) and the Middle-way Consequence School (Prasangika). The Middle-way Autonomous School was founded by a disciple of Nagarjuna, Bhavaviveka or Legdenje in Tibetan. One of his followers was the bodhisattva Shantarakshita, and their lineage is known as the Middle-way Autonomous School.

Within the Middle-way Autonomous School, four major schools developed. The first of these is the Middle-way Autonomous school compatible with the Sutra (Sautrantika) School's tenets. In Tibetan this school is called the *Dode tang-tun-ki U-ma Rang-gyupa*. This school came about first through Legdenje/Bhavaviveka's commentary, *Tokke barwa* (*Tarkajvala*, *The Blaze of Reasoning*) on Nagarjuna's *Uma-tsawa-sherab* (*Pranjamila – The Roots of Knowledge*). This first commentary was on the words of Nagarjuna's text. Writing a commentary on the words of the text means he expanded upon the words Nagarjuna had written. So, for example, when Nagarjuna wrote something like "I take refuge in the Buddha," he described what the "I" meant, what "take" meant, what "refuge" meant, what "in" meant and what "Buddha" meant.

Following this he wrote a commentary on the meaning of *The Roots of Knowledge's*, called the *Sherab Drönme* (*Prajna-paradipa*, *The Light of Wisdom*). This text did not focus on the words Nagarjuna had used, but on their meaning. The content of these commentaries, the aspect of Madhyamaka they show, became known as the Middle-way Autonomous School compatible with Sutra.

The second sub-school of the Middle-way Autonomists is the Middle-way Autonomists compatible with Mind-only (Chittamatra). This school is slightly different to the Middle-way Autonomous School compatible with Sutra. It was founded by the bodhisattva Shantarakshita, or Shiwatso in Tibetan, who was a follower of Legdenje/Bhavaviveka. His name means "he who lives in peace." His student's name was Kamalishila, the great master Kamalashila. Many people have heard his name. Their lineage, the Middle-way Autonomists compatible with Mind-only, is still based on Nagarjuna's *Uma-tsawa-sherab* (*Pranjamila – The Roots of Knowledge*); however, the "Mind-only" school that this Middle-way school is compatible with has the basic philosophy that everything is a manifestation of mind. Sometimes when we are debating, some of the other Buddhist schools like Rangtong will say the Shentong view is Mind-only. It is similar but it is not quite the same.[23]

The philosophical lineage of these masters forms the content of quite a few important commentaries on Nagarjuna's *Roots of Knowledge*. There is one written by the bodhisattva Shantarakshita called *Umagyen* (*Madhyamaka-lamkara*, *An Ornament to the Middle Way*), and Kamalashila also wrote three very, very enlightening, comprehensive texts based on the meditation practices of Madhyamaka. They are called the *Gomrim sum* (*Bhavana krama*, *The Stages of Meditation*), and describe three stages of meditation. The content of all these texts is known as the Autonomist school compatible with Mind-only and it is still part of the Madhyamaka.

The third sub-school is similar to the Mind-only school, but also quite similar to the Consequence school. You will remember that I said the Rangtong Madhyamaka has two main lineages: the Autonomist and Consequence lineages. I will explain what those words mean later. Still, even though this school is similar to the Consequence lineage it is still an Autonomist school. It is called, the Autonomist school that asserts proofs by means of illusion like reasoning. In Tibetan it is called the *Juma rigpa drup pa*: *juma* means illusion, *rigpa* means cognitive reasoning and *drupa* means to establish – they use cognitive signs or methods to verify their view.

Where does this lineage stand? They say that everything from the lowest form to the highest enlightenment is just like a dream, like an illusion, like magic. Some philosophical texts say this position was put forward by a disciple of Vasubandhu named Vimuktisena (Namdrölde) and a disciple of Shantarakshita named Haribadra, Senge Sangpo in Tibetan, but other scholars have questioned this assertion. The main thing to remember about this school, their main stand, is that everything, equally, is like an illusion, a dream.

The fourth Middle-way Autonomist School is the Middle-way Autonomist School that accords with the Particularist (Vaibhashika) School. In Tibetan it is called the *Chidramawa-tang-tun-ki U-ma Rangjupa*. *Chidra* means "specifically," and *mawa* means to speak or teach. The master who started this school was the arhat Upagupta, Drachomba Nyerbe in Tibetan. He wrote commentaries on the three basic teachings of the Buddha – the tripitaka of Vinaya, Abhidharma and Sutra – not Tantra. He interpreted these teachings in his own way, very clearly. He was an arhat so for him to interpret the Buddha's teachings in his own way was different from an ordinary person like us trying to interpret the Lord Buddha's teachings. First he attained arhathood, and then he manifested the tripitaka in his own way, slightly differently than the way others had interpreted it.

This roughly covers the sub-branches of the Madhyamaka lineage known as the Autonomists. In order to understand the name "Autonomists" we need to look at Pramana. When you study Madhyamaka you also have to use the teachings and terminology of Pramana. If I say, "Here is a glass of water," I have to prove there is a glass of water, that there is a glass with water inside; that this is a glass of water like any other, the water is like other water and the glass is like other glasses. From the perspective of Pramana, you cannot simply say that this is a glass of water, then not show that it is a glass of water. It could be a photograph of a glass of water. It could be a glass of vinegar that looks like water. It could be a glass of white wine or Vodka that looks like water. It is a very simple statement, "Here is a glass of water," but we don't necessarily know it is true. Pramana has many ways of defining and coming to conclusions. Through Pramana we can say that this is indeed a glass of water.

Pramana is a very advanced subject. As already mentioned, there are seven main Pramana texts: the *Commentary of Valid Cognition*, the *Discernment of Valid Cognition*, the *Drop of Reasoning on Valid Cognition*, the *Drop of Logical Reasoning*, *Analysis of Relationship*, *Establishing an Alternative Continuum* and *The Science of Debate*. The first three of these are the main texts and the last four are the "limbs" or secondary texts. Each one of these texts is enormous.

There are many ways to explain Pramana but one of the simplest is through the *tsul-sum,* the three modes of proof. If we were going to make the statement, "there is, or has been a fire on the mountainside because there is smoke," for example, we need to apply these three modes of proof to our statement in order to confirm it. The first part of our statement is the subject "fire on the mountainside," the second part is the sign, in this case smoke, and the third part is our assertion that if there is smoke there has to be, or have been, a fire. The fire may not be active now but if there is smoke there has been, or is, a fire. Nowadays it may be that stuff restaurants use in dishes that looks like smoke but doesn't come from a fire — let's forget about that. It is not smoke. It is steam. We are not saying that there is a fire on the mountainside because there is steam, so our statement is still okay.

In order to prove our assertion we apply the three modes of proof to it: the *chog chö* (the premise), the *je kyab* (the forward pervasion) and the *dog kyab* (the reverse pervasion). The premise is the statement "When there is fire there is smoke." The forward pervasion is that "If there is smoke there will be, or has been a fire." The reverse pervasion is the opposite, "If there has been no fire there will be no smoke."

An Autonomist asserts these three modes; they make a stand on these three principles. The Tibetan form of Autonomist, *Rangju,* means "an independent argument." As I said earlier, some of the Autonomists make a stand similar to the non-Madhyamaka Sutra school, others take a stand similar to the non-Madhyamaka Mind-only school, and yet others' view is similar to that of the Particularists, another non-Madhyamaka school.

The non-Madhyamaka schools are the Particularist school,[24] the Sutra and the Mind-only school.

The Particularist school was based on a particular text, with a different approach called the *Chedrag Shetso Chenmo, The Great Ocean of Commentary.* The Sutra school is based on the original Sutra teachings of Lord Buddha, rather than any commentaries made on them by great masters, which are only used in a secondary capacity. Even commentaries like the root texts of Nagarjuna and Aryadeva are not considered that important. They place an absolute importance on the Sutras, and only look into other texts as commentaries on these Sutras. They focus on the command rather than the commentaries on the commands.[25]

"Mind-only" means that no phenomena, from hell to heaven, are separate from our mind. They are mirror like projections or manifestations totally reliant on our mind. They are the mind's reflections – nothing more, nothing less. Within the Mind-only school itself there are also quite a few different definitions and beliefs. Not as many as within the Madhyamaka, but quite a few. I will not go into those here though.

We can look at the Mind-only school through the three modes of proof. The subject is all phenomena, everything. Not everything "else" okay? Then the second part, the sign is that "All phenomena are only manifestations of the mind and non separable from the mind." The third part, the assertion, would be "Phenomena only occur through the karma created by the mind and acted out through body and speech." They would say that all of the things happening outside only happen because of the karma created through the body and speech by the mind – it all boils down to the mind. This is the simplest way to give a definition of the Mind-only position.

There are also further ways to split hairs in the Mind-only school but I will only briefly go into this here. In the Mind-only school they divide all phenomena into three groups: *kuntag* (that with an imaginary nature), *zhenwang* (that with a dependent nature) and *yongdrub* (that with a perfectly existent nature). An imaginary nature is something that is only a projection of mind. For example, we call the things we put our feet in "shoes." We could call them hat or jacket but in the beginning the English people decided to call them shoes. Tibetans call them *lham* and in India we use the Hindi word *jut*. These labels are all *kuntag,* imaginary natures. "Dependent natures" are things that come into existence due to something else, another force. These phenomena are nothing within themselves but are perceived, utilized, consumed and affected positively and negatively by the mind. The other power is the power of the mind; all phenomena are influenced by the power of the mind. The "perfectly existent nature" is that there is nothing other than the projection of the mind. This is the Mind-only school's definition of emptiness.

An imaginary nature is also void of a dependent nature. They are not the same thing. When I say this is a nice long table, this idea is an imaginary nature. My seeing this as "a nice long table" is influenced by my perception of what "nice," "long" and "table" are. There is nothing more to it, and nothing less to it, than my idea, it is not the dependent object – the thing that is a table – itself.

These three aspects are the Mind-only school's basic philosophy. I won't go into their philosophy any further; otherwise you will get confused. I hope you are not already confused. If you are confused, there is not much point in discussing these philosophies. But let's try looking at one more school anyway. We have finished the Autonomist school in a superficial way and some of you are confused, so perhaps we should look at another school.

The other main Madhyamaka School, the other main lineage of the Madhyamaka, is the Consequence School. To make defining the Consequence school as simple as possible for you, we need to look again at the Autonomist School. By definition the Autonomist school has a belief. This belief is based on three things, the three modes of proof. However the Consequence school does not hold onto anything. The Autonomist school is an "offence" school, and the Consequence school only has defense. The Consequence School does not say, "We believe in this, we believe in that." Instead they react to what other people say. They examine the consequences of what other people say. The Consequence philosophy examines what other people put forward and comes to conclusions about them, rather than stating their own beliefs. The Autonomist school will say they believe something, and the Consequence school will not – this is their main difference. Of course both schools believe in Buddhahood, bodhichitta, all of these things, but not as particular dualistic belief systems.

The Consequence lineage also has many branches: There is the *Gel bä jö bä tal jur*, a consequence that exposes contradictions; the *Drubche Drubcha dang tsung pä ma drub ba*, the non-application of the means of proof due to the presupposition of the premise; and the *Gyumsten sum gyi go ne zhen kyi drag bä je bag*, the inference through the popular conventions of others established by way of the three reasons. From among these I think we will look at the simplest way to understand this school, the "Consequence that is an inference established through the popular conventions of others," *Zhen kyi drag bä je bag*. This Consequence school would only say that everything is impermanent when somebody else said they were permanent. They would use the philosophical principles, the Pramana principles and techniques, to prove that everything is impermanent because somebody else believes they are permanent. This Consequence school itself, however, would not make a particular, dualistic assertion. For them this is like creating conditions for ourselves. It becomes like target practice: when you shoot an arrow it is only ever at a little target, you limit yourself to the little bull's-eye. You are only happy when you hit that little bull's-eye with your arrow, you lose all the opportunities to be happy that may come from hitting something else. If you don't aim at a bull's-eye, however, and don't particularly aim at anything else, whenever you hit anything you will be happy. Those who put forward the Consequential position do not create bull's-eyes for themselves. They only make comments about, and react to, other people's points of views.

The Autonomists are different, they believe in the three principles I mentioned earlier. If something fits these principles, it is okay; if it doesn't, they will dismiss it. It isn't really this simple, but I have simplified its description. Generally, the Madhyamaka is divided into these two groups, the Autonomist and Consequence Schools.

Pramana

Now we come to Pramana. Pramana is an entire subject in itself. Based on the Sutras and the Abhidharma, it is basically a tool to understand them properly. Let us take karma for example, cause and result. It is a very basic subject but it is still very difficult for people to believe that everything is a cause and a result. Pramana makes it easier for people to understand this by using common sense. To look at something specifically, how can there be today without yesterday? There can never be "no tomorrow" as long as there is a today. Or another example, if you plant rice seeds, rice will grow. If you plant orange tree seeds, orange trees will grow. Orange trees don't grow when you plant rice seeds. Through these examples karma, cause and result, becomes simple, common sense.

Why does each one of us have different tastes, likes and dislikes? Something that is exactly what you don't like may be exactly what somebody else likes. Take paintings for example. I did an exhibition of my paintings. Some of them were so bad I wanted to burn them, but the organizers said, "These are beautiful, I want to exhibit these." I thought these paintings were terrible, but other people thought they were wonderful. When I showed other people some paintings that I thought were really beautiful, really nice, they said, "I think we should skip these."

Why do these things happen? Of course we can say it is because we grew up in a particular culture, a specific environment, we were taught this and that, exposed to different things and this is how we came to have differences, but it doesn't stop there. Conveniently this line of reasoning stops at birth, although this process doesn't. How could it stop there? If we had the ability to go further back than our birth we would find out that our past doesn't stop conveniently at our birth, that nothing stops conveniently anywhere. Everyone has existed for a very, very long time and goes on forever. If you could trace yourself you would trace forever. There is no end to it, if you got tired of tracing where you have come from and stopped, that would be one thing, but if you wanted to continue tracing your history you could continue doing so forever.

Pramana helps us to get these things right. Another example is the concept of a god as a creator. I am quite sure that most of you know that in Buddhism we believe in all the gods but we don't believe somebody created us. Yet we understand and appreciate the creator concept because we consider ourselves equal to the highest power and believe we created ourselves. If we have done something good yesterday we feel good today. If we have done something bad yesterday we may end up in jail today. We created the situation we are experiencing now. In our past lives we created a connection with our parents and the rest of our family, so in this life we ended up with this couple we call daddy and mummy. The same process applies to our brothers, sisters, cousins, nephews and all the other kinds of people around us. In our past lives we have also developed connections with the other people here. Relationships called teacher-student, guru-disciple, friend, husband and wife, are all productions of our many past lives. We don't believe it is arranged by somebody like a chessboard: no one is playing games with our lives. We don't believe in that kind of creation, but we believe in creation.

Creation is accomplished by the ultimate essence within us, an essence equal to the essence of any god you can think of. I don't know too much about other gods, but for example the essence of the Hindu god Shivaji. In Tibetan Shivaji is called, *Wang-chug chenpo* (Mahashvara, Shiva). In our prayers we say "Chenrezig tu wang chug lha chenpo," "The emanation of the bodhisattva Avalokiteshvara, the great god Shivaji." In this way it is quite easy for me to understand the belief that one god creates, one god maintains and one god destroys. I understand this by interpretation, I have read it and heard it many times, but I don't have the lineage of Hindu teachings from a guru so I cannot preach this to you or verify it for you. Still I have lived in India since I was six years old; I have no problem with this interpretation, unless we take it literally. Unless we think there are three guys sitting up there above us: one creates us, one maintains us, and one destroys us. That doesn't make sense.

If, on the other hand, we go one step further and interpret these three aspects – creator, maintainer and destroyer – as our essence, then we could say it represents the way we are created the minute we don't recognize our limitless, primordial wisdom. We are constantly created this way, and we are constantly maintained this way. I teach you, I learn, I rest, I get sick, I take medicine, and I am well, not like yesterday. In this way my essence manifests and is maintained. If you want to call this essence "god" I don't have a problem with that, but for me it is more than just "god," it is our limitless essence. It creates, it maintains and in the end it destroys because we have to defeat and destroy our egos in order to become Buddhas. If I can't defeat my ego, my attachment, my jealousy, my pride, I can never become a Buddha. My awakening essence has to defeat these things.

This essence works like the Hindu deity Narasingha, the fourth avatar (incarnation or manifestation) of Shiva, who took the evil king Hiranyashasipu onto his lap. The evil king had a shakti (power) that stopped him being killed by any weapons while he was on Earth. So the destroyer picked him up and put him on his lap: this way he was not on the ground. Then instead of a weapon he used his hand to open his chest. Likewise, whatever shakti our ego has cannot be compared to the shakti of our primordial wisdom. Our primordial wisdom can rip through it, destroy it and reveal itself, reveal the primordial wisdom that is within.

I hope I am not playing Hindu guru here. Please forgive me all the Shankara Archaryas and Mahapanditas. I have no right to interpret these things in this way. I can only speak from the point of view of the Buddha's teachings and especially the Vajrayana teachings I have learned. From this point of view I have no problem with a creator, a maintainer and a destroyer but I can never believe or accept that there are guys up there, existing dualistically. That they are just like us, if they are prayed to they get happy and help, and if they are not prayed to, they become unhappy and punish us. I cannot accept that if we listen to them, they do nice things for us and if we don't listen to them, they punish us. I cannot believe this sincerely. It is okay for other people to believe this, but I cannot. It is dualistic and I don't believe in a dualistic Buddha.

Sometimes people say to me, "God will be happy if you do this," and I don't argue with them. At other times people say to me, "God will be unhappy if you do this," and I don't argue with them either! Still for me these comments do not make sense. God, this most supreme, limitless being, should not have any likes or dislikes, they shouldn't have any preferences. When I say "god" I only think of the highest of high, and from my perspective this is the manifestation of the Buddha, always perfect and equally regarding all. How I receive and perceive this, how it benefits me, depends on what kind of a vessel I am. If I am a clean vessel, when the milk of blessing is poured in, it will stay pure. If I am a dirty, sour vessel then even the snow lion's milk will become sour in me. We say that the snow lion's milk is the most powerful, the most precious milk, but the minute it touches my sour vessel it will go bad. The Buddha's blessings work in the same way as the snow lion's milk.

I don't mind saying "god;" this is not a problem for me. One is spelt G, O, D. The other is spelt B, U, D, D, H, A. There is no difference to me; it is just a different language with a different terminology. Buddha's blessings are there for all sentient beings at all times. It is not as if Buddha only hears us when we shout loud enough and that when we whisper Buddha cannot hear us. We are dualistic, so we think we have to sing, we have to shout so Buddha will hear us. This is okay. This is correct in a way, because it means we are doing everything we can, shouting as loudly as we can, singing as beautifully as we can so that the Buddha will respond to us – it makes sense. Still, it is because of us that we need to do this, not because of the Buddha.

The Buddhas are like Consequentalists, not offensive. They do not promote themselves. They do not do anything dualistically. They are just like the sky, providing at all times, for all. We receive from them, each of us individual vessels, according to our own capacity. An example of this is an Indian tradition. Perhaps those of you who are not from India will not know this, but here in India people believe that one sour lemon and a few hot, green chilies put together can ward off other peoples' jealousy. In Hindi people say, "Anka band jata hai," "To bind the evil eye." We don't want other people to say, "He has a nice car, he has a nice house," because we believe it brings bad luck. You see the results of this belief everywhere; a shoe polisher sitting on the corner of a street with virtually nothing will have some chili and lemon hanging next to him and a Mercedes car that costs $75,000 to $85,000 will also have chili and lemon hanging right there on its windshield. Very big mansions with ten acres of land surrounding them will hang chili and lemon at their door and very small shopkeepers who have nothing but a few potatoes and vegetables worth only a few dollars will also use them. It is very interesting the way we perceive things.

For me, the way we receive the Buddha's blessings is the same way that Christians receive "God's grace," and everybody has their own reasons for requesting it. If I only had a little shop, instead of putting lemon and chili on it to protect myself from others' jealousy, I would be depressed, thinking that others would look down on me because I had nothing. Still the people who live at this level know that other people living in the same way may be jealous of them having a little place like that. This shows me that the way we perceive things is an illusion. It is really all illusion. The other day when I was driving the car, there was a kid selling these clumps of chili and lemon and I bought five! It was very interesting. I don't know where I will put them, I haven't hung them anywhere, but I bought five of them.

Pramana is a very, very important tool for understanding Madhyamaka. Madhyamaka has to be understood along with Pramana in order for its subjects to become interesting and rich. For beginners who have not been exposed to these concepts they can seem very complicated. This is why, when I wrote my notes a long time ago, I wrote that "My head was turning like an umbrella meant for the noble ones." The subject is so deep and vast, this is what happened when I attempted to understand it myself.

If you look at the Vinaya, then the Abhidharma, then Madhyamaka, Prajnaparamita and Pramana, you will see all of these are very big subjects. In my monastery in Himachal Pradesh, for example, monks study and debate every day for nine years to complete their studies of these five texts. Even then they only learn some of these five texts. There are five texts, but each of them has many sections. In these nine years they only learn the symbolic basics of these five texts. Just learning this takes nine solid years. They only have a one or two month holiday a year. During the time they are studying they only have one day off a week; apart from this every day they have several classes and debate until about eleven o'clock at night.

It is quite something when they debate. They get very excited. Those of you who don't know about debate may think the monks are fighting. The little, thin ones have no chance, the big ones pick them up and throw them aside. The little ones keep trying, itching to say something, their mouths are itching but they never get the chance to say anything because the big ones throw or push them to the side. It can look very unruly and a little aggressive but it never actually turns into a fight. At least I have never seen anybody get into a fight. Our first group graduated this year after nine years of study, there were nine graduates. Right now there are 108 or 109 of them studying like this every day but I think for you here that this much is enough.

To review, Madhyamaka means "the Middle-way." A simplified way to explain the Middle-way is to say that everything is neither this nor that and the essence of everything is limitless and beyond any dualistic limitation. The Middle-way does not mean being a Swiss National! It doesn't mean being neutral! It means everything is neither this nor that and has a limitless potential. Everything is perfect beyond description. The essence of everything cannot be described by an exact example, so any example used to describe it remains just that, an example. We can say mind is empty and limitless like the sky, but that is not exactly what it is. If we said this we would have to add that it is as luminous as the sun, as solid as a vajra and illusory like a rainbow. We have to use many examples because if we say mind is solid like a diamond, for example, this implies something eternal and if we say mind is empty like the sky that implies nihilism – both are wrong, so to get at the view of the Middle-way we have to give many examples.

This is the Middle-way position. The Shentong view of the Middle-way is that mind is everything – the essence of everything – and that this essence has no limitation. This is the specific emphasis Shentong puts on the Middle-way. I think that maybe it is time to stop here because we may have gotten more than our fill. If you have any questions, you can go ahead with them. I am sure you have a lot.

QUESTIONS

Question: Earlier you said that Buddha-nature is in each and every one of us and it is always there. Could you also say that Buddha-nature is permanent?

Rinpoche: I could say that. I am a proponent of Shentong, so I can say that. If I had to choose out of these two, permanent and impermanent, I would say the Buddha-nature is permanent. However, I would also answer that it is beyond being permanent or impermanent. I have to say it is more than permanent but if you only give me these two choices, permanent or impermanent, I have to say permanent. If after that you asked for further clarification I would say it was more than permanent because being "permanent" is related to being "impermanent," it is dualistic.

Even the proponents of Rangtong Mä-gag though, would say the essence of the mind is not solid or dualistically existent. They could not say the essence of the mind is dualistically existent, so we are actually saying the same thing. The essence of the mind is not dualistically existent; it has no dualistic existence. It is a non-dualistic reality – unspeakable, incomparable, ineffable and indescribable – but there. This is why if you only give me these two choices, permanent or impermanent, I have to say it is permanent. But if you were to give me more choices, I would say it is more than permanent.

Question: In Buddhism there are only two proofs accepted, two Pramana, actual experience and inference. Experience means I see something and an inference is for example, "Where there is smoke there must be a fire."

Rinpoche: Sir, Who told you Buddhism only believed in these two?

Question: I have heard verbal testimony that what is written in a book is not accepted as evidence. In many other religions they say, this is written in the Bible or the Koran or in Veda, so this is absolute truth. But Buddhism says that if it is written in a book it need not be truth. This is a very important difference. I understand that you don't accept verbal testimony as an evidence of truth.

Rinpoche: You are very intelligent and have made things quite interesting. I appreciate that. I agree with you in the main, but it is not quite like this. We also have belief without using reasoning. When we have total faith and trust in something we do not need to use reasoning. If we have total faith, total trust in the Buddha, then we don't have to have a reason. It is the same thing as taking aspirin when we have a headache, we don't know what is in it but we have faith in it anyway, so we take it and get well. In Buddhism we have this kind of faith also.

If it is necessary we use reasoning, and we have very profound reasoning. In Pramana, Madhyamaka, Abhidharma, Prajnaparamita and Vinaya reasoning has been clearly and thoroughly implemented. We use reasoning but it is not as if we don't believe without reason. Another thing we need to consider is that this reality we see here, that we believe to be reality, is only the reality of a human being on planet Earth, in this solar system. Reality is not exactly like this. I am not talking about this from an enlightened level necessarily, but also from an unenlightened level. Other human beings, from a totally different environment but the same state of mind – the same human realm – might not even see our reality. They may come here and not even see us. The wall here may not impede their movement. If they have eyes they may see completely different things, but maybe they don't even have eyes. This reality that we are experiencing depends on a lot of conditions.

Right now we all see everything in here similarly, not exactly the same but similarly. We call this *kal-nyam,* a similar fortune. Our similar situation is one of those things that are not solid but are a reality. Similar sorts of conditions and karma have bought us together on this planet. We have this commonality between us, therefore we call it a *kal-nyam.*

We should also consider things like my ownership of this booklet. The minute I got it, it became mine. Before I got it, it was not mine.

If I had taken it before I got it that would have been stealing. The moment after I received it, taking it was not stealing. If I own something and take it with me I do not accumulate the bad karma of stealing. What is the difference between these two situations? All of the aspects involved are categories of reality. We call them non-associated compositional factors, *demin duche*. They are there, but you can't put your finger on them. I paid ten dollars and I got my diary or notebook. But what is that? What stops me from being a thief when I give the shop owner ten dollars before taking this book? You cannot really put your finger on it. You cannot see this kind of thing through inference or experience, so they do not belong to the categories you mentioned.

Another thing to consider is our motivation; we learn and reason because we want to believe. Once we believe, we don't need to use reasoning. We use all of this reasoning, like Pramana, to develop faith. If we have faith without knowing any of this, this is very good, but if we don't have faith without knowing all of these subjects, we can use them to acquire faith. This option is available to us.

We also believe in the Buddha's *Ka*, his commands. In the same way you said people believe things because the Bible says it, the Bhagavad-Gita says it, or the Koran says it, we believe in things because the Buddha's commands say it. These commands are not condensed to one book, however. The correct words of the Buddha, written down by his disciples, run to over a hundred volumes. They run to over a hundred volumes because so much is explained within them. If the Buddha did not explain as much it might be in one volume. We believe in these words of the Buddha, but using this word "believe" does not mean these commands are not clear: they are very clear.

When Buddha talks about emptiness for example, he said, "Form is emptiness, emptiness is form." If he had just said "Form is emptiness," we would only have one perspective. We would be stuck because this would not be emptiness, it would be solid. When he then went on to say, "Emptiness is form," it made it a lot clearer for us. Then when he says a third or fourth thing, it becomes even clearer. In this way we really believe in the Lord Buddha's commands.

We also consider the great masters who wrote the commentaries contained within the *Tenjur*, like Nagarjuna, to be enlightened beings, not just scholars. We consider their teachings pretty close to the Lord Buddha's teachings. These masters were arhats, mahasiddhas, mahapandits and we believe they were all enlightened.

All of this means I only partially agree with what you said, as I think we have to add a few things to it. As far as belief is concerned, we are not that different from those who believe in the Bible, the Koran or the Bhagavad-Gita. The Buddha told us that if you have faith, that is very good. If you don't have faith then you should learn and question. You should make sure these teachings are like gold by burning, rubbing, cutting and weighing them. In this way you will learn they are gold, and treasure them. I think that is how it is. Your question was very deep. I appreciate it. Thank you.

Question: You mentioned that one of these lineages believes that everything is a manifestation of the mind. Can you elaborate on that?

Rinpoche: The Mind-only school believes this. This is one of the very basic Buddhist philosophical lineages. These basic lineages are the Particularists school, the Sutra school, the Mind-only school and the Madhyamaka schools. Another basic philosophical lineage is the Theravadan lineage. The Mind-only and Madhyamaka are Mahayana lineages. The Mind-only school is quite highly considered, but it isn't considered the top lineage. The Mind-only school is derived from the four main Sutras that are associated with it, the *Semtsam do zhi*.[26]

What the Mind-only school says is that everything, from the most basic to the highest phenomenon, is just a manifestation of mind. When your mind is pure, a pure land will manifest. When your mind is impure, a hell manifests; when your mind is so-so, a situation like ours manifests. This is a simplified way to describe the philosophy of the Mind-only school. There are actually many levels, aspects and branches of the Mind-only school. For example, there are the *Zung-Dzin Drang Nyampa*, the proponents of an equal number of subjects and objects, and the *Gonga Che Tselwa*, the Half Eggists. The Half Eggists, say that subject and object are like one boiled egg cut into two, actually the same thing. These two branches, and many others, all have their own unique views.

Question: I also have a question on the Mind-only school. Does it refer to relative and ultimate worlds or only relative phenomena?

Rinpoche: When we say it refers to everything from the most basic to the highest phenomenon that means from relative to ultimate truth. The Madhyamaka doesn't say this exactly.

Student: Even primordial wisdom?

Rinpoche: Yes. This is what the Mind-only school would say. These schools go from a grosser philosophy to a subtler philosophy, step by step. First there is the Particularists school, then the Sutra school, then the Mind-only school and then the Madhyamaka school. Progressing from one to the other is sort of like climbing. However, the Mind-only school may not say this.

Question: *Tsema* is translated in many English works as "valid perception." Could you elaborate on this? Do only Buddhas have Tsema?

Rinpoche: No. "Tsema" is basically the opposite of the word *Tsema Mayinba*, non-valid cognition. If they say you are Mr Agawul, that is a non-valid cognition. You are not Mr Agawul. You are a lady so you cannot be Mr Agawul. If you are called your correct name, your surname and everything else clearly, that is a Tsema, a valid cognition.

There are also different kinds of Tsema/Pramana. There is a *Ngönsum Tsema*, a direct valid cognition, which means for example what we can see and hear. A *Ngönsum* is something we experience here; what we can hear, what we can see, what we can really perceive. Another kind of Tsema/Pramana is a *Jebak Tsema*, an inferential valid cognition. This means you presume something based on a valid sign.

From the noise of maintenance on the roof going on now, for example, I can presume they are drilling. I can't perceive what they are doing directly but my inferential valid cognition is that they are drilling. I make this inferential valid cognition when I come to know they are drilling through hearing their drills so many times; they go drrrrrrrr then stop, pull the drill out then try to make another hole drrrrrrr, then after making holes with a drill they are putting nails into them to hang pictures on or something. I can infer this – it is an inferential valid cognition. In an inferential valid cognition you use your logic to ensure your thought is a Tsema/Pramana.

Seeing you all here is a direct valid cognition, a *Ngönsum Tsema*, a direct valid cognition. What we think about, like the drilling they are doing upstairs, is a *Jebak Tsema*, an inferential valid cognition. This is it simply, but generally the monks go into much more detail in their studies of these texts. For example, the Gelugpa lineage is very famous for making Tsema/Pramana the main theme of their studies and when they study the *Tse-ma-kun-du / Pramana Samuccaya / The Compendium of Valid Cognition*, they spend at least six months focusing on its first two sentences. These first two sentences are: *Tsema gyur ba dro wa la pen bä zhe, Tön ba desheg job la gö chag stel lo.* "What became of valid cognition, [the truth]? Wishing to benefit other sentient beings, I bow my head to the teacher who has reached peace, the protector." The word *ton pa*, teacher, means one who shows, it means a Buddha. *Desheg* is short for *dewa shepa*, the one who has reached peace and also means Buddhahood. To define each of the words in these two sentences clearly they will debate for at least six months. Those who go through Drepung, Sera and Ganden, the three large Gelugpa monasteries, spend many months studying these words. The rest of the text follows on from these sentences pretty quickly but many months are spent on these two sentences, starting with the definition of *Tsema gyur ba*, "valid cognition" and "became." Is this what you are asking?

Student: In these two sentences, the benefactor is the teacher?

Rinpoche: Yes. They will look into this, they will ask, what does that mean? What is the definition of benefit? How can a Buddha benefit others? How does it happen? Does a Buddha have a wish, and if so is the Buddha dualistic? If he has a wish he is dualistic. If he is dualistic he is not Buddha. After these six months of debate, to make it very simple for you, they will conclude that the ultimate truth unfolds and becomes. Prince Siddartha became what any of us can become, he reached his destiny – this is "what becomes of valid cognition," *Tsema gyur ba*, what becomes of the truth. It means he did not just learn or discover truth but with the intention to benefit others he became truth. This means that after enlightenment the Buddha is non-dualistic but he benefits others spontaneously because his original motivation was to benefit all sentient beings.

Millions and millions of eons ago the Buddha Shakyamuni, before he was a Buddha, was a beggar in another universe with just a handful of food, but when he met the Buddha of that land he was so inspired he offered his meager bowl of food. Offering this bowl he said, "May I become like you, in order to make everybody like you." This was the first lineage of enlightenment Prince Siddartha received, many, many, many, many, billions and billions and billions of lifetimes ago, and as a result of this original intention, after he finally achieved Buddhahood all of his power manifested, and manifests, spontaneously for the benefit of others.

This is the end result of their debates, but it takes a long time to get to this point. If we just jump to a simple conclusion it doesn't really sink in as well as if we had debated it thoroughly. We say, whatever the subject is, you truly understand it when you have to carve it into your ribs and the inside of your skull. By debating, by really scrutinizing and drilling through these topics you receive true lessons.

Another example is the debate over the word *tön ba*, which means "the one who shows the path." The Buddha showed us the path, but what path? The path leading where? The path that leads to what has already been reached? The next two words after *tön ba* are *dewa shegpa*, "one who has reached ultimate peace." These words refer to someone who has reached the ultimate, limitless peace and harmony and is showing us the path he traveled.

Job means to protect, help and save. It means the Buddha is a savior, a protector. He is a savior because although all of us have the same potential as him, we don't know we are suffering in samsara, wandering from heaven to hell. Sometimes we are born as a god, then when our god karma finishes we are born in hell. Then when our hell karma is finished we may be born as a god again, or a human being. We go up and down, wandering everywhere, getting nowhere. The Buddha saves us from this wandering, protects us from the suffering of samsara, the suffering of going in circles.

The next word is head, *gö*, "to whom I bow my head." The head is the highest part of our bodies. In order to bow down we have to be humble, we bow to the Buddha for this reason. We do not bow because the Buddha is our boss, we do not bow because if we don't we may lose our job. We bow to the Buddha because he became enlightened for us and all his wisdom and power is to benefit us by helping us become like him. Bowing means submission, devotion. If my ego thinks I am better or equal to someone, I will not bow to them. This bowing marks the conclusion of these two sentences.

These debates show how Tsema, in detail, is a very elaborate subject but from a commonsense point of view it is very simple. It is about the confirmation of relative truth, and by confirming relative truth and exposing its fallacy, ultimate truth will be revealed. Relative truth in itself is not the ultimate truth. When the fallacy of relative truth is revealed, ultimate truth is revealed. It is just like the questions about primordial wisdom relating to ignorance. When the fallacy of ignorance is revealed, the secret, the unspeakable, is revealed and spoken. This is what Tsema/Pramana does.

Nothing is forbidden when you are debating, there is nothing you are forbidden from saying, but your motivation has to be to learn. If you understand Tibetan you will hear them trying to prove, for example, that the Buddha is not enlightened. This would be forbidden in many other religions, to say something like, "God is not god," but in Tsema/Pramana debate you have to address things like this. The people debating may even try to use all the terminology and meaning of the texts, even the words of the Buddha himself, to prove that Prince Siddartha was not enlightened. The person debating this knows that Prince Siddartha is enlightened but his job in this instance is to debate that he is not. This is very enlightening and gives those debating a lot of freedom.

These days a lot of the younger monks would rather go and debate than sit and do pujas. In my monastery, it is a little difficult to get monks to do pujas, there are about sixty, almost seventy monks who do this. When it comes to learning debate and philosophy though, I can't accept any more monks – we are full. Some of the rooms that are meant for two people now have four people sleeping in them. I have six teachers and that is not enough.

We recently had the annual Karma Kagyu higher Buddhist study group come together at Sherab Ling: around 300 monks came and spent a month debating and discussing. It has become a very, very big thing by our standards. In South India there are monasteries that have 7000 monks but in the Himalayas we don't have this kind of capacity.

It is very interesting and very good. Debate makes you feel free to explore the Lord Buddha's teaching but it is not mandatory. If you have faith, devotion and trust you don't have to spend your time doing all of this, you can just practice and meditate. Still I thought you should go through a little of this, have a little taste of it, so I have shared this with you. Next we will move into a discussion of practice.

ENLIGHTENMENT
*Calligraphy by
Tai Situ Rinpoche*

Chapter 4

BUDDHIST PRACTICE

REFUGE

REFUGE REFERS TO TAKING refuge in the Buddha, dharma and sangha. Our Master, the Buddha, is our ultimate refuge because our ultimate aim is to reach Buddhahood. We take refuge in the Buddha because we believe in his teachings, and we wish to follow him.

We take refuge in the dharma as the path. The dharma is the Buddha's teaching, the path that he has shown us. The Buddha taught in order to help all sentient beings become free from the suffering of samsara, just as he had. He taught so that we could also attain enlightenment and become free of the effects of conditioned existence, just as he had.

Taking refuge in the dharma means taking refuge in the Lord Buddha's teaching. It means learning the Lord Buddha's teachings, contemplating their meaning and, after we have understood them, implementing them. It means applying them in our day-to-day lives, over and over again, until we become Buddhas. The dharma is relevant right up until Buddhahood. Only then has the purpose of learning the dharma been completed. Until then we should continue to learn the dharma.

The sangha by definition – or more specifically the holy, extraordinary sangha – are the bodhisattvas such as Avalokiteshvara, Manjushri and so on. Of course we take refuge in them, but the sangha is also the community of fully ordained monks and nuns and those lay teachers who guide us. We take refuge in the sangha as our guides and friends.

It is from them that we receive the dharma's unbroken lineage transmission, and through this lineage that we receive the dharma. So only through them will we truly understand the Lord Buddha's teachings. First the Buddha taught the dharma himself and his disciples heard, understood and practiced it. Then these disciples taught the dharma, and their disciples heard, understood and practiced it. This process of passing dharma from master to disciple – uninterrupted, uncorrupted, unchanged – has continued for the past twenty-five centuries of Buddhist history. What Lord Buddha taught has been re-taught again and again by all the masters of the past to all the disciples of the past until the masters of the present and is now being passed on to the disciples of the present. It has not been changed or corrupted – it is the pure teachings of the Buddha. This purity is only possible through the continuation of an unbroken lineage of transmission, the lineage the sangha passes down.

When we wish to receive the teachings of the Buddha the sangha become our teachers. We depend upon the sangha because until we become enlightened they will help, protect and assist us. When we have doubts they are there to answer our questions. In times of distress they help us dissolve our confusion, encourage and bless us. This is taking refuge in the sangha, and we need to do this until we attain Buddhahood also.

Our gurus represent all three: the Buddha, dharma and sangha. They themselves are the sangha, the teachings they transmit to us are the dharma and as the origin of these teachings is the Lord Buddha and their lineage is unbroken, they speak the words of the Buddha. The dharmakaya, sambhogakaya and nirmanakaya are all represented through these teachings. In a practical manner, this means our gurus represent the Buddha, dharma and sangha.

In this way we take refuge in the Buddha, dharma and sangha and with this understanding we formalize our Buddhist beliefs by participating in the refuge ceremony. In this refuge ceremony, we first make three prostrations towards the altar that represents the Buddha, dharma and sangha, then we sit on our right knee and hold our hands together. This is the same physical posture the Buddha's first five disciples adopted during the first turning of the wheel of dharma. To remember the Buddha, to remember his first turning of the wheel, we sit in this posture. After his enlightenment the Buddha Shakyamuni gave refuge to five ascetics, and through this they became his first disciples. Later, of course, the Buddha had countless disciples and beings continue to become his disciples up till this day, 2500 years later. By taking refuge in the Buddha, dharma and sangha we confirm we are one of these disciples.

The refuge ceremony consists of recitations, but its most important part is the act of confirmation. In the ceremony we make very clear that our refuge is in the Buddha, the dharma and the sangha. Merely reciting things after the preceptor is not enough; we have to confirm that we take refuge truly and whole-heartedly under the Buddha, dharma and sangha. This perception is extremely important, it is the basis for refuge.

The text for the refuge ceremony begins, "I take refuge from today onwards, as long as I live, in the Buddha, the dharma and the sangha." This is the essence of the recitation. After this we request the lineage, through the preceptor, to grant us refuge. The most important thing to remember during these recitations is that you are receiving refuge in the Buddha, dharma and sangha because you wish to become a follower of the Buddha.

The lineage of refuge, which began when Lord Buddha gave refuge to those first five disciples, has continued for the past 2500 years uncontaminated, unbroken and uninterrupted. I first received it from my supreme master His Holiness the 16th Karmapa. Since then I have continued to renew my refuge with many masters. I last renewed my refuge with His Holiness the 17th Karmapa, when I visited his monastery while he was in Tibet. This is my refuge lineage and when I conduct the refuge ceremony the participants become part of it. They join the ocean of countless beings who are the Lord Buddha's followers and receive his blessings. This is what it means to receive the transmission of refuge.

So when I give refuge, I am continuing the lineage that the Buddha started, that is all. I am able to give refuge because my master gave me refuge. It is not as if I am giving it on my own behalf. Those taking refuge are like the light bulb on the ceiling and I am like its switch, but the light does not really come from the switch, it comes from the powerhouse, and Buddha Shakyamuni is the powerhouse. The reason the light comes on is because there is an unbroken line from the powerhouse to the switch and then to the bulb. Likewise the lineage of the Buddha continues unbroken through to those taking refuge.

This lineage continues because of two things: devotion and compassion. Masters should have compassion for their disciples and disciples should have devotion to their masters. If this is the case, the line will not break. When these are missing, the line breaks and no matter how intensely you push the switch the light will not come on, it will not shine. You can beg the switch as hard as you like, and you can change the light-bulb a hundred times, but the light will not come on. There may be nothing wrong with the switch or the bulb, but if the line is broken the light will not come on. Fortunately for us the line is unbroken and we can still receive refuge. Still I do not want people to misunderstand and think that I can give refuge myself. I can only give refuge because of my lineage.

When we take refuge for the first time we also have a small lock of our hair cut from the crown of our head and offered to the altar of the Buddha. After this, blessed water is poured on us. This symbolizes that we are sacrificing our body, speech and mind to become enlightened for the benefit of all sentient beings. This is not a bodhisattva vow, but our refuge vows also involve this concept. This ritual also symbolizes that our taking refuge is serious because our head is without question the most important part of our body and the crown is the highest, most sacred part of our head. We call this the *dra-pul*: *dra* means hair, and *pul* means "the highest offering" – it is a symbolic gesture. At this stage you also usually receive a dharma name if you don't have one, and this somehow symbolizes that you are a follower of Lord Buddha in this particular lineage.

When taking refuge we also say prayers for bodhichitta to develop. It is appropriate for us to add these prayers of aspiration because even though refuge is fundamental for Buddhists, as followers of Vajrayana Buddhism we also need bodhichitta. In order to receive the transmission of bodhichitta you need to take the bodhisattva vow, but when taking refuge with a preceptor it is very positive to have the bodhisattva attitude. This is why we say, "I am taking refuge in the Buddha, dharma and sangha because I wish to help all sentient beings become free from samsara. To do this I wish to become a Buddha and to do that I wish to become a follower of the Buddha." To add this kindness, this compassion, this bodhichitta, to our motivation is very beneficial. We should be clear that this, in itself, is not the bodhisattva vow though.

After we say our final recitation of the refuge precepts we should try to make it very clear to ourselves that we have taken refuge in the Buddha, the dharma and the sangha and that we are followers of the Lord Buddha. We should also think that we will do our best to be a sincere, happy, positive and helpful Buddhist and respect all other religions and ideas, because they are all derived from the primordial wisdom of others. We should think that we are Buddhists and as Buddhists we will respect everyone.

At the end of the refuge ceremony the preceptor says *tab yin no*, which means something like, "It is complete," but is very hard to translate. Those taking the vows reply, "*Lek so.*" This literally means "good."

Having performed this refuge ceremony we officially become Buddhists. In my opinion it does not mean we have changed anything, though. According to our teachings each and every one of us is already more than Buddhists – essentially we are Buddhas. Still, in taking these refuge precepts we have decided to follow the path the Buddha taught in order to fully develop our destiny, the ultimate potential we all have. For this reason we participate in the living lineage of the

Lord Buddha's teaching and this begins with taking refuge in the Buddha, dharma and sangha.

Of course, many of us may have been born into a Buddhist family; our parents are Buddhists, so we become Buddhists through birth. We may have been born into Buddhist families but we don't personally become Buddhists until we take refuge in the Buddha, the dharma and the sangha. This is our way of confirming that we are truly Buddhist individually.

Precepts

By taking refuge we commit ourselves to the Buddhist path. In order to progress on the path we need to conduct ourselves accordingly. For this purpose we take precepts. The five precepts for laypeople are not to kill, not to steal, not to engage in sexual misconduct, not to lie and not to take anything that intoxicates you. When you take these precepts you can take one, two, three, four or all five of them. The person giving the vows says a prayer that includes all of them and you mentally take the ones you want to take. When taking these precepts it is better not to bite off more than you can chew. Only take the precepts you think you can keep for the rest of your life. There is no point taking precepts that you don't think you can keep, just make a wish to be able to take them in the future.

We need to be very clear about what the vows are. "Not killing," in the context of the vow, only means not knowingly, intentionally killing something. Otherwise drinking a glass of water would be breaking this vow, squashing lots of bugs every step we take would be breaking this vow, breathing in germs would be breaking this vow, and taking medicine to make our stomachs okay would also be breaking this vow. We shouldn't pretend that these things don't count, but we have to be very clear in our mind that our vow is to not go out there and kill something intentionally. We still have to take medicine, we still have to eat food, and we still have to drink water. We just have to face the reality that the things we do to survive, even drinking a glass of water, are not one hundred percent okay. Even if we grew our own vegetables we would need to spray them and therefore harm insects, otherwise insects would eat them and there would be nothing left for us.

We have to do these things to maintain our body but they are not one hundred percent okay. This is why the Buddha called our bodies *Sakche dugden che pungbo*, "A stained heap of the truth of suffering." To maintain this heap of flesh and bones, we have to feed, water and protect it. By maintaining it in this way we are creating karma; there is no way to avoid that. When we take life beyond this maintenance though, this is "killing" as described in this vow. So we need to be very clear about what we are actually saying when we vow not to kill.

When we say we are not going to steal, we again run into similar problems. Everything in this world belongs to everybody, everything. Birds, gods, asuras, ghosts, animals, human beings, everybody owns everything, but we push everybody else aside and make out as if things are really ours. Take a tree, for example: it is a home and food for birds and insects, it shelters monkeys and apes, but we cut it down and turn it into nice tables. My house, for example, is full of wooden furniture. I like wooden furniture. We need to recognize that this is also stealing because it is taking something that belongs to everyone.

This is also true for milk. Cows do not voluntarily give us milk; they make it for baby cows. Taking milk is actually stealing – we tie the baby cow somewhere and the mother cow somewhere else so we can milk her. This is not what we are vowing not to do, though, and we have to be very clear about these things. When we say "I am not going to steal" this only means that we are not going to knowingly take somebody else's money or property when it has not been intentionally given to us. It does not mean we are not going to eat cheese or vegetables or drink milk.

The next vow is not to lie. Every morning when we meet our friends they ask us how we are and we say, "I am fine, thank you." This is a lie. Nobody is fine, everybody has problems. There is nobody on this Earth who does not have any problems whatsoever, but we don't talk about these things; we just say, "I am fine." When we take this vow we are not promising to refrain from this kind of lie, we are talking about intentionally lying to gain something for ourselves, regardless of the consequences to others. We are talking about twisting things so that we fool others and get what we want.

There are also good lies. Say for example there were three big macho men teasing one little thin guy and they have hammers, chains and everything but the thin guy manages to get away from them because being smaller means he can run faster. Say then that this thin guy was hiding in a big dust bin next to us, and the three big macho men, with all their weapons, were to ask us where the thin guy was, should we tell them the truth? Would that be a good idea? I think it would be better to lie. I think it would be better to tell them he went somewhere else. Then, after the three macho men have left I think it would be a good idea to tell the thin guy in the dustbin that they have gone and he should run the other way. We shouldn't be naive about the truth or telling lies. We say we are not going to lie, but we do not mean this literally, we mean that we are not going to tell lies for our own purpose with no consideration for others. The worst from among these types of lies is the spiritual lie, to lie about your spiritual accomplishments, but I don't think you have to worry about that. This is something I need to worry about as someone teaching the dharma.

To refrain from sexual misconduct is the next precept. There are many details within this vow but what it really boils down to, if you are not celibate, is that you will only have sex with your partner. Anything outside of this relationship is sexual misconduct.

The last precept is not to take anything intoxicating, except as medicine. It is not okay to take intoxicants for entertainment, or any other reason apart from medicinal ones. If your doctor tells you that you should take a drug, you should take it, even if it is intoxicating. For example, the medicine I am taking at the moment to get rid of my running nose makes my pupils a little bigger than usual. Still it is okay for me to take it because I am ill. If you are sick, take medicine, the Buddha permitted this. This doesn't mean we can use this exception as an excuse though. It doesn't mean we can have a little glass of wine to go to sleep just because our doctor suggested we do so. It is only if we are suffering from a genuine illness and have medicine prescribed by a doctor, that it is okay if that medicine intoxicates us.

As I said, you can take one, two, three, four or five of these precepts. Taking these precepts benefits us more than simply not engaging in these actions. By taking these precepts we are intentionally not engaging in these activities, and this is much, much more beneficial than not engaging in them by accident. If you already behave as if you have these vows, then taking them makes your behavior more meaningful. These vows come from a lineage and taking them means you have the opportunity to make your natural behavior more noble and sacred.

AVALOKITESHVARA (CHENREZIG) PRACTICE

Now we will learn one of the practices of the bodhisattva Avalokiteshvara. Avalokiteshvara is a bodhisattva because he said so. He took a vow not to attain enlightenment until the last sentient being attained enlightenment; that is, to remain as a bodhisattva forever. This action was also symbolic as it represented compassion. Compassion is only relevant until the last sentient being attains Buddhahood. We do not need compassion for Buddhas – we need devotion to them. If I were to write a letter to Buddha I would not sign off, "Yours sincerely, with compassion, Tai Situ." I would write "Yours sincerely, with devotion, Tai Situ." Compassion becomes irrelevant only when the last sentient being reaches Buddhahood. This means Avalokiteshvara, as a representation of compassion, is relevant until the last sentient being reaches Buddhahood.

These are the two aspects of Avalokiteshvara. He is not just one person called Avalokiteshvara who decided not to become a Buddha until all sentient beings have reached Buddhahood. He is also the symbolic representation of compassion. We describe Avalokiteshvara as the father of all the Buddhas because compassion is the father of all the Buddhas.

There are many Avalokiteshvara practices: two-armed Avalokiteshvara, four-armed Avalokiteshvara, thousand-armed Avalokiteshvara, red Avalokiteshvara, white Avalokiteshvara, and many more. The great goddesses White and Green Tara, along with the twenty-one Taras, are manifestations of Avalokiteshvara and – as I mentioned – Wangchuk Chenpo (Mahashevara, Shiva), the great god of Hinduism, is also described as a manifestation of Avalokiteshvara. In our prayer we say "Chenrezig tu wang chug lha chenpo," "The manifestation of Avalokiteshvara, the great god Shivaji."

The thousand-armed Avalokiteshvara came about because many eons after taking his vow, through his wisdom, Avalokiteshvara assessed how many beings had already attained Buddhahood and how many were still suffering in samsara. The sentient beings suffering in samsara were countless and the beings who had attained Buddhahood were also countless. The sentient beings suffering in samsara were hopeless though, and seeing this Avalokiteshvara became discouraged and almost broke his vow. Now originally, when he had taken his vow, he had promised that if he broke his vow his body would fall into a thousand pieces so when he became discouraged this is exactly what happened, his body broke into a thousand pieces.

Through the blessings of all the Buddhas and bodhisattvas, however, he was transformed into his thousand-eyed, thousand-armed form. The thousand eyes represent a thousand Buddhas, and the thousand arms represent a thousand Chakravartins, universal monarchs who are the patrons of the Buddhas. This is the way the thousand-armed Avalokiteshvara manifested.

Another time, when Avalokiteshvara again gazed on all sentient beings and saw how many countless sentient beings were suffering in samsara, he shed two tears. These two tears transformed into Green and White Tara, two manifestations of Avalokiteshvara. They vowed to play the role of enlightened mother to all sentient beings, helping them to attain Buddhahood and fulfill Avalokiteshvara's original aspiration. Green Tara and the twenty-one Taras manifest to help sentient beings, in particular to liberate them from types of fear or aspects of suffering. This is the Anuttarayoga aspect of Avalokiteshvara.

I believe that many people in East Asia consider Avalokiteshvara to have a female form and be white in color. I can't be a hundred percent sure but I presume this is White Tara, a manifestation of Avalokiteshvara. To be sure you would have to go to a lineage master of that particular practice, scholars and many other people. I am drawing conclusions here, because I have no authority and don't know for sure, but for me this is what Kuan-Yin is, White Tara, Avalokiteshvara in female form.

Avalokiteshvara's practices, as with all dharma practices, have three parts. The first of these is refuge and bodhichitta. We have to focus on refuge and bodhichitta every time we practice, otherwise we may forget the purpose of our practice. To make sure we know clearly why we are doing a practice we start by saying the refuge and bodhisattva prayers. These two prayers together make up four simple sentences. These two sentences are the refuge prayer:

SANG GAY CHÖ DANG TSOK KYI CHOK NAM LA
Until I reach enlightenment, I take refuge in all the Buddhas,
JANG CHUB BAR DU DAK NI KYAB SU CHI
And in the dharma and all the noble sangha.

The next two sentences are the bodhichitta prayer:

DAK GI JIN SOK GYI PAY SÖ NAM KYI
By the merit of accomplishing the six perfections
DRO LA PHEN CHIR SANG GAY DRUB PAR SHOK
May I achieve Buddhahood for the benefit of all sentient
   beings.

Bodhichitta is peace. Sometimes I feel people misunderstand, or do not understand clearly, the difference between basic compassion and bodhichitta. If you are able to spend a few hours doing something for somebody you don't even know people might call you a bodhisattva. They may say, "Oh, he or she is so kind, they are a bodhisattva." This is not necessarily so. A kind person is not necessarily a bodhisattva. Being kind is very good, being a compassionate person is very good, but it does not necessarily make us a bodhisattva. A bodhisattva has to be kind and compassionate for a reason. A bodhisattva is kind and compassionate in that they are working to establish all beings as Buddhas. In this way bodhichitta is very specific.

As a Vajrayana Buddhist whose ultimate aim is to reach Buddhahood, not just nirvana but Buddhahood, we must have bodhichitta. We cannot attain Buddhahood unless we wish to attain Buddhahood. We cannot attain it by mistake or accident. It has to happen intentionally. The intention must be to become a Buddha for the benefit of all sentient beings. If I were to wish to become a Buddha just for my own reasons, it would never happen. This intention would make my Buddhahood limited, private, but Buddhahood cannot be limited. By definition Buddha is limitless. This means that Buddhahood has to be attained by a limitless purpose – the limitless freedom and liberation of limitless sentient beings. Bodhichitta, therefore, must be focused on enlightenment in this way.

The next section of the practice is the visualization of the four-armed Avalokiteshvara.

> DAK SOK KHA KYAB SEM CHEN GYI
> On the crown of my head and that of all sentient beings pervading space,
> CHI TSUK PAY KAR DA WAY TENG
> On a moon, on a lotus, is a HRI.
> HRIH LAY PHAK CHOK CHENREZI
> From the HRI on the lotus appears the Noble one, Chenrezig.
> KAR SEL Ö ZER NGA DEN TRO
> He radiates clear white light.
> DZAY DZUM THUK JAY CHEN GYI ZIK
> He gazes with compassionate eyes and a loving smile.

CHAK ZHI DANG PO THAL JAR DZAY
He has four hands. The first two are joined in prayer.
Ö NYI SHEL TRENG PAY KAR NAM
The lower two hold a crystal rosary and white lotus.
DAR DANG RIN CHEN GYEN GYI TRAY
He is arrayed with silk and jewels.
RI DAK PAK PAY TÖ YOK SOL
He wears an upper robe of doeskin.
Ö PAK MAY PAY U GYEN CHEN
His head ornament is Amitabha, Buddha of Boundless Light.
ZHAB NYI DOR JAY KYIL TRUNG ZHUK
His legs are in the vajra posture.
DRI MAY DA WAR GYAB TEN PA
A stainless moon is his backrest.
KYAB NAY KÜN DÜ NGO WOR GYUR
He is the essence of all those in whom we take refuge.

Following the refuge and bodhichitta prayer we visualize Avalokiteshvara. On the crown of our head, and the heads of all sentient beings pervading space, there rests a white lotus and moon disc. Standing on the moon disc is a HRI, a syllable letter: from this HRI comes the noble supreme Avalokiteshvara. He is luminous white, radiating five-colored light and grace. He is smiling charmingly, with compassion, and gazing at sentient beings with compassionate eyes. He has four arms; the upper two are joined together and the lower two hold a white lotus and crystal mala. He is beautifully adorned by precious jewels and silks. A deerskin that symbolizes compassion covers his upper body, worn over his left shoulder.

Some people have a hard time understanding why a deer skin should represent compassion, but the particular deer whose skin Avalokiteshvara wears was a bodhisattva manifesting as a deer who sacrificed his life for the benefit of all sentient beings. Hence this deerskin represents compassion. It is not as if the deer was killed and Avalokiteshvara is now wearing its skin.

Avalokiteshvara's crown jewel is the Buddha Amitabha. He actually has five crowns representing all five Buddha families, but on top of these is the Buddha Amitabha. Avalokiteshvara sits in the vajra asana and a stainless moon supports his back. This means there are two crystal moon discs in this visualization: one is used as the seat underneath him and the other behind him as a backrest. Avalokiteshvara, in this basic visualization, is the essence of all sources of refuge.

This is this practice's main visualization. Following this visualization, we praise the Lord Avalokiteshvara:

JO WO KYÖN GYI MA GÖ KU DOK KAR
Oh Lord of whitest form, not clothed by any fault,
DZOK SANG GAY KYI U LA GYEN
Whose head a perfect Buddha crowns in light,
THUK JAY CHEN GYI DRO LA ZIG
Gazing compassionately on all beings,
CHENREZIG LA CHAK TSAL LO
To you, Chenrezig (Avalokiteshvara), I prostrate.

There is no specific visualization that accompanies this praise; we should maintain the visualization we already have and mean what we say when we say it. In this prayer we supplicate the Lord Avalokiteshvara, whose white body is not clothed by fault and whose head is adorned by the perfect Buddha Amitabha. Avalokiteshvara looks upon all beings with compassionate eyes. In Tibetan this second-to-last sentence actually contains the Tibetan name of Avalokiteshvara, *Chen-re-zig*. *Chen* is the honorific word for eye. Ordinarily we say *mik*. The two syllables *Chen-re* together mean the entire face, or the eye itself. *Zig* is the verb "to look." To understand Tibetan syllables and words you have to look at their spelling, not only their sound. The *zig* here has four letters in Tibetan that make one syllable and means "to look." If this syllable were only to contain the first three of these letters, and not the final letter "sa," it would still be pronounced the same but it wound mean tiger or leopard. So here where it says, *Tuk jay chen gyi dro la zig*, "Your compassionate eyes look on all beings," the *chen*, "eyes," and the *zig*, "look," are the same syllables that are in the name Chen-re-zig.

Following this there is a longer prayer to Avalokiteshvara:

SOL WA DEB SO LAMA CHENREZIG
I pray to you, Lama Chenrezig.
SOL WA DEB SO YI DAM CHENREZIG
I pray to you, Yidam Chenrezig.
SOL WA DEB SO PHAK CHOK CHENREZIG
I pray to you, Perfect Noble One Chenrezig.
SOL WA DEB SO KYAB GÖN CHENREZIG
I pray to you, Lord Protector Chenrezig.
SOL WA DEB SO JAM GÖN CHENREZIG
I pray to you, Lord of Love, Chenrezig.
THUK JAY ZUNG SHIK GYAL WA THUK JAY CHEN
Buddha of Great Compassion, hold me fast in your compassion.
THA MAY KHOR WA DRANG MAY KYAM GYUR CHING
From time without beginning beings have wandered
ZÖ MAY DUG NGAL NYONG WAY DRO WA LA
In samsara, undergoing unendurable suffering.
GÖN PO KYAY LAY KYAB ZHEN MA CHI SO
There is no other refuge but you, Lord Protector!
NAM KYEN SANG GAY THOB PAR JIN GYI LOB
Please bless them that they achieve the omniscient state of Buddhahood.

This prayer starts by supplicating the Lama Chenrezig. A lama is a guru. It continues with a prayer to the Yidam Chenrezig. A yidam is a deity, the sambhogakaya aspect of the Buddha. Then it continues with a prayer to the Noble Chenrezig, the Lord Protector Chenrezig and the Lord of Love Chenrezig. These refer to more specific characteristics of Avalokiteshvara.

Up until this point we are asking Avalokiteshvara to bless ourselves and other beings; from here on we make specific prayers on behalf of the six realms.

THOK MAY DÜ NAY LAY NGEN SAK PAY THÜ
By the power of accumulating negative karma from beginningless time,
ZHAY DANG WANG GI NYAL WAR KYÉ GYUR TAY
Sentient beings, through the force of anger, are born as hell-beings
TSA DRANG DUK NGAL NYONG WAY SEM CHEN NAM
And experience the suffering of heat and cold.
HLA CHOK KYAY KYI DRUNG DU KYAY WAR SHOK
May they all be born in your presence, Perfect Deity.
OM MANI PEME HUNG

This first prayer is for the sentient beings in the hells. We pray to Avalokiteshvara to help them become free from this suffering. This prayer accords with the last syllable of Avalokiteshvara's mantra OM MANI PEME HUNG. HUNG represents the compassion of Avalokiteshvara that purifies the karma of sentient beings committed through anger, and this leads to the liberation of hell-beings from the suffering of hell. In this prayer we start at the lowest realm, the hell realm represented by HUNG, and work our way through the realms represented by ME, PE, NI, MA before reaching the highest realm, the god realms represented by OM.

In this first prayer that relates to HUNG and the hell realms we reflect that because sentient beings have accumulated negative karma since beginningless time, they are born in hell through the force of anger and experience the extreme suffering of heat and cold. We then pray that they may be liberated from this suffering by being born in the presence of the perfect deity, Avalokiteshvara. OM MANI PEME HUNG.

THOK MAY DÜ NAY LAY NGEN SAK PAY THÜ
By the power of accumulating negative karma from
 beginningless time,
SER NAY WANG GI YI DAK NAY SU KYAY
Sentient beings, through the force of greed, are born in
 the realm of hungry ghosts
TRAY KOM DUG NGAL NYONG WAY SEM CHEN
NAM
And experience the suffering of hunger and thirst.
ZHING CHOK PO TA LA RU KYAY WAR SHOK
May they all be born in your perfect realm, the Potala.
OM MANI PEME HUNG

This prayer is about those in the preta or hungry ghost realms. We are not praying to them though, we are praying for them – there is a big difference. We do not pray to the hungry ghosts, we pray to Avalokiteshvara for the hungry ghosts. These beings, having accumulated negative karma since beginningless time, are born in this realm through the force of greed and experience the suffering of hunger and thirst. We pray that they may be liberated from this suffering and all be born in Chenrezig's perfect realm, the Potala. This means we are requesting Chenrezig to liberate all sentient beings from the suffering of the preta realms. OM MANI PEME HUNG.

These verses don't translate very smoothly because Tibetan and English do not match exactly. In Tibetan, for example, instead of asking someone, "How are you?" we will say, "*Cherang kusu depo yin bä?*" *Cherang* means "your," *kusu* is the honorific way to say "body," *debo* means comfortable, *yin* means are, and *bä* is a question particle. A direct translation would be, "Your body comfortable, yes?" This shows the difference between the languages and how when prayers are translated almost word for word that they do not sound very smooth.

THOK MAY DÜ NAY LAY NGEN SAK PAY THÜ
By the power of accumulating negative karma from
 beginningless time,

TI MUK WANG GI DÜ DROR KYAY GYUR TAY
Sentient beings, through the force of stupidity, are born as animals
LEN KUK DUG NGAL NYONG WAY SEM CHEN NAM
And experience the suffering of dullness and stupidity
GÖN PO KYAY KYI DRUNG DU KYAY WAR SHOK
May they all be born in your presence, Protector.
OM MANI PEME HUNG

This is a prayer for those in the animal realm. It describes how sentient beings have accumulated negative karma through ignorance and because of this are reborn in the animal realm: remembering this we pray to Avalokiteshvara to free them from their suffering. This is the verse of the prayer that relates to the syllable PE.

Animals really are ignorant. I like them but they are very ignorant. People raise them so they can slaughter them by the thousands for food and they just sit there waiting to be slaughtered. If they were intelligent they would know they were going to be slaughtered and would use their superior physical strength to fight back. Animals are many times more physically strong than human beings. Without protective clothing or tools, we cannot even fight with small animals like cats if they really want to challenge us. As animals suffer from ignorance, however, humans can raise them and use them as slaves, while hardly giving them anything, and they will still sit there passively. This is the definition of ignorance.

It doesn't mean animals are bad. I consider animals to be very good, pure and genuine. Dogs, for example, are like very good people. In fact, if dogs are treated with respect they are more loyal than most people. When a dog steals food from you, they don't do so maliciously, they just see food there and think, "Oh my poor master forgot to give it to me." They have very good hearts I think.

THOK MAY DÜ NAY LAY NGEN SAK PAY THÜ
By the power of accumulating negative karma from beginningless time,

DÖ CHAK WANG GI MI YI NAY SU KYAY
Sentient beings, through the force of desire, are born
in the human realm
DREL PONG DUG NGAL NYONG WAY SEM CHEN
NAM
And experience the suffering of excessive activity and
constant frustration.
ZHING CHOK DAY WA CHEN DU KYAY WAR
SHOK
May they all be born in the Pure Land of Dewachen.
OM MANI PEME HUNG

The next verse describes how accumulating negative karma since beginningless time has caused sentient beings, through the force of desire, to be born in the human realm. In the human realm we experience the suffering of excessive activities and constant frustration. Sentient beings in the human real are said to suffer from *drelwa* and *polba*. *Drelwa* refers to a state of busyness, and *polba* to the non-fulfillment of greed. In order to alleviate this suffering we pray that all humans may be born in Amitabha's pure land of Dewachen, Sukhavati in Sanskrit. OM MANI PEME HUNG.

THOK MAY DÜ NAY LAY NGEN SAK PAY THÜ
By the power of accumulating negative karma from
beginningless time,
TRAK DOK WANG GI HLA MIN NAY SU KAY
Beings, through the force of envy, are born in the realm
of jealous gods
THAB TSÖ DUG NGAL NYONG WAY SEM CHEN
NAM
And experience the suffering of constant fighting and
quarrelling.
PO TA LA YI ZHING DU KYAY WAR SHOK
May they all be born in your realm, the Potala.
OM MANI PEME HUNG

This prayer is for those beings in the asura or demigod realm. I think it can also be called the realm of the titans in English. It describes how sentient beings, through the force of jealousy, are born in this realm. Here they experience the suffering of jealously fighting and quarreling. To ease this suffering we pray that they may be born in the Potala. OM MANI PEME HUNG. The demigods do not have it as good as the gods, but they do have certain powers and abilities. This situation means they are always jealous of the gods and fight with them even though they can never win.

THOK MAY DÜ NAY LAY NGEN SAK PAY THÜ
By accumulating negative karma from beginningless time,
NGA GYAL WANG GI HLA YI NAY SU KYAY
Sentient beings, through the force of pride, are born in
the realm of gods
PHO TUNG DUG NGAL NYONG WAY SEM CHEN
NAM
And experience the suffering of change and falling.
PO TA LA YI ZHING DU KYAY WAR SHOK
May they all be born in your realm, the Potala.
OM MANI PEME HUNG

This last verse is a prayer for the gods. It describes how, by the power of negative karma accumulated since beginningless time, sentient beings through pride are born in the realm of the gods and experience the sufferings of change and falling. The highest of realms, and births, is the god realm.[27] Gods suffer because they know the future and the past, and when their karma to be a god is coming to an end they can see where they will be born next, which is a lower realm due to the exhaustion of their virtuous karma in being a god. This causes them to suffer immensely. This prayer, then, is for the liberation of all the gods from the suffering of samsara. To alleviate this suffering we pray that they may all be born in Avalokiteshvara's realm, the Potala.
OM MANI PEME HUNG.

As you can see, these six verses show us the meaning of the mantra OM MANI PEME HUNG, which is how it relates to the six realms.

Following this, the prayer becomes much more personal.

> DAK NI KYAY ZHING KYAY WA THAM CHAY DU
> May I myself, through all my existences,
> CHENREZIG DANG DZAY PA TSUNG PA YI
> Act in the same manner as Chenrezig.
> MA DAK ZHING GI DRO NAM DRÖL WA DANG
> By this means may all beings be liberated from the impure realms,
> SUNG CHOK YIG DRUK CHOK CHUR GYAY PAR SHOK
> And may the perfect sound of your six-syllable mantra pervade all directions.
> PHAK CHOK KAY LA SOL WA DEB PAY TÜ
> By the power of this prayer to you, Most Noble and Perfect One,
> DAK GI DÜL JAR GYUR WAY DRO WA NAM
> May all beings to be trained by me take karma and its effects
> LAY DRAY HLUR LEN GAY WAY LAY LA TSÖN
> Into account and practice skillful acts diligently.
> DRO WAY DÖN DU CHÖ DANG DEN PAR SHOK
> May they take up the dharma for the good of all.

We pray that wherever we are born our deeds will equal Avalokiteshvara's, liberating beings from impure realms and spreading the perfect sound of the six syllables in the ten directions. We pray that in this, and all future lives, our activities will be like Avalokiteshvara's activities – liberating sentient beings from the lower realms and helping them to become free and happy. We pray that the sound of OM MANI PEME HUNG, the sacred syllables, will pervade all directions. Sometimes we say "ten directions," which is another way of saying everywhere. The ten directions are the north, south, east, west, north-east, north-west, south-east, south-west, up and down.

The prayer continues, "By the power of this prayer to you, most noble and perfect one, may all beings who are trained by me take karma and its effects into account and practice skillful acts diligently. May they take up the dharma for the good of all." Here we ask that by the force of praying to Avalokiteshvara all sentient beings who become subject to our influence will respect and sincerely follow the teachings on cause and result. We pray that they will live moral, ethical lives and that by diligently practicing these virtues everything they do will benefit sentient beings, according to the dharma. We pray that all sentient beings live according to the dharma and that we live according to the dharma for the benefit of all sentient beings. We pray that all of our followers, anybody who encounters us in the future, will live according to the dharma for the benefit of all sentient beings.

When we translate this verse it becomes a little unclear. Its meaning is quite simple but if we cannot see this meaning the verse's wording may make things complicated for us. This happens with many translations, I will give you an example. One of our most precious texts is Gampopa's *Tharpa Rinpoche Jen*. It has been translated many times and the translations are very good. Sometimes, however, the translation of its title does not give us exactly the same meaning as the Tibetan original. Often it is translated as the *Jewel Ornament of Liberation*, which is okay, but that does not have exactly the same meaning as *Tharpa Rinpoche Jen*. Literally translated *Tharpa Rinpoche Jen* would be the *Ornament of Precious Liberation*, or the *Beautifier of Precious Liberation*. There is not much difference between the titles *Jewel Ornament of Liberation* and the *Ornament of Precious Liberation*: it is just that the latter is more precise. In Tibetan, the *Jewel Ornament of Liberation* would be written *Tharpe Rinchen Jen*. But it is not *Tharpe Rinchen Chin*, it is *Tharpa Rinpoche Jen*, in which *Tharpa Rinpoche* means precious liberation and *Jen* means ornament. An ornament makes something more beautiful and in this text "precious liberation" is made more beautiful, more understandable, more approachable, more easily appreciated, clearer. In a similar way to the slight change in this title, through translation, this Chenrezig prayer has become a little less clear. However, I hope now through my explanation it has become clearer for you.

After this personal prayer, the visualization continues:

> DE TAR TSAY CHIK SOL TAB PAY
> Having prayed like this one-pointedly,
> PHAK PAY KU LAY Ö ZER TRÖ
> Light shining from the sacred form
> MA DAK LAY NANG TRÜL ZHAY JANG
> Removes all impure karma and ignorance.
> CHI NÖ DAY WA CHEN GYI ZHING
> The outer realm becomes the realm of bliss (Dewachen).
> NANG CHÜ KYAY DRÖ LÜ NGAK SEM
> The body, speech, and mind of all beings
> CHENREZIG WANG KU SUNG THUG
> Become the perfect form, sublime speech, and pure
>   mind of Chenrezig.
> NANG DRAK RIK TONG YER MAY GYUR
> All knowledge, sound, and appearances become
> inseparable from emptiness.

Until this point we have been using the same visualization, but now it changes. When it says, "Having prayed like this one-pointedly," it refers to the prayers we have already made. Through the power of these prayers, light radiates from the body of the sublime Avalokiteshvara, purifying impure karma, appearances and deluded minds. That is, Avalokiteshvara blesses and purifies the impure karma of the body, speech and mind of all sentient beings. The outer realm transforms into the pure land of Dewachen, Sukhavati, including its inhabitants whose body, speech and mind are transformed into the perfect form, sublime speech and pure mind of the mighty Avalokiteshvara. As light radiates out from Avalokiteshvara, whatever it touches in the whole universe is transformed.

The last sentence of this visualization is quite important. It says *Nang drak rik tong yer may gyur*. That is, "All knowledge, sound and appearances become inseparable from emptiness." Appearance, sound and awareness are indivisible from emptiness. Whatever you hear, see and are aware of becomes non-dualistically Avalokiteshvara. Your mind and Avalokiteshvara's mind, your body and Avalokiteshvara's body, your speech and Avalokiteshvara's speech all become non-dual. In the beginning of this visualization there is a lot happening; light is radiating, and everything is transformed. Once it has been transformed, however, it is one in absolute harmony and union – non-dual. Trying to remain in this state we recite the mantra OM MANI PEME HUNG.

OM MANI PEME HUNG is the mantra of all Avalokiteshvara's forms, including the thousand-armed, six-armed, four-armed and two-armed forms. Some forms' mantras add other syllables to these six, but the four-armed Avalokiteshvara's mantra is simply OM MANI PEME HUNG. In groups, after saying OM MANI PEME HUNG for a little while, we usually sing it for a little while, because it may inspire us. If you are practicing this at home though, you don't have to sing. When we sing the mantra we cannot repeat it as many times as when we say it, so if we are practicing at home we should say the mantra and repeat it more times than when we are in a group.

The mantra of the thousand-armed Avalokiteshvara is not the same as that of the four-armed mantra, but in essence they are the same. If you recite the mantra of the thousand-armed Avalokiteshvara this will enable you to connect with this form of Avalokiteshvara also. His mantra is, NAMO RATNA TRAYAYA NAMO ARYA JNANA SAGARA BEROTSANA BAYUHA RADZAYA TAT'HAGATAYA ARHATEH SAMYAK SAMBUDDHAYA NAMA SARWA TAT'HAGATEBEH ARHATBEH SAMYAK SAMBUDDHEBEH NAMA ARYA AWALOKITESHRAYA BODHISATOYA MAHASATOYA MAHAKARUNIKAYA TAYATA OM DHARA DHARA DHIRI DHIRI DHURU DHURU EETAH WEETAH TSALEH TSALEH TRATSALEH TRATSALEH KUSUMEE KUSUMA WAREY EELEH MEELEH TSEETEHDZOLA MAPANAYA SOHA.

The thousand-armed Avalokiteshvara is the main bodhisattva deity of the fasting practice, the Nyungne. Hopefully, in the future you will be able to do lots of Avalokiteshvara practices including the Nyungne fasting practice. This is a very, very sacred, precious practice that I hope you will do from time to time. Many of you may already be doing the Nyungne practice from time to time, but those of you who are not should, it is a wonderful practice. You can really feel inspiration and blessing by doing the Nyungne practice. Physically you feel cleansed and mentally you feel blessed. It is not that easy though.

The concluding visualization is:

DAK ZHEN LÜ NANG PHAK PAY KU
Everyone appears in the form of Chenrezig;
DRA DRAK YI GAY DRUK PAY YANG
All sound is the sound of his mantra;
DREN TOK YESHE CHEN PÖ LONG
All that arises in the mind is the great expanse of wisdom.

After reciting this mantra, as we conclude the practice, we dissolve the visualization. This is translated here as, "Everyone appears in the form of Chenrezig; all sound is the sound of his mantra; all that arises in the mind is the great expanse of wisdom [the great jnana]." The "great jnana" is primordial wisdom. Here we visualize that Avalokiteshvara dissolves into ourselves and all sentient beings with everything becoming inseparable from Avalokiteshvara.

After this dissolution, we should sit for a little bit, maybe a few seconds, maybe a minute or so. When we manifest again, we should do so as Avalokiteshvara, with the outer universe as the mandala of Dewachen, all thoughts as the compassionate wisdom of Avalokiteshvara and all sounds as OM MANI PEME HUNG. This does not mean brainwashing ourselves, it means maintaining pure perception for as long as we can and trying to say OM MANI PEME HUNG whenever we have a free moment during the day. At other times we should do what we have to naturally, comfortably and simply try to feel the presence of Avalokiteshvara at all times.

When we are new to the dharma there is a tendency to take things extremely seriously and literally and this is not very healthy. We have to sit back a little bit and take it easy. Everything is okay, everybody is Buddha, everything in its essence is a pure land, but being practical, a little bit of pragmatism is necessary. We can't all of a sudden become totally different – it doesn't work. Even if we pretend everything is different, it is not. We still need our common sense. We just have this other outlook at the same time as a bonus. When we see somebody who is not very nice to us, we can still do everything we can to avoid harm, trouble or bad feelings from them. At the same time though, deep inside we know that in essence he or she is no different from Avalokiteshvara, and this is our bonus.

Also, when we are walking, if we see a really dirty place it is not as if we should purposefully walk straight into it saying it is a pure land. We should avoid it, but deep inside we should know that in essence it is a pure land. We should know that in essence there is no difference between this dirty place and the very clean apartment or house in which we live. Relatively, however, there is a very big difference. If you go somewhere dirty, your clean home will become dirty, and more importantly, because of attachment to your clean home you will stay in samsara.

We may be like the yogi in the story about the two great Vajravarahi practitioners. One of them had a very beautiful mala, and the other didn't. Both of them practiced so well that Vajravarahi sent them stairs of red light to lead them up to the pure land of Akanishta. The one who did not have a nice mala went straight up to Akanishta, but the one who had the nice mala got half way up and realizing he had forgotten his mala came down to get it. By the time he had collected it the stairs had gone. Our very nice homes may be our beautiful malas, but knowing deep inside that the essence of everything is the same, we should try to maintain the presence of Avalokiteshvara in all aspects of our life.

> GAY WA DI YI NYUR DU DAK
> Through virtue of this practice may I now quickly
> CHENREZIG WANG DRUB GYUR NAY
> Achieve the All-seeing One's great state.
> DRO WA CHIK KYANG MA LÜ PA
> And to this same state may I come to lead
> DAY YI SA LA GÖ PAR SHOK
> Every being, not one left behind.

After arising from our state of oneness we move on to the next stage of the practice, the dedication. The dedication at the end of this practice is very short. It says, "Through virtue of this practice may I now quickly achieve the all-seeing one's great state. And to this same state may I come to lead every being, not one left behind." This is the realized state of Avalokiteshvara. We ask that we ourselves become like Avalokiteshvara and all sentient beings also become like Avalokiteshvara. This is our prayer and also our visualization. There are many other dedication prayers that we can add to this, for example the Mahamudra and Amitabha dedication prayers.

So this is a nice, short, neat Avalokiteshvara practice. As you know there are many other practices in our lineage also. It is a rich lineage, with abundant practices: so many Tantras, so many deities, so many bodhisattvas, so many mantras, so many sadhanas. The purpose of all of these practices, however, is to realize Buddhahood to benefit all sentient beings. This is the only purpose of any practice. On the way we may also have to clear physical, mental or environmental obstacles from our path, but our ultimate goal is to reach enlightenment for the benefit of all sentient beings.

There may be those of you who have decided to follow the tradition of practicing exactly step by step through the preliminaries and deity practices. This is wonderful, this path is very clear, in this lineage everything is laid down for us. Still, if you only did one practice wholeheartedly, like OM MANI PEME HUNG, I can guarantee you that you could still reach Buddhahood. OM MANI PEME HUNG represents the bodhisattva Avalokiteshvara and it purifies all the karma we have accumulated through countless lifetimes. The bodhisattva Avalokiteshvara's compassion manifests as OM MANI PEME HUNG to purify all the karma we have accumulated through pride, jealousy, attachment, ignorance, stinginess and anger over countless lifetimes. It purifies all of the causes and conditions for the suffering of samsara and if all our karma and defilements are purified then we are left with pureness itself, our ultimate essence, the tathagatagarbha – the Buddha-nature.

This means that OM MANI PEME HUNG is the simplest, easiest, most complete and convenient practice for everybody. I sometimes get the feeling that when I tell some of my disciples that they should only practice OM MANI PEME HUNG, this does not make them very happy. Then I realize that they think it is too simple, it is a practice for peasants who do not know how to read or write. This is absolutely wrong. OM MANI PEME HUNG is for everybody. It is also a practice for intellectual, learned people who know how to read and write.

Nobody can attain Buddhahood without overcoming the five – or as outlined in this practice, the six defilements; nobody can attain Buddhahood without purifying all their karma, it is impossible. Therefore I would say that on top of the practices you have from your guru, in any extra time you get – on the bus, the airplane, the couch or in the restaurant waiting for your food to be served – you quietly say OM MANI PEME HUNG. You have plenty of time in these situations. Don't come and tell me that you don't have any time. As I mentioned earlier, only 150 years ago, to communicate with your relatives on the American or African continent would have taken a very long time, and now you can do it in a moment and correct their spelling. All you need is one little gadget, one laptop, and you can actually see the person you are talking to. You may, of course, hear what they are saying after their lips have already moved, because the technology is not yet that good, but these are small problems.

This is how we live. We had so much time before, why don't we have more time now? We are saving so much time with all these gadgets that we should have more time, but we feel busier. It must be in our heads. Many people even work harder on their holidays than they do at work! They plan their holiday, they make schedules and they have so much luggage. They pack, unpack, pack, unpack, pack and unpack. They check out of one hotel and into another, get out of one taxi and into another. They spend time waiting in lines in airports and their plane or train is late so they have more problems. They then come back home relaxed and say they had a wonderful two-week holiday! They say they feel good, rejuvenated when there is actually less stress going to work.

When you are working you just drive from your nice home, only half awake with a nice, flat bottomed cup of coffee in front of you that won't spill but still you drive slowly. Then you park in your own parking spot, go into your office and sit in the comfortable chair that you carefully chose after visiting many different furniture shops. You may have secretaries and all kinds of people working for you. You may sit there, look at what people write, change it a little, sign a few things, and still you say, "It is so tiring. I need a holiday."

Other people may not be the boss, their situation is even better. As an employee you only have to think from eight o'clock to five o'clock. You show up at eight o'clock, do whatever you are supposed to do and at five o'clock you are finished, you can go home or do whatever you like. Being an employee is actually less stressful than being an employer, but people don't like being an employee; they want to be the employer, they are really looking for trouble. It is all in our head. That is why I am saying all of this, because it is just all in our head.

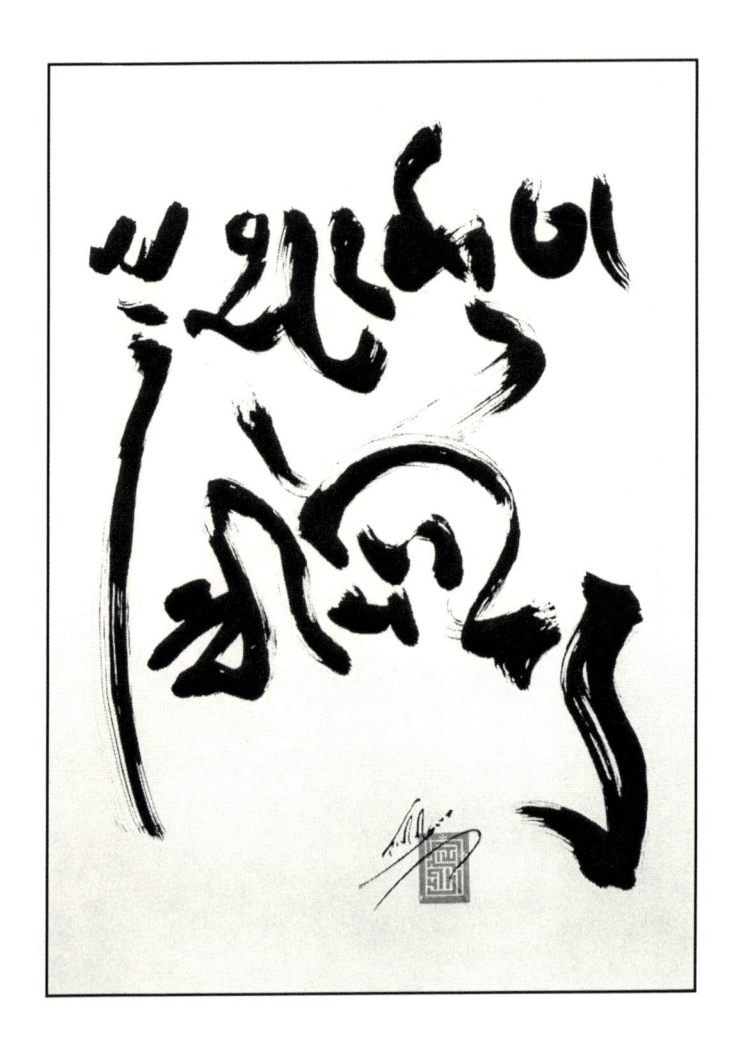

BODHICHITTA
Calligraphy by
Tai Situ Rinpoche

Chapter 5

THE SEVEN POINTS OF MIND TRAINING

NOW I WILL TEACH ON THE *Lojong Ton Dunma*, which has been translated into English as the "Seven Points of Mind Training." "Mind training" sounds a little strange. It is a translation of the Tibetan word *Lojong*. *Lo* means thought or perception and *jong* means purifying. It is not brainwashing, or any of those kinds of mind training. It is trying to see clearly by putting ourselves in other people's shoes. In this way we come to understand why others behave in certain ways. We come to understand that, just like us, nobody else wants to suffer. We come to understand that it is not only we who suffer, it is not only we who would like to be happy – everybody wants to be happy. This is a simple thing, a very simple thing that we can find out through practice. The Seven Points of Mind Training is a text with seven chapters; each of these chapters is on a particular subject but they are all related to each other. It is focused on the practices of bodhichitta, compassion, loving-kindness, impartiality and joy.

The lineage of this teaching was taken to Tibet by the great Indian master Atisha Dipankara who received it from his master Jowo Serlingpa. Many historians think Serlingpa was responsible for, or involved in, the building of the great stupa at Borobudur in Indonesia. This teaching is Serlingpa's. He gave it to Atisha Dipankara, who then took it to Tibet where it was passed down through the Kadampa lineage. Within the Kadampa tradition, Atisha's disciple Geshe Dromtonpa held this lineage and passed it on to three of his great disciples, especially Geshe Potowa. In our lineage the first Jamgon Kongtrul Lodro Thaye made commentaries on this text, but it had been one of our main practices even earlier than that.

We can look at the "Seven Points" of this text's title as its seven chapters, and they all describe the practice of bodhichitta. They describe how our mind – which at the moment is stained and defiled by ignorance, attachment, anger, jealousy and so on – can become pure. How our mind is essentially stainless and through practicing Lojong its temporary stains or obscurations are purified and its essential stainlessness is revealed. In order to purify something, there has to be an essence that remains after the process of purification. When we purify our minds the pure essence that remains is "ultimate bodhichitta." It is revealed, through the purification methods and practices that in this case we call "relative bodhichitta." Relative bodhichitta is our method of purification and that which becomes pure and stainless through this practice is ultimate bodhichitta. Ultimate bodhichitta is the goal of our relative bodhichitta practice as well as its foundation, its ground.

The process is similar to cleaning dirty clothes. The clothes may have stains – ink, ketchup, dirt – but they are on or in clothes that can be cleaned. The clothes are not the stains. If we use soap, water or other substances we can clean them, revealing the clothes' cleanliness. If the clothes were made of dirt, you could not clean them. If you cleaned ink itself, for example, when you finished there would be nothing left, nothing would be revealed. If the ink had a diamond in it though, when you cleaned away the ink it would reveal the diamond.

At the moment we have so much dirt, grease and ink surrounding us we don't even look like ourselves, but with a strong hose, soap and a brush we can reveal ourselves. This is what Lojong does. It doesn't mean altering our thinking. Altering our thinking is like brainwashing. It is not that. Instead we are purifying our perception so that our true essence can be revealed. In this way it is not really "mind training." "Mind training" is a literally correct translation of Lojong, but it may confuse us. We cannot train ourselves to be Buddhas, or bodhisattvas. We cannot take a crash course in talking, acting, looking and thinking like a bodhisattva. We can train to become a soldier and become very efficient at performing certain physical activities for a short period of time, but afterwards, through the stress of these activities, our knees, elbows and necks will be worse than everybody else's. Soldiers may have been trained to perform a specific purpose, but old soldiers need a lot of physiotherapy. They need their oversized muscles and sprained joints fixed, they need to be loosened so everything works. If there are lots of old soldiers around, physiotherapists do a good trade.

Saying "mind training" for Lojong is okay, but it makes me feel a little uncomfortable. I have even noticed that people introduce me by describing the monasteries I have "trained" in and the masters I have "trained" under. Somebody also once sincerely and politely asked me, "How many years of training does it take to become a Rinpoche?" It does not happen like this. I wasn't "trained." I learnt, received transmissions, practiced and purified myself. Even though I have voiced my worries about using this word "training," as so many people have translated the Tibetan term "Lojong" as "mind training" I will continue to use it. I just wanted to make it clear that you cannot train somebody to be a Buddha.

The Seven Points are briefly:
1. A bodhisattva's preliminary practices.
2. A bodhisattva's main practice.
3. How a bodhisattva should transform negative circumstances into positive circumstances.
4. A summary of an entire life's practice.
5. Assessing how well your practice is progressing.
6. What bodhisattva practitioners shouldn't do.
7. What bodhisattva practitioners should do.

These last two points end up being the same thing; if you do one thing, you don't do another and if you don't do something you do something else. They are similar instructions, but in this text they are taught separately so their points can be described clearly. This makes the "Seven Points of Mind Training" as a whole a simple, clear, complete work.

I will not go into great detail on these seven points because I am only going to teach them for a day but I will not, hopefully, have to leave out any important, crucial points.

1: The Preliminaries, Which Are a Basis for Dharma Practice[28]

First, train in the preliminaries.

Bodhichitta: The first of these seven points is the preliminaries. The first of these preliminaries is the development of aspiring bodhichitta and the taking of the aspiring bodhisattva vow. Aspiring bodhichitta is the wish to practice the bodhisattva's way and as a result reach Buddhahood. The second part of the development of bodhichitta, the actual bodhichitta and the actual bodhisattva vow, involves engaging in the activities of a bodhisattva, dedicating ourselves to their practices. Aspiring bodhichitta is like thinking, "I would like to go to the moon." Actual bodhichitta is like putting on a space suit, getting inside a space shuttle, pushing the start button and traveling to the moon.

In the *Bodhisattvacharyavatara,* Shantideva says, "Wishing to depart and setting out upon the road, this is how the difference is conceived." That is to say that aspiring bodhichitta is like wishing to go somewhere and actual bodhichitta is like taking off on your first steps, actually moving in that direction. When you go to the moon you cannot walk there, you have to strap yourself tightly to a seat, but it is the same process. Likewise, as a preliminary practice, a person should take both the aspiring and actual bodhisattva vows. In our lineage these vows are sometimes taken separately and sometimes together.

There are many aspiring and actual bodhisattva vows, but the basic aspiring vow is "Not to exclude any sentient being from your bodhichitta." This means, for example, that even if somebody tried to chop us into pieces, we might be very upset and angry, but if we had the chance to make that person a Buddha right then we would do so without hesitation. We should not tell someone we would not lead him or her to Buddhahood because they cut us into pieces: this would be breaking the aspiring bodhichitta vow. We are not vowing not to shout, scream, kick, push and try to run away from them, we are vowing not to exclude them from our sacred vow to attain Buddhahood for the benefit of *all* sentient beings.

The people who have been most kind to us and those who have hurt us the most are all included within this commitment. If someone who has been horrible to us has a chance to become a Buddha right now, and a person who has been most kind to us does not, we need to help the person who has been horrible to us. When we have the aspiring bodhichitta vow we cannot say, "He could become a Buddha right now but I am not going to help him do that because he was nasty to me. Instead I will find a way to make my dear friend a Buddha first." We cannot engage in divine corruption.

This is the main aspiring bodhisattva vow. The actual bodhisattva vows are many, but I think that the practice of the six paramitas somehow covers them.

The next set of preliminaries is the four contemplations. These are:
1. The Precious Human Life.
2. Death and Impermanence.
3. Karma, Cause and Result.
4. The Suffering of Samsara.

Precious human life: The first of these contemplations, the precious human life, is very important. We all have a precious human life but we take it for granted. We overlook or dismiss our basic privileges and potentials. Appreciating what we are and what we have should be the first thing we concentrate on. Someone once asked me, "How can you say 'a precious human life'? Every day the human population increases. There are over five billion human beings on Earth, how can they all have a precious human life?" I replied that I had said "precious human life," not "general human life." A human life is defined as "precious" when it has eighteen specific qualities.[29]

In contemplating the precious human life, you contemplate each of these eighteen qualities. If I were to explain them all to you now it would take too long, but you can read about them in books such as the *Torch of Certainty*, where each of them is explained very clearly. Having read this you can contemplate each of them, one by one. If you find you have all eighteen qualities then your human life is precious. If one, two or three of them are missing you should contemplate these points until you acquire them. Through this practice your life will be made precious.

From another point of view, not only human but every life is precious and everyone should be allowed to live happily. From this perspective we do not separate out one type of life from another. When we talk about a precious human birth we are saying it is precious in the sense that if you utilize it you have all the conditions you need to attain Buddhahood. Those that don't have all of these qualities still have a precious opportunity, they are not "less" than those with them, they just need to develop, one way or another, the qualities that they are missing.

When we discover we actually have a precious human life we should appreciate it, we should be very grateful for it. We may even become euphoric about it, but as being euphoric does not help us very much we should move on to the next contemplation – death and impermanence.

Death and Impermanence: This thing we have, this precious human birth is so great, so precious but we could loose it in the snap of a finger. All the doctors, physicists and scientists in the world could check us from head to toe but they still could not sign a piece of paper saying they were one hundred percent sure we will be alive tomorrow. They may be certain we will not die from naturally occurring lung or heart failure but if we pressed them they would stop short of signing a legal document guaranteeing we will still be alive tomorrow, especially if signing this form made them vulnerable to large fines and the like. Anything can happen to any one of us at any time. We could lose our precious human life in the snap of a finger – it is impermanent. Everything is impermanent. I cannot even be sure that I will walk out of this room alive. I cannot be sure that I will wake up tomorrow morning, I just don't know. I presume I will walk out of this room because I walked into it but death and impermanence are with us all the time. Death is like life's shadow – they are always together.

Karma, Cause and Result: Once we understand death and impermanence we need to understand cause and result. People commit suicide when they do not understand the process of cause and result. They think they have a big problem, which is really a little problem, and jump out of a window or under a subway train. They think they have a big problem and hang themselves or take an overdose of sleeping pills. In these ways many people don't seem to mind dying, they seem to have recognized that everybody will die, but to cause their own deaths they must not have thought about karma. People take their own lives all over the world in every society because they do not understand that dying is not the end, it is the beginning. Our past karma brought us here and it and our present karma will bring us our future. Someone may be fifty million dollars in debt and try and avoid this by jumping out of a window but this will only make their problem worse. They may not have to pay off that life's fifty million dollar debt but in future lives they will have to pay off a one hundred and fifty million or a two hundred million dollar debt. In this way they are worse off than if they had not killed themselves.

When we look at karma, cause and result, we also realize that when something wonderful happens to us we should be grateful to everybody. Why? Because if it was not for everybody else how would we have accumulated the good karma that caused this wonderful thing? If there were only one person floating in space how would they accumulate good karma? There would be no one else towards whom they could have compassion, devotion, patience or generosity. Floating in space they may be able to accumulate some merit by developing a meditative state, but really their accumulation of merit

– including the positive things they must have done to have a precious human life – depend on everybody else.

Karma, cause and result, also continues into our future lives. Doctors and scientists are constantly trying to develop medicines that will make us live longer, and their ultimate goal, of course, is immortality. They are trying to develop new knees, eyes, brains, hearts, lungs, kidneys and the most difficult organ to make – livers. They have already made a heart but they cannot find a way to make a new liver yet. When they do manage this it will be a great achievement. Thousands and thousands of researchers and scientists take years and years, spending millions of millions of dollars trying to make our lives a year longer, ten years longer or even a hundred years longer. Some people even have their heads cut off when they die, then immersed in special preserving chemicals and put inside head banks so that they can be revived when the technology becomes available. Even more interestingly, they have their pets' heads, their cats' and dogs' heads, put into these banks and pay for the service yearly, hoping they or their pets will be revived in the future.

People make such a big deal about immortality, but if you look at karma closely we are all immortal; only our bodies are mortal. Our minds are immortal, they have never died, they were never born, they were never children, teenagers, grown-ups or elderly. They are beyond these limitations, they are immortal and so are we. We do not have to worry about living for ten more years, we are countless eons old and we will go on forever. The problem is that we want to be here forever in the same form as we appear in now. We will continue but as what we are, not how we appear. What we are are Buddhas, we have limitless potential, freedom and liberation. Wouldn't it be better to forever manifest this full potential? We don't really want to go around forever in this limited way – searching and struggling, having ups and downs – we don't really want to continue this way. Once we know this then the next thing to look at, after karma, is the suffering of samsara.

Suffering of Samsara: In samsara, even if we create good karma it does not mean we will be free from suffering. Good karma makes us rich, powerful and famous but do you think being rich, powerful and famous necessarily makes us happy, comfortable, joyful and nice? If you have ten elephants you have to feed ten elephants. If it takes six hours to clean them, then immediately after you have finished cleaning them you would have to start feeding them again. In the same way, being rich does not mean we are necessarily enjoying ourselves. It does not necessarily mean we don't suffer. The more we have, the more we are at risk of losing. Being rich means you have more things you have to worry about losing. If I was a multi-billionaire, for example, and I made one small mistake – I didn't keep track of my financial flow or something – it could cost me millions of dollars. On paper some people are worth thirty or fifty billion, and when they make one small mistake – even if they oversleep, do not pick up the telephone or give a wrong instruction – they can loose two or three million dollars.

Imagine how disciplined and hard working very wealthy people have to be. Imagine how much stress and pressure they experience. I have some friends who are multi-millionaires and often they do not have access to very much of their own money. It is as if they have less than no money because all they have is tied up in debts and new projects. If you have $10,000 in your pocket, that is yours, you can spend it, but these people cannot behave like this. Before they spend anything they have to look at their whole financial system and see if their budget can handle it. They have to find a place they can take the money from so that their cash flow will be okay, their accountants will know where the money went and that they are not breaking the law, so they won't get locked up. Being rich is an enormous job that causes a lot of stress for those involved. In this way even those who are very rich suffer intensely.

Being powerful is even worse. However much power you have, you also have that much responsibility. You cannot have power without responsibility. People respect you only as long as you fulfill your responsibilities. What happens when you don't fulfill your responsibilities? We can't count on our ten fingers how many people either lose or gain positions of power in a week. There are only seven days in a week, but there are more than ten people every week who lose their positions of power. The higher they climb the harder they fall. The more powerful you are the more pressured and responsible you have to be.

Another problem with having power is that many people will be nice to you for their own benefit. They are not really being nice, they are only trying to get something from you. If you are not mature enough to recognize this you may think they are really being nice to you, only to fall flat on your face when you find out the truth. In these ways being powerful also involves a lot of suffering.

Then there is fame: when you are famous people who have nothing to do with you have opinions about you. You do not know them, but they know you. You have enemies you have never met, friends you have never met. It must be very confusing. Famous people suffer because of this all the time. Then there is the problem of staying famous. Being famous is one thing, but staying famous is incredibly difficult. Famous people may become infamous, or un-famous. Very few people manage to stay famous and die famous.

In these ways the result of good karma − health, money, power and fame − still bring suffering, as of course does bad karma. When people have nothing to eat or wear, when they have no friends or they are abused like a doormat with everyone cleaning their shoes on them, this is all the result of bad karma. As long as we are in samsara − no matter where we are, whether we are rich or poor, famous or a nobody, powerful or powerless − none of us are exempt from suffering. We have a saying in Tibetan, "The king cries on the golden throne in the palace, the beggar cries under the tree on a bed of stone, the tears are the same."

The suffering of samsara is the same for everybody. This is why we need to look at samsara after we have examined karma, cause and result, otherwise we will carry on trying to create good karma and end up a slave to it. If we constantly try to create good karma but only so we can be luckier, richer, more famous and more powerful there will be no end to our suffering in samsara. If, on the other hand, we understand the suffering of samsara, we will seek to become free from all its aspects.

After contemplating these four thoughts, we realize that no matter how much we improve our external conditions we will not overcome the suffering of samsara unless we cultivate and mature our inner being. We have all kinds of gadgets, but they can't help us overcome the suffering of samsara. The way we used to boil water was quite hard work, nowadays we just plug in an electric kettle and it boils the water. The water is clean and our hands are not covered in ash and soot from making a fire and carrying blackened pots. Has it helped us overcome the suffering of samsara though? There are even stories of people taking overdoses of pills and dying on very beautiful beds in big mansions with all kinds of gadgets around them. At the same time another person who lives in a slum with ten kids, cooks on an open fire and always has dirty feet, hands and clothes, is still laughing. The gadgets haven't made a difference to the rich person's happiness. You may also find the opposite, a happy person in a mansion and an unhappy person in a slum, but you cannot point at the gadgets and say they are what made the difference. If we look at these types of situations we will come to know that it is the development and maturity of our inner being that is most important.

It is not that I am against gadgets. I use a microphone when I teach because it saves me from having to shout. To be honest though, I still tend to shout because I have been giving speeches since I was a teenager and when I began I did not have microphones. Unless I am teaching a large audience it doesn't really matter whether I have a microphone or not, I am used to speaking without them. Still, outer developments like microphones help us. Cars help us. If I had to walk from my home to the places I teach I would not arrive until the day after I was supposed to begin teaching. If I were to ride a horse, myself and my five or six helpers would each need a horse, with a few extra pack horses to carry the food we would have to stop and cook, and the tent that we would have to set up and sleep in. There might even be robbers waiting in the bushes so we would need guards with weapons to protect us. Traveling from one place to another would be very complicated. Now that we have cars all we have to do is drive and the traffic police take care of us. Perhaps someone will honk their horn occasionally but that is a bit like music anyway, and we get where we want to on time, well almost on time.

For all these reasons contemplating the four thoughts is a very important aspect of Buddhism, especially Vajrayana practices. They are also important here in these Mahayana Lojong practices. They form the second part of the preliminary practices. After contemplating all these things properly we will come to the conclusion that the most important thing is our inner development. This is what mind training is all about.

Shamatha: Shamatha (Shinay in Tibetan) is another preliminary practice. In layman's language, Shamatha means calming down. At present our minds are totally under the influence of everything that happens to us, but through methods such as breathing meditation we are able to calm our minds down. We are able to temporarily calm the emotions and memories that mix us up. This means we are temporarily able to remain in peace and harmony. It is a very important part of the preliminary practice. Without good Shamatha it is very hard to practice anything efficiently.

There are many Shamatha methods but the one most commonly used is breathing meditation. Concentrating on our breath when it is even and quiet is a very convenient and efficient method. We breathe anyway, and when we are calm we breathe calmly. When we are not calm we do not breathe calmly. An angry person's breathing is so short they can hardly talk. They cannot finish a sentence without it becoming distorted – their whole system is distorted. An angry person may try to hide their anger but if you watch for these signs you can tell. When we are jealous our faces and our breathing change, so that no matter how hard we try to hide it, people will still know we are jealous. When we are proud, no matter how we try to hide it the curl of our lips will give us away. Complexes, whether they are inferiority or superiority complexes, also show in our voice, in our face, we can't hide them. All our emotions are the same: when we are influenced by them we change and our breathing changes.

If we are able to practice Shamatha in any of these states though, we will calm down immediately. We may not act on our anger, jealousy or pride but still it in itself is a defilement that Shamatha can help us get rid of temporarily. Shamatha cannot help us get rid of them permanently but getting rid of them temporarily is a good start. If you are able to pacify your smaller defilements in this way, gradually you will be able to pacify your larger and larger defilements until you are able to pacify your greatest defilements. At the same time you will be strengthening your qualities, they will go from being weak to quite significant to great. In this way we can see how important Shamatha is as a foundation practice.

How this works is, for example, if you are a businessman or woman and you oversleep, forget to call somebody back or give the wrong instruction, you could have a big problem and therefore start to worry. If you drive yourself crazy by worrying and try to fix the problem in that state it will not work. If I try to find something in my notes while I am hurriedly mixing them up, I will not find anything. If on the other hand I put them all down on the table, relax and calmly look through them, I will find it. If we calm down and relax we will be much more able to handle our mistakes.

2: THE MAIN PRACTICE, WHICH IS TRAINING IN BODHICHITTA

[Ultimate and Relative Bodhichitta]

Ultimate Bodhichitta
Regard all dharma as dreams.
Examine the nature of unborn awareness.
Self-liberate even the antidote.
Rest in the nature of alaya, the essence.
In post-meditation, be a child of illusion.

Relative Bodhichitta
Sending and taking should be practiced alternately.
     These two should ride the breath.
Three objects, three poisons, and three seeds of virtue.
In all activities, train with slogans.

Begin the sequence of sending and taking with yourself.

The second point has two parts, relative and ultimate bodhichitta, which comprise the main practice of this Lojong text.

Relative Bodhichitta

The main practice of relative bodhichitta is known as *Tonglen* (giving and taking). *Tonglen* is a term that is used in other practices but is mostly associated with the Seven Points of Mind Training. *Tong* means "give, send or let go." *Len* means "take or receive."

This practice itself can also be done in many ways. One of the best ways is first to sit comfortably, do a good Shamatha practice – perhaps breathing meditation – then when your body and mind are calm visualize your dear parents in front of you. They are surrounded by all other sentient beings, your enemies as well as your friends and relatives. Another way is to first practice Tonglen with you dear ones then gradually progress to including more and more beings. Whoever you visualize, you see yourself giving them all your good karma as you breathe out and breathing in all their suffering, pain and bad karma – everything they don't want. When you breathe it in you then dissolve it. By doing this you see that you are making them free from suffering, you are making them happy and this makes the idea of giving away your wisdom and positivity easier. Accompanying our out and in breath with these ideas is one form of Tonglen.

Using breathing to practice Tonglen is a simple, basic, beginning practice but Tonglen does not always have to be practiced with breathing meditation. It can also be about simply giving things away, sending them away, and dedicating all our goodness and positivity to the purification of sentient beings' negativity and the relief of their suffering. This is also Tonglen. Yet another way to practice Tonglen is when we are sick. When we have a cold or some other illness we can view this as the suffering of other sentient beings and see ourselves taking on this suffering. We can think, "May my suffering take away the suffering of others. May my suffering purify others' suffering." Likewise when something wonderful and joyful happens to us we can dedicate this to others. We can send this out to others.

In India we have a custom of giving out sweets (*mithai*) when there are holidays or something nice happens. We at least try and make other peoples' mouths sweet when something sweet has happened to us. We say please take some, don't refuse because we want to share our happiness with passers-by and strangers. On these special holidays people will stop me as I drive to my monastery, and not only me but anyone else who passes by. They have put up tents with food inside and they give away all kinds of food, juice and water, even the very poor ones at least have water, and they want you to stop there and have a meal. If you were to be polite and stop every time you were asked to, you would end up eating twenty meals in one day! This does not always happen, but on special holidays and during special seasons it does, especially in the Punjab. I am not saying that they are necessarily practicing Tonglen, I don't know if they are or not, I am just saying that Tonglen practice is a little like this tradition. When something good happens to us, sharing it with others is Tonglen.

Relative bodhichitta practices also include seeing ourselves, in our visualizations and dedications, as a wish-fulfilling gem, a medicinal plant, or a river that quenches the thirst of everybody on its banks and cleans their clothes. A river provides so much; it is the home to so many fish, frogs and all kind of life-forms. It provides electricity for big cities and becomes a place for picnics and holidays for those seeking to relax after working hard during the week. They may even work harder during the week so they can get away on their boats at the weekend. Bringing all this happiness is like being a manifestation of the Buddha. So seeing ourselves manifesting as a river, a light or medicine is another aspect of relative bodhichitta practice.

We could also envision ourselves as a vehicle that fulfills the wishes of great bodhisattvas. This is a sacred practice because it also involves devotion and therefore less of our ego. If we pray, "May I be the vehicle for White, Green and the Twenty-one Taras to liberate sentient beings from samsara," this is another way to practice relative bodhichitta. Or maybe we could pray to be a vehicle for Manjushri to provide wisdom, Avalokiteshvara to provide compassion, Medicine Buddha to provide health.

Relative bodhichitta in our day-to-day life when we are not on our meditation cushions means trying to maintain the perception and presence of inner compassion, joy, impartiality and loving-kindness as we walk around carrying out our daily activities. It means, for example, not thinking, "How dare he say such a thing," when someone insults us. It means thinking instead, "May this insult purify any negative karma I have with this person. I have definitely said something nasty to them, perhaps a long time ago, so may them saying this resolve any residue from my previous actions." When somebody does something nice to us on the other hand, then we can think, "This is the result of something good I did for this person and now they are returning the favor. I appreciate it, and may they also accumulate good karma by being nice to me." This means that this positive experience is not wasted either. It stops being about payback and becomes a sacred exchange, a sacred relationship in itself. These are all post-meditative relative bodhichitta practices.

Ultimate Bodhichitta

The definitions of relative and ultimate bodhichitta are simple. Ultimate bodhichitta is non-dualistic; relative bodhichitta is dualistic. It is dualistic in that we do something for others: we take on others' suffering and give them our happiness. This view is dualistic. It is relative bodhichitta. Ultimate bodhichitta is non-dualistic.

Ultimate bodhichitta practices are usually meditation, but in the Seven Points of Mind Training they are taught in two stages: meditation and post-meditation. The meditation stage is also taught in three stages:
1. Preparation.
2. Actual meditation.
3. The Conclusion.

Preparation: We begin meditation by sitting down nicely in front of our shrine, or wherever we feel is a proper space to meditate. We say refuge and bodhichitta prayers while envisaging all the Buddhas and bodhisattvas above and around us. This is just something we do for our own sake because the Buddhas and bodhisattvas are above and around us all the time whether we envisage them or not. Everything is part of the limitless manifestation of Buddha, everything! Nothing is a secret to the Buddhas and bodhisattvas, but as we are dualistic, un-enlightened people we purposefully envisage and invoke them.

After this we do whichever Shamatha practice we usually do, breathing meditation or whatever. Then we think about and appreciate bodhichitta. It is like the sun which shows everything, a cleansing river that quenches everyone's thirst, the sky that provides space for all and the medicine that heals all suffering and pain. Thinking on bodhichitta in detail involves contemplating compassion, loving-kindness, joy and impartiality. It means wishing that all beings attain the limitless freedom, happiness, joy and harmony that they seek in the same way we do. If we searched we could not find one sentient being in the universe that likes to suffer or does not want to be happy: these are universal quests. Bodhichitta is the greatest provider for these quests, it is a limitless resource. When we sit down to meditate we need to appreciate and recognize this.

Then if we know it we should say the Seven Branch Prayer, The *Yenlag Dün*.

CHAK TSEL WA TANG CHÖ SHING SHAK PA TANG
Prostrating, offering, confessing,
JE SU YI RANG KÜL ZHING SOL WA YI
Rejoicing, beseeching and praying,
GE WA CHUNG ZE DAG GI CHI SAG PA
Whatever little virtue I have accumulated from these,
THAM CHE DZOG PE JANG CHUB CHIR NGÖ WO
I dedicate to the perfect enlightenment.

These seven braches are:

1. <u>Prostration</u>, which is easy to understand. It means bowing to the Buddhas and bodhisattvas.

2. <u>Offerings</u> are also easy to understand: we make offerings to all the Buddhas and bodhisattvas.

3. <u>Confession</u> is confessing all our wrong doings, whether we remember them or not.

4. <u>Rejoicing.</u> We rejoice when we appreciate the wisdom and compassion of all the Buddhas and bodhisattvas, as well as the happiness of sentient beings. It is the opposite of jealousy. Jealousy is an evil thing, it is appreciating other peoples' suffering and disliking their happiness. This joy is its opposite.

5. <u>Requesting the Buddhas to turn the wheel of dharma.</u> This needs some explanation. The Buddha Shakyamuni said that the enlightenment of a Buddha is rare indeed but still countless sentient beings attain Buddhahood in every moment. He said that the number of sentient beings who attain enlightenment in one moment could not be counted by the grains of sand in the river Ganges. From its source to the ocean, how many grains of sand would there be on the banks and bottom of the Ganges? There are countless grains of sand and this number of beings become enlightened in every moment. A moment is the shortest measure of time, less than a snap of the fingers. If this many beings attain enlightenment in every moment and enlightenment is still seen as rare, this shows us how many sentient beings there are. Beings are so numerous, universes are so numerous, that even if one sentient being from every million galaxies attained Buddhahood once in a million years the number of beings becoming enlightened in each moment would still be uncountable. Space is endless and filled with countless sentient beings of all kinds.

Buddhahood is the full maturation, the full development of the ultimate, limitless potential that manifests as limitless freedom, harmony and liberation. It is natural for sentient beings to achieve Buddhahood because they have the potential to. This term we use, "Buddha," came about because Prince Siddhartha attained Buddhahood in India and therefore we use a Sanskrit word for this state. Tibetans use the word *Sangye* but I think everybody uses a word that is at least related to the original Sanskrit word "Buddha."

Our idea of enlightenment should not be limited to this name though, it should not be limited to the image we have of Prince Siddhartha. All Buddhas do not look like Prince Siddhartha. Prince Siddhartha was a human being on planet Earth, in this solar system, in this galaxy. On Earth, where he attained enlightenment, humans have two hands, one head, two eyes, one nose with two holes, two ears, hair on top, hands with five fingers, five toes on two feet, two legs and one central part of their bodies. In other universes humans may look totally different to Buddha Shakyamuni, they may attain enlightenment and not look a thing like Prince Siddhartha. They will manifest in whatever way they consider perfect, the most majestic way for them to look in those circumstances. "Buddha" does not only refer to Prince Siddhartha the Buddha, it also includes those who have reached the same level of ultimate liberation elsewhere and at other times.

When we sincerely request "Every Buddha achieving enlightenment right now" to turn the wheel of dharma, we are performing almost the same role as the gods who asked Shakyamuni Buddha to teach. The king of the gods came down from heaven, sat in front of the Buddha and offered him a conch shell while another of the gods offered him a dharmachakra – a golden wheel with a thousand spokes. This wheel, along with the two deer that came out of the forest to sit near him, are where we get the emblem of Buddhism from. Buddha Shakyamuni then went on to turn the wheel of dharma in Varanasi when he taught the Four Noble Truths. If we sincerely request the countless Buddhas who are attaining enlightenment right now to turn the wheel of dharma, we are doing the same action as the king of the gods.

Ultimately the distance between the Buddhas who are achieving enlightenment and us does not matter, but our request will not be exactly the same as that of the king of the gods because we are dualistic and from a dualistic perspective here is not there – we don't see any Buddhas in front of us. If we visualize these Buddhas though, ask them sincerely to please turn the wheel of dharma, it will be a similar action.

6. <u>Asking Buddhas not to enter into paranirvana for the benefit of sentient beings</u>. Many Buddhas are also about to enter into paranirvana, or to use simple language they are about to die. When the karma for beings to see a Buddha's nirmanakaya has finished, Buddhas enter into paranirvana, this is the death of a Buddha. Buddha Shakyamuni died at the age of eighty-one. There are as many Buddhas dying now as there are Buddhas becoming enlightened. Here we request them to live longer so they can benefit sentient beings by giving them the opportunity to meet a living Buddha.

7. <u>Dedicating the merit of the other six branches</u>. This is the last of the seven branches. Here we dedicate the merit of the first, second, third, fourth, fifth and sixth branches. Along with this merit we also dedicate all our other merit and wisdom to the Buddhahood of all sentient beings.

This was the seven branch prayer and completes the beginning section of the ultimate bodhichitta practice.

Practice of Ultimate Bodhichitta

With the completion of the preliminaries you are supposed to have reached a quiet, calmly abiding state of mind. In this state you then dissolve everything into emptiness by viewing all objects outside yourself as if they were a dream. They are nothing more than how our mind perceives them and the mind that perceives them does not have any solid, tangible reality either. Neither external objects nor our mind, which is internal, exist. They do not exist but they are there. In this way they can only exist beyond dualism.

Dualistically we can never find anything that is truly substantial. External objects are atoms in some kind of combination but even these smallest objects are made up of their parts. Even atoms need to have seven parts: four sides, a top, a bottom and a center. When other similar atoms are attached to it the object may become bigger and bigger, but if something has seven parts it cannot be the smallest object in existence, its seven parts have to be smaller than the object and again each of these parts must have seven sections. In this way objects can get smaller and smaller and smaller forever. There is nothing in any of these parts that really exists.

The mind, for its part, is superficially like a river. You may be able to bathe in the river Ganges today but if you went to the same spot tomorrow the "river" you bathed in yesterday will have flowed out to sea. You cannot bathe in the same river Ganges twice. Another example is a butter lamp. It looks the same but it doesn't stay the same even for a split second, it keeps on burning. Time, is also like this. What is the present? If we try to find the present moment it is just like searching for the "real" atom. "Now" has to have three parts: one closer to the previous shortest moment of time, another closer to the future shortest moment of time and another in the middle of the two. So really this middle part of the smallest moment of time is "now." But this also could be divided into three, again and again, which means we cannot find "now." We cannot find a moment of mind in a dualistic context. Time, mind and all realities are baseless in this way, absolutely baseless, but they are here.

As practitioners of the Mahayana, as practitioners of Lojong, we are also seeking to remain in the non-dualistic state when we practice ultimate bodhichitta. Philosophically and scientifically we can prove that nothing exists, but that does not necessarily help us. Even if we know nothing is here we are still happy when something nice happens and upset when something not so nice happens. Just proving philosophically that "nothing is here" doesn't help us. At the core of all of this is a non-dualistic state of mind above and beyond something or nothing. You cannot point at something and say it is your mind, you cannot grasp at anything, but you cannot say your mind is nothing either. If the mind is nothing, who or what is asking questions about the mind? Who could come to the conclusion that the mind is nothing? It cannot be nothing and it cannot be something, it has to be above and beyond "nothing" and "something."

This core that is beyond "nothing" and "something" is the ultimate bodhichitta. We say it is *khor sum nampar mi-tokpa* in Tibetan, "free from the three circles." These three circles are the object, subject, and the interaction between the subject and object. For example, a paramita by definition means to reach beyond, but what does "to reach beyond" mean? What, for instance, does the generosity paramita mean? Does it mean we need to make everybody rich? Or does it mean we have to spend everything we have? The generosity paramita actually means reaching beyond the idea of a giver, a recipient and the act of giving. Seeing the giver, recipient and action non-dualistically, without these three circles, is the definition of the generosity paramita. This is true not only for the generosity paramita but also the morality, diligence, patience, meditation and wisdom paramitas. Ultimate bodhichitta and ultimate emptiness are the same thing. In Tibetan "ultimate emptiness" is called *dondam thong nyi*: *dondam* means ultimate, *thong nyi* means emptiness. Ultimate bodhichitta is *dondam jang chup chi sem* or *dondam jang chup sem*, the ultimate mind of enlightenment; they mean the same thing.

When we do the practice of ultimate bodhichitta, or ultimate emptiness, we first dissolve reality, then ourselves into emptiness. What remains is the limitless non-dualistic state of being and we stay in this state for as long as we can.

To do this, first relax, physically and mentally relax. Don't try to stop your thoughts but don't follow them either, just let them come and let them go. When you reach a relatively calmly abiding state, then maintain that state with awareness. In that state everything is in absolute harmony. Sounds are just like echoes and images just like dreams. Then remain in a continuous state of awareness of the present.

Meditating for even a short time in this way you may get a glimpse or a taste of this ultimate, non-dualistic state. You may not want to come out of it, but you have to.

This ultimate bodhichitta is the ultimate essence of bodhi, enlightenment, within each one of us. In this very brief, simple meditation we somehow feel comfortable, relaxed and in harmony. It is as if there aren't any problems anywhere, as if everything is perfect and in harmony. It is a very good feeling. We are still dualistic of course. We are only glimpsing a little piece of limitless. It is like we see the space in a glass, but not the limitless space outside the glass. Limitless space, like our mind, has no center, no edge, no beginning, no end – it is all-pervading.

When practicing these meditations it is much better for beginners to do more, shorter sessions rather than one long session. If you practice this way you will actually progress. Once you have progressed then you can do fewer, longer sessions. Of course it depends on the individual, but many times beginners treat calm abiding merely as a relaxant. There are many relaxants available these days but some people like calm abiding meditation better than pills. They may even become so involved in being relaxed that they are not really doing an ultimate bodhichitta practice, just stress management. We are not doing calm abiding meditation to manage our stress. We are practicing calm abiding and ultimate bodhichitta meditation to attain Buddhahood for the benefit of all sentient beings. We need to be truly and sincerely progressing, not just trying to feel good. We may feel good, but that is a bonus. We are allowed to feel good, there is nothing wrong with it, but if we are doing our meditation in order to feel comfortable then we are doing it for the wrong reason.

I can describe this feeling that we may become attached to. From head to toe we feel as though there is no sickness, no disease, no discomfort – everything feels absolutely perfect. Even if I have a cold, in meditation it is as if I am swimming in an ocean of honey – perfect. If we get attached to this state though, we are back to square one. It is as if our meditation fulfills no greater purpose then a daily dose of relaxants, and this should not be the case. In order to stop this happening shorter sessions are recommended for beginners, as is taking refuge and developing relative bodhichitta at the beginning of each session and dedicating merit at its conclusion. These things remind us exactly why we are meditating. We can get lost in bad things, we can also get lost in good things, but we should try not to get lost anywhere.

We also need to be aware that usually, when we begin to meditate, we fall into one of two categories: those that tend to fall asleep or those that cannot calm down. I am not worried about those who fall asleep. If you fall asleep when you try to meditate it means you know how to relax. I do worry about those who cannot calm down though. If someone cannot calm down when they meditate it shows they don't know how to relax and meditation can have an adverse affect on them. If people fall asleep when they meditate they are not likely to go crazy through meditating, but those who cannot relax need to be guided carefully otherwise they can develop mental problems.

The most important thing to learn about meditation in the beginning is how to relax. Usually meditation is not done vigorously. When we meditate we should be relaxed.

There are some exceptions, tantric meditations that should be done vigorously and involve specific breathing and exercise techniques, but these should not be attempted by beginners. Calm abiding meditation, which we should do in the beginning, is not vigorous, it is calming. We concentrate in these meditations but not like a fighter pilot flying through mountains. They have to concentrate intensely or they will hit something and die. This is not the kind of concentration we need in meditation. The concentration we need in meditation is like looking at the vastness of the sky. If we are able to concentrate in this way, we will succeed in this kind of meditation. I feel it is necessary to explain this because I know lots of people who meditate and some of them have been, to put it politely, affected. It is important to remember to first relax, have a calmly abiding mind and then base our ultimate bodhichitta meditation on this.

For those of you who fall asleep easily there is a simple remedy – keep your eyes open! It is a very ancient, original, skillful technique for not falling asleep. Another thing that may help is looking up. If you are looking up with your eyes open it is hard to fall asleep. If you start thinking too much and becoming agitated you can close your eyes and bend your head down a little. These techniques help because our body functions on many levels and the subtle functions that make us think one way or feel another are affected by our posture.

Our diet also affects these subtle functions. Those of you who have lots of thoughts and no peace of mind should really consult your doctor. I don't want to be responsible for anything happening to you. These days I have to be very careful. I might be liable! Still generally speaking, eating food that is a little heavier may make us feel a little bit more substantial and grounded. Those of you who tend toward sleep, on the other hand, may want to cut down on substantial foods. Eating lighter foods and less of them will help you feel a bit lighter.

There is also a connection between these two types of people and high and low blood pressure: those with high blood pressure find it harder to relax and those with low blood pressure fall asleep easier. Blood pressure does not necessarily connect to what you eat: thin fit people can have both high and low blood pressure as can unfit, fat people. They do not necessarily correlate with our diet.

Hopefully, through knowing all of this you will be able to figure out when something is wrong with you when you are meditating. If you fall asleep each time you meditate you do not have to think, "Something is wrong with me!" You will know it is just a physical or environmental condition. Actually nothing is wrong with you, you are ultimately perfect but due to some environmental conditions things are sometimes good and sometimes not so good. Things are sometimes conducive to meditation and sometimes less conducive to meditation. Knowing these things is very helpful.

The other thing to remember is that there are no ghosts disturbing you! Having ghosts disturb you is very convenient, isn't it? Anything that does not work out we can blame on the ghosts. Anything that is wonderful we can say is the work of an almighty god and anything unbecoming are the ghosts. Then it is all good, it has nothing to do with our ego. The only problem is that it is not true. Our ego is very tricky, its games are impeccable. We always have to be aware of ego's games. We are experts at playing games with ourselves, we need to try to do this less.

Dedication: The third part of the meditation is its conclusion, the dedication. Here we dedicate the merit from our meditation on ultimate bodhichitta to the realization of ultimate bodhichitta, which is Buddhahood, by all sentient beings. This conclusion is always the same. The conclusion of every Buddhist practice is a dedication.

Post-Meditation: In post-meditation, in our activities, we should try to retain some aspects of whatever state we reached in our meditation on ultimate bodhichitta. If, for example, we did this meditation in the morning, when we finish it and start doing regular things – going to the office and so on – we should try to retain the perfectly harmonious state of our meditation. This will automatically affect the way we do things. Normally most of us do things in a stressful manner, but if we are in this calm abiding state we can do the same things without causing ourselves stress. If I were to calmly put my glasses down on the table and then pick them up again I could do so without any stress. If, on the other hand, I were to do the same action hurriedly because I was worrying about something it could make things more difficult. I might even put my glasses on incorrectly and not be able to see.

In this way, if we try to maintain this calmness, if we try to do things clearly with awareness, we will achieve much more, less stressfully. Our daily activities will become a practice for us. We can do this when we are driving, talking, eating – doing anything. We eat breakfast every morning but many times we do not even remember what we ate. We eat lunch and do not remember what or how much we ate – was it too much or too little? If we manage to maintain our calm abiding state we will taste every sip of our tea and orange juice and taste every slice of our bread. We will know what we are eating and we will enjoy eating it. It will make eating a harmonious and healthy thing, a practice even. Nobody can even drink a glass of water perfectly until they reach Buddhahood. I may drink a glass of water every day but I am not going to do it perfectly until I become a Buddha.

Instead of actually trying to retain this state we could pretend to be calm. We could act very holy, sacred and reserved even though our minds are chaotic. We could do this, but it would not help. It is not easy to maintain this state during our ordinary activities; I did not mean to suggest it was, but we should know how important it is. If we try to do it and sometimes manage and sometimes don't, that is okay. We have been in samsara for countless lifetimes and to get where we are we have done okay – we all have a precious human life. There is no reason for me to think that in my past life I, or all of you, did something unbelievable, unimaginable or impossible in order to have a human birth now. We have done okay, so we are okay.

We need to remember that everything we experience, the good and the bad, is a result of what we have done in the past. This means we could experience all sorts of things. The rain that fell in the ocean a million years ago and the rain that fell in the ocean yesterday are both still in the ocean. Our karma is the same, it is not lined up like an army – "Right, left, right, left" – with one piece of karma finishing and another starting. Karma's results manifest through the force of karma. Which results will manifest now or later and in which way depends on the force of the karma that caused them. The outcome of our past lives is what we experience now. My past lives are like an ocean of milk and I am its butter. It is the same for all of you, you are the butter of the ocean of milk that is your past lives.

3: Transformation of Bad Circumstances into the Path of Enlightenment

The Paramita of Patience

When the world is filled with evil, transform all
  mishaps into the path of bodhi.
Drive all blames into one.
Be grateful to everyone.
Seeing confusion as the four kayas
Is unsurpassable shunyata protection.
Four practices are the best of methods.
Whatever you meet unexpectedly, join with meditation.

This third point of the Seven Points of Mind Training is taught in two parts: thought and action.

Thought: When we are practicing relative bodhichitta we need to know that every negative circumstance we experience has everything to do with us. If something has nothing to do with me it will not happen to me. If something happens to me it has everything to do with me. Someone else may do something to me that causes me to suffer but it still has everything to do with me. This does not mean we should blame ourselves for everything, it means we should recognize the core of the problem. If I have a problem then it has everything to do with me and I have everything to do with it.

We should not blame ourselves for what happens but we definitely should not blame only others. Blaming others may make us feel good, but please do not do it seriously or wholeheartedly. It is not okay. If I had never hurt anyone, ever before, there is no way anyone would ever hurt me. I have everything to do with what that person does to me. Although this is also true for any positive situations we may experience, here we are learning how to deal with negative circumstances. Understanding that any negative experience we have has everything to do with us is the first step in developing the right "thought" for this practice.

If we know this we can stop negative experiences from becoming a cause or condition for us to experience more negativity. Instead of reacting to these situations badly, and thereby creating the causes of more suffering, we can do our best to find a solution to these situations or just endure them, depending on what kind of problem it is and how easy it is to solve. We may have no choice but to solve it because we may not be able to endure it. It is like catching a cold. If I have the capacity to endure it all I need do is sit there, drink lots of hot water and take no medicine. I can get rid of the cold that way. If I do not have the capacity to endure the cold though – if I have to give a series of teachings for example – I can take a lot of pills so I can talk without sneezing, coughing or having my nose run. There are different ways to handle things in different situations.

The next step is to recognize that the source of all our suffering is ego. When we say circumstances have everything to do with us, we mean they have everything to do with our egos. Through my ego I indulge in desire, anger, jealousy, pride and so on and their result is my suffering. When we reflect on our experiences in this way our "thoughts" of relative bodhichitta become more detailed.

The "thought," as it relates to ultimate bodhichitta, means knowing that ultimately nothing is happening. Even the worst thing that could happen to us is only happening relatively – ultimately, nothing is happening. I will give you a very stupid example. Let's say I was in a helicopter in Hawaii and I wanted to take photos of a volcanic eruption so I told the pilot to go closer to the lava. The pilot would tell me it was too hot and too dangerous, but let's say that I ignored this and asked him to take me closer anyway. Finally, let's say, I lost consciousness and fell into the volcano. My pilot would not be able to do anything. As I have fallen into molten lava there is no way medics could come and treat me. My mortal body would be completed consumed by Madam Peli (the Hawaiian goddess of the volcano). Hopefully the pilot will have made a video-recording of the incident, otherwise he might get into trouble but apart from that there would be nothing else for him to do except go home, relax and tell the story.

Relatively all these things have happened but from the point of view of ultimate bodhichitta nothing has happened. My mortal flesh, blood and bones might have been completely consumed by Madam Peli but my mind cannot be burned by anything. Even if it was 10,000 degrees nothing could happen to my mind and therefore from the perspective of ultimate bodhichitta nothing has happened to me. Even the worst possible thing that could happen does not happen ultimately. We cannot experience this view right now because even a pinprick hurts us. Even the New Delhi winter weather makes us sneeze and shiver. We may not be able to do much with this understanding technically but deep inside it can make a big difference. When something terrible happens to us, knowing that nothing is happening to us ultimately can make a big difference.

Without this perspective, falling into the mouth of an active volcano on the big island of Hawaii would be a big problem. At only fifty years old I would be completely, ultimately finished. If I know that ultimately nothing has happened, though, this makes a very big difference. We can avoid pinpricks and other problems but when they do happen knowing ultimately that nothing is happening, that ultimately everything is above and beyond this, is very healthy. It gives us perspective and with perspective we can transform negative circumstances into a positive condition for the path.

To summarize, we can transform all situations into the path by relating our experiences to relative and ultimate bodhichitta. Everything we experience has relatively everything to do with us and is ultimately not happening. These two truths are essential to understanding this chapter.

Action: There are also actions that transform negative circumstances into the path to liberation. Tonglen is obviously something that transforms negative situations. When something bad happens to us Tonglen becomes easier to practice. If we are sick and lying in hospital, for example, somebody near us may be screaming, somebody over there may be crying and somebody over somewhere else may be struggling to breathe. We will most probably be surrounded by suffering and may even be in pain ourselves or be attached to tubes and undergoing different types of treatment. In these situations Tonglen is no longer a joke or a game. It is not just our imagination, it is reality. This makes it easier to pray with sincerity. If we can see others suffering and we are suffering ourselves then we can pray that our illness consumes the illnesses of everybody else in the room sincerely and vividly.

When other negative situations happen to us, if we lose money or face a lawsuit for example, generating compassion towards our tormentors can turn them into great opportunities to practice Tonglen. That is if we are still able to do this. This does not mean, though, that we should just sit there when these things happen and do nothing. It means that deep inside our hearts, as practitioners of bodhichitta, we should have compassion for our tormentors. He or she is committing bad karma, so we should have compassion for them. The way we deal with individual situations can vary: sometimes we may endure them, other times we may solve them and in yet other situations it may be best to challenge our persecutors. In all these situations though, as practitioners of bodhichitta, we should be thinking, "I don't want them to be a persecutor," instead of thinking, "I don't want to be victimized." Bodhisattvas challenge destructive activity because they think they can stop people from becoming a killer, thief or liar instead of worrying what is happening to them personally. Depending on the situation they may stop perpetrators from acting with malice towards them for this reason or try to stop them but not be able to.

If we are going to endure these situations we should endure them in a healthy way. That is, we should endure them thinking, "May this suffering I am experiencing be the suffering of all sentient beings including that of my tormentor. May I suffer on behalf of all of them." In any of these situations, how well we respond to them depends on how genuine, how pure our motivation is. We cannot generalize about what to do in these situations but we can say that whether our actions are effective or ineffective, appropriate or inappropriate depends on our intention at the time.

Another type of action we can engage in is accumulating merit. Normally we would do this by being generous towards the Buddha, dharma and sangha and by doing charity work for the needy, but there are other ways to accumulate merit. In the Vajrayana and in these Mahayana teachings they mention the offering of mandalas. When we offer mandalas we offer the whole universe – including the sun and the moon – to all the Buddhas and bodhisattvas so that the merit we generate from this can be a cause for all sentient beings to attain Buddhahood. I read somewhere once that one of the Kadampa master Tsongkapa's main practices was offering mandalas. Tsongkhapa was the master who built Ganden monastery, and after he did this the Kadampa lineage became the Gelug lineage. Tsongkapa himself was a yogi so he did not have any gold or silver to offer in his mandala. Instead he used stones and a stone plate and he is supposed to have worn out thirteen stone plates by making mandala offerings. I don't know if this is an historical fact or his disciples' devotional exaggeration, but it is very inspiring.

Offering mandalas like this is a very pure way to accumulate merit. With a pure practice lineage and the right visualization it is almost as if you are offering the whole universe to the Buddhas and bodhisattvas. It is a tremendous way to accumulate merit. As sentient beings we have the right to every piece of the universe, it belongs to each one of us equally, so we are not offering something that does not belong to us and this is the only way we can do this. We cannot put the whole universe in an envelope and give it to Buddha, offering a mandala is the only way to do it. It is a very sacred way to accumulate merit.

Confession is another very important action. When we experience negative circumstances we have an insight into the similar types of negative karma we must have committed in the past and can confess them. If, for example, we get sick and experience pain all over our body this roughly speaking means we have previously beaten up lots of people. If we lose a lot of money and become poor this means we have stolen others' property. If people misunderstand us and do not respect us this means we have lied and slandered others a lot. Through the result we can see the cause and then we can confess our previous negative deeds by saying something like, "I confess all my bad karma from all my past lives. Whatever it was that I did to others that caused them to suffer like this I confess it along with all my other negative deeds."

Confession is not just saying we are sorry though. We also have to promise never to perform this kind of deed again and engage in positive actions that we will then dedicate to all sentient beings attaining Buddhahood. If our confession has all these different elements within it, it is complete. We should not confess in the same way a little child begs their father, "Please, please don't beat me with the newspaper, I will never do it again." It is not like the Buddha is beating us and therefore we are afraid of the Buddha. Confession means having genuine regret for what we have done and hoping that we will never conduct ourselves in this way again. We should also hope that others will not conduct themselves in this way again; that is, they will not create the causes and conditions for suffering. When we add these other aspects we have a more complete definition of remorse and confession.[30]

Interestingly, this text then talks about making offerings to spirits. Sometimes people can be problematic for us and sometimes spirits can be. I find people from all over the world very receptive to the idea of spirits and ghosts so I try not to talk about them too much. All this talk of ghosts and spirits is only half true and half superstitious paranoia so I will not go into this section in too much detail. There are, however, certain problems that are caused by spirits and we can appease them by making special offerings to them. These offerings are not made with devotion but with respect, appreciation and compassion. We are not bribing them, we are more acknowledging that we have done negative things to them in the past, that we have intruded into their space, and because of this they have become annoyed and have done something similar to us. We are saying to them, "Now I have done something for you please leave me alone."

Whether we should make offerings to spirits or not depends on our specific situation. Not every headache is caused by spirits. Every time we trip and fall down the stairs it was not necessarily spirits, but sometimes things that happen are caused by spirits, and this text is referring to these instances.

It also talks about requesting the dharma protectors to protect us by making offerings to them. This is important. There are wisdom protectors like Mahakala that manifest from the Buddha's wisdom, but there are also worldly protectors. Many of these worldly protectors are just powerful gods and spirits who have taken vows from Buddhas and bodhisattvas to protect people who practice dharma or are just generally in harm's way. When we make offerings to them, usually cups of tea, we remind them of their vows. We say, "Hey! You took a vow from Buddha remember. It is your job to protect me now that I am in trouble. Please have this cup of tea and do your job, protect me. I am sincerely trying to practice dharma and have encountered a problem here."

These activities are ways we can transform negative circumstances into positive circumstances, but their most important part is to have the motivation of ultimate and relative bodhichitta. The key to this chapter is to remember that every bad thing that happens to us has everything to do with us, and that whatever is happening is only happening relatively, not ultimately.

4: Showing the Utilization of Practice in One's Whole Life

The Paramita of Diligence

Practice the five strengths,
The condensed heart instructions.
The Mahayana instruction for ejection of consciousness at death
Is the five strengths: how you conduct yourself is important.

This is explained as the five strengths in two different situations: while we are living and when we are dying.

Living: The first strength is bodhichitta itself. Its strength is similar to the force with which we hit a golf ball: the first drive sends the ball where we want it to go. In Tibetan it is called the *penpä tob*: *penpä* means throwing, *tob* means strength. The strength with which you throw something is what makes it reach its destination. If we wish to end up as Buddhas, we have to have the strength to project ourselves in that direction right from the beginning. This strength is bodhichitta. It is the thought, "I wish to become a Buddha so I can lead all sentient beings to Buddhahood." This is our driving force, our first strength.

The second strength is our constant practice of relative and ultimate bodhichitta. In Tibetan we call it the *kom bä tob*. *Kom bä* means to acquaint ourselves with something, to get used to it, so this refers to practice itself. It refers to getting used to bodhichitta.

The third strength is the *kar bö sabön tob*. A *sabön* is a flower's seed and *kar bö* means white. This means we should always do our best to encourage relative and ultimate bodhichitta, to let them manifest from us and continue to grow like a planted seed. Our bodhichitta should progress from a shoot to a bush, to a flower and finally to fruit. If relative and ultimate bodhichitta are constantly cultivated and practiced they will flourish like this and come to fruition.

The fourth strength is the *sunjinpä tob*. *Sunjinpä* means to defeat. We do not have to defeat anyone outside ourselves though, just our egos. It is our ego that harms us so we have to do our best to achieve victory over it. Our ego manifests, as I have said many times, as attachment, greed, anger, jealousy, pride and so on. If we cut the supplies to our attachment, jealousy, anger, then we can defeat our ego. After all, the essence of our ego is primordial wisdom, so when our ego is defeated it will transform into primordial wisdom. It is not as if our ego is our number one enemy, because it is actually the other side of our perfect essence, but when we do not know this, that is ignorance, and a by-product of this ignorance is the ego.

Ignorance, ego, the "I," duality are all different names for the same thing. Doing our best to minimize its negative aspects is the fourth strength. We need to do this to the best of our capabilities even when we are just beginning to practice. We need confidence at the beginning though, and if we desperately do away with our entire ego we may also lose our confidence. We don't want to throw the baby out with the bath-water. We need to get rid of the water, but we want to keep the baby in the bath. That is, we need to keep our confidence and get rid of our ego. If we were to get rid of our confidence at the beginning as well this would not be very good, so we need to take things step by step. Eventually even our ego's more positive forms, like our confidence, have to be transformed, but we should not worry about this right now. We have to overcome the bad, negative parts of the ego before we start on the nice, good, friendly parts. For now we need a little bit of the positive, friendly ego to overcome the negative, bad ego.

The fifth strength is the strength of aspiration, *mön lam kyi tob* in Tibetan. Finishing our positive actions with a dedication of merit covers this strength.

Dying: Another way to look at the five strengths is how they relate to death. All of us will die one day, there is no question about it. Each one of us would like to live as long as possible. I don't know about this living for 10,000 years business, but we would like to live for a long time. Sooner or later, though, we will die, and when that time comes we need to know how to handle it. In this text, it shows Lojong practitioners how to use these same five strengths at the time of their death.

The first strength we need to focus on at this time is the strength of white seeds. In relation to living it was explained as the third strength, but when we are dying it should be the first strength we concentrate on. In this context it means, first, overcoming the fear of death. These days doctors do not usually say, "We have tried everything but there is no hope, you are going to die," but if a doctor told me this I would appreciate it greatly. If a doctor says that to you, you should appreciate it. These days they are much more likely to say, "You will be okay, we are trying hard. This can be done, that can be done, take this pill, go to sleep." Still, when we know ourselves that we are dying, the first thing we need to do is overcome our fear of death. The simplest way to overcome this fear is by knowing the truth about death. Death is merely the separation of our mortal body from our immortal mind; the mind never dies, only the body does. Our body may be broken, sick or ruined and therefore not a conducive environment for our mind, so it has to separate from our body. When our mind can no longer function in our body and leaves it, this is death.

If we know this we will not have any strange ideas about what death is, we will know it is not a frightening and unspeakable thing. Naturally we should do our best to stay alive, we should go to the best doctors, the best hospital and do everything we can to stay alive, but when nothing works we should be able to say, "Okay, now I am going to die." We should be able to overcome our fear of death by knowing exactly what death is. We have died and been born countless times in the past. This life is only one of many lives we have led, and our death will be just one more death. Of course we should try to live as long as we can, but when our doctors tell us we are going to die we should remember what death is and not be afraid.

The next thing we should do, which is still part of the first strength, is to take care of unfinished business. This is also very important. We have to let go of all our sentimental things. Any dolls from childhood, anything we do not feel we can part from we should part from. We should write a will, call all our friends and make it very clear who gets what so that after our death the living will not fight with each other over our stuff. Instead of being busy being frightened we should be busy taking care of unfinished business. If we are in a coma, that is a different story, we cannot take care of unfinished business when we are in a coma, but really we should be ready for death at all times. Otherwise, when we die problems may come up, and we should try and stop this from happening. This is our responsibility. If we do not deal with this unfinished business, the suffering people endure because we did not will be our responsibility.

The second strength is the strength of aspiration; in the order of strengths we should develop in life, this was number five. Here we should collect our energy and use it to take refuge and develop bodhichitta sincerely. We should practice *dana* (generosity) by performing charitable acts, every positive thing we can do we should. If people follow this instruction it enables them to die in a positive, happy, healthy, meritorious environment.

The third strength to practice at the time of death, which was the fourth strength when it was described as a practice for life, is the strength of being victorious over the ego. How you want to practice this at the time of death depends on you. If you wish to be born again for the benefit of all sentient beings then you can wish for that. If you wish to be born in a pure land, attain greater realization and then benefit sentient beings in a greater way then you can wish for that. Whatever aspiration you have should be an antidote to your ego and ignorance, though, and this can only happen with the limitless intention of working for the benefit of all sentient beings.

The fourth strength, which in the previous section was the first strength, is the strength of projection. In this case we need to make sure that our intention is strong enough to carry us to wherever we wish to be reborn. This means we should strongly aspire that after our natural death we will be able to pass through the in-between state and birth accompanied by relative and ultimate bodhichitta.

At the time of death the fifth strength is the strength of habit – practice. According to these teachings, this means that we need to start engaging in the fifth strength now. We need to start practicing relative and ultimate bodhichitta now. When the doctor tells us that we are going to die we may not have the time to practice relative and ultimate bodhichitta, so we need to start practicing it right now and keep practicing it as long as we live.

This is a very specific teaching on dying that was given by Atisha Dipankara and is presented here as the fourth point of the Seven

Points of Mind Training. It describes how practitioners of mind training should behave when they experience the last moments of life, when the doctor tells them they are about to die. These guidelines were given to Atisha by his guru Jowo Serlingpa in relation to the five strengths.

At the same time as doing these practices, if we are able to remain in the state of meditation on ultimate bodhichitta that we have discussed, this would of course be enormously beneficial. When the doctor has told us we are going to die, when we have written our will and taken care of everything, there really isn't anything else to do. We can sit there, relax and meditate on the nature of our mind. We can enter into the state of ultimate harmony and peace that we call samadhi. Many great masters, including those I have seen die with my own eyes, have remained in this state for many days after they were clinically dead, looking just as if they were alive. Then when they were really ready to leave their bodies they became like a corpse. Some of them even died in the meditation posture and stayed sitting in it for two or three days. They were able to do this because they died in samadhi; that is to say when the separation of body and mind took place they were able to recognize the nature of their mind. We should also try to practice this at the time of death.

The last thing I should mention with regard to dying is that if you cannot die doing any of these things at least try to die with a positive thought. Do not lie there thinking, "Why me! Why me!" Instead try to focus on how you have done your best, the doctors have done their best and your relatives have done their best so now you can relax and die peacefully without any uneasy feelings towards anybody. Relax and go. Of course if you can do the Lojong practices or the ultimate bodhichitta meditation this would be better, but if you cannot it is better to die with a positive thought than a negative one.

5: Assessing How Well Your Practice is Progressing

The Paramita of Meditation

All dharmas agree at one point.
Of the two witnesses, hold the principal one.
Always maintain only a joyful mind.
If you can practice even when distracted
You are well trained.

There are many ways to assess how well our mind training practice is going but the simplest is to check and see if we are less jealous, angry, greedy and hateful. If we are less like this our practice is going well. In other words, if we have less ego our practice is progressing well. If these negative states are decreasing we should also have more positive states like compassion and devotion. If we have more clarity and less confusion and neurosis our practice is going well. If we have more of the negative things and less of the positive things we are not doing so well. This method of assessment is very simple but its details are numerous. I don't think we should go into these details very much though because I don't think assessing ourselves too much at this stage is very helpful. Most of us are still so influenced by our egos that when we assess ourselves we only see what we want to see.

6: Disciplines of Mind Training

The Prajna Paramita

Always abide by the three basic principles.
Change your attitude, but remain natural.
Don't talk about injured limbs.
Don't ponder others.
Work with the greatest defilements first.

Abandon any hope of fruition.
Abandon poisonous food.
Don't be so predictable.
Don't malign others.
Don't wait in ambush.
Don't bring things to a painful point.
Don't transfer the ox's load to the cow.
Don't try to be the fastest.
Don't act with a twist.
Don't make gods into demons.
Don't seek others' pain as the limbs of your own happiness.

This point talks about the samaya of mind training, the *Lojong gi damtsik*. This means it describes what we should not do. The next chapter talks about the *Lojong gi labcha*, advice for mind training. This means it describes what we should do. But these two approaches are so closely connected that it is difficult to completely separate them.

Their basis is the maintenance of the bodhisattva vows. Taking the bodhisattva vow is the beginning of Lojong practice; after this we primarily need to maintain its main precept: to never exclude any sentient being from our motivation to attain Buddhahood. On top of this we should also respect, appreciate, cherish and uphold the lineage of the bodhisattva and its teachings without contaminating it.

The second important thing is that no matter what state we think we may have realized through Lojong practice, we should always behave properly. "Behaving properly" means that we should do our best to make sure that our actions do not harm or confuse others. In order to stop ourselves doing this we need to be mindful and aware of our actions.

Another objective of our practice should be to stop favoring certain sentient beings over others; our Lojong practice should be equally on behalf of all beings. Our motivation should not have any bias. These are the three main parts of the Lojong samaya.

The text gives lots of other helpful advice too. It tells us, for example, to "Finish what you start." This means developing the good habit of continuing with what we have started until it is finished before we start something else. We should adopt this approach rather than starting many things, shifting from one to another and not completing any of them. Clarity and consistency is very important for a Lojong practitioner, for any practitioner actually, but especially for a Lojong practitioner.

Another thing it mentions we should avoid doing is exhibiting our practice to others. If we have to teach dharma, we have to teach dharma, but apart from that nobody needs to know whether we are a good practitioner or not. This should not be important to us. We should do our best but nobody needs to know that we are doing our best. It is not something we need to exhibit to others, they do not need to know how much we practice, or how great a practitioner we are.

It also advises against "looking for other people's faults." Everybody, including ourselves, has lots of potential and good qualities. We also have a lot of faults. Digging into others' faults, however, does not benefit us in any way. As we always look for others' faults through our own negative perceptions, it could also harm us. A thief, for example, will always worry about his things being stolen. He thinks others will steal because he steals. Liars do not trust anybody's word. They lie all the time so they think everybody else lies. In this way we can see that looking into others' problems and shortcomings is not helpful.

Then there is the advice not to have "too many expectations," even with your practice. If we expect too much from our practice, this in itself can become an obstacle. If we wish or expect to accomplish this or that then even things that may have been relatively easy will become difficult. Expecting too much of ourselves may even stop us making small gains.

Yet another piece of advice is to "be less sentimental." This means having fewer gentle attachments, fewer things we are sentimental about. I will tell you one of my secrets. I have a teddy bear! It is very small and filled with sand. I have had it since I was eight or nine.

Everyone must have something like this that they are gently attached to. It is not only my teddy bear that I feel this way about, I have many other pieces of memorabilia that I feel sentimental about. We can still have these things, we can still appreciate them but we should not be too attached to them because it makes us neurotic. We all have defilements but the last thing we want to be is neurotic. Being gently attached to our fame or fortune may also cause us to be neurotic. We really need to grow up and overcome our neurotic aspects. We can keep sentiment's healthy aspects but we need to try to overcome its neurotic ones.

I told you a story of how destructive this kind of sentiment can be earlier. It was the story in which two lamas were practicing Vajrayogini and when the stairs of light leading to Akanishta descended one of them went straight up but the other forgot his beautiful mala and only made it halfway up before he came back to collect it. By the time he had collected his mala the stairs had gone. My teddy bear could become my mala! We really need to overcome the neurotic aspects of our attachment to sentimental things. We can be easy on ourselves while we do it but we should be mindful of these things.

We should also refrain from holding grudges. If somebody did something nasty to us we could remember this and make ourselves feel bitter about it by thinking about it again and again. As a result of this we may say bad things about that person, drop damaging hints about them or wish them ill. This kind of behavior is something that Lojong practitioners should try to overcome. No matter who did bad things to us or what these were, we should not hold a grudge that may cause us to experience resentment or try to extract revenge.

Lojong practitioners should never wish anybody suffering no matter what they have done. Lojong practitioners should not blame other people for their mistakes. We should not do something bad and then say it was someone else. Nor should Lojong practitioners go against the law of karma, cause and result, *le-ju-dre* in Tibetan. They should never be deceitful. I will give you a stupid example. Let's say you are selling butter brought from 100 kilometers away. If people know that when you bought the butter it cost five rupees but now you are selling it for ten that is okay. Your customers will probably understand that you had to transport the butter and need to make a profit so they will happily pay the extra five rupees instead of traveling 100 kilometers to get it themselves. If, on the other hand, you secretly mix bananas into the butter to deceive your customers and give yourself larger profits, that is very bad. Practitioners of Lojong should not ever do this kind of thing.

These kinds of ethics are extremely important in Mahayana and Vajrayana practices. They should become our day-to-day life principles. We should never cross their boundaries. We should never pretend untrue things are true, or that true things are untrue. This is very important. To what extent we can keep these ethics depends on our individual capacities, but we should do our best.

One of the last things the sixth point says we should refrain from is becoming proud. We should do our best not to become proud. Having a little bit of positive pride is okay, but we should never become so proud that we look down on others. No matter how successful or celebrated we become we should do our best not to look down on or be disrespectful of others. Even if we become the highest of the high we should respect the lowest of the low.

7: Guidelines of Mind Training

Post-meditation

All activities should be done with one intention.
Correct all wrongs with one intention.
Two activities: one at the beginning, one at the end.
Whichever of the two occurs, be patient.
Observe these two, even at the risk of your life.
Train in the three difficulties.
Take on the three principal causes.
Pay heed that the three never wane.
Keep the three inseparable.

Train without bias in all areas.
It is crucial to do this pervasively and wholeheartedly.
Always meditate on whatever provokes resentment.
Don't be swayed by external circumstances.
This time, practice the main points.
Don't misinterpret.
Don't vacillate.
Train wholeheartedly.
Liberate yourself by examining and analyzing.
Don't wallow in self-pity.
Don't be jealous.
Don't be frivolous.
Don't expect applause.

The last, the seventh point of the Seven Points of Mind Training, is similar to the previous point but deals with what we should cultivate, as opposed to what we should abandon. We should start by trying to have Lojong as the background for everything we do. When we are eating food we can practice Lojong by thinking that we are eating food to maintain our health and strength so that we can continue to benefit others and eventually attain Buddhahood. When we take medicine, when we talk to others, when we go shopping, when we do business, when we are employed by someone, in every situation the backdrop – our purpose – should be bodhichitta.

If you are an employee, for example, you can bring bodhichitta into your work by reminding yourself that you are working to earn a living so that you can make the best of your life and you want to make the best out of your life so you can progress towards enlightenment for the benefit of all sentient beings and eventually become a Buddha. As Lojong practitioners bodhichitta should always be present in whatever we do. That is the first thing.

The second thing it advises us to do is remember that all the negative things that happen to us have everything to do with us. I have explained this already. The third piece of advice is to remember others when we do something selfish. If, for example, we have a nice meal in front of us, we should not forget to offer it to the Buddha, or the beings that were involved in bringing the vegetables or meat to our table. The meat was once a sentient being's hand, shoulder or ribs. Bugs were killed to stop them devouring the growing vegetables. We should remember these things. When we are enjoying something we should remember what was involved in bringing this enjoyment to us and sincerely pray for all those who helped make it happen.

Some people may think this way of thinking is hypocritical, but I don't. If we don't eat we die and we don't want to die, we want to live as long as possible. Looking at our situation clearly and doing the best we can is not hypocrisy. If we had a spiritual realization that meant we did not have to eat or drink, and we still ate and drank, then maybe that would be hypocritical but none of us has reached this state. There are practices in our lineage that enable people to live on stones. I have read texts on this but have never done it. I would not know how to digest them. Apparently one pebble takes many days to digest and it is very healthy. There are descriptions on the different types of pebbles and the individual properties the yellow, red, black and green pebbles have. The texts describe how to eat them and the exercises and herbs that will make you able to digest them. There is a whole practice describing how to digest pebbles, but I will not take you on a long ride through it. That may become a trip for you, a pebble trip.

Instead what we should remember is not to get lost in whatever kind of happiness or suffering we experience by looking at the big picture. However happy, fortunate, rich and comfortable we may be, we cannot be limitlessly comfortably and happy. When we look at the bigger picture it will stop us becoming proud about our experience or lost in it. Whatever suffering we experience cannot be the worst kind of suffering so we should not get lost or overwhelmed by our little problems. We should know that the kind of problems other sentient beings encounter, the kind of problems we ourselves might encounter, can be a hundred times worse than what we are encountering now. That is the fourth thing.

The fifth piece of advice is to "be aware of all the advice that has already been given." The sixth is to "always remember the antidotes to each of the obstacles." This has also been mentioned earlier. The seventh is to "appreciate the three things that we already have." The first of these three things we need to appreciate is having and being part of a lineage. The second is the teachings of the Mahayana, the bodhichitta. The third is having the conditions to implement the teachings we receive. If we really wanted to implement all the Mahayana teachings, then we really do have the time and ability to do it.

It goes on to say that we should use our body, speech and mind in whichever ways we can for our own and others' betterment. Our mind is the boss and our speech and body are its attendants. We need to use these attendants, make use of their abilities, for good and beneficial purposes.

The next piece of advice is specifically to be positive to those who are negative to us. Being positive to those who are positive to us is easy but being positive to those who are negative towards us is very difficult. This is why it advises us specifically to be compassionate, respectful and understanding to those who are not nice to us.

It also advises us to be positive with ourselves. Instead of getting frustrated with our faults we should appreciate the fact that we have recognized them. If we find a particular weakness, instead of thinking, "Oh my goodness, how terrible I have this weakness," we should think, "How wonderful I have recognized my weakness." We should try to appreciate the recognition of our weaknesses rather than being disappointed in finding them.

We should also "always try to be patient, diligent and mindful." This means being mindful, aware, diligent, patient and tolerant in positive as well as negative situations. Never be impatient. If you are waiting in a line and somebody pushes in front of you, even if saying, "Hey man, the end of the line is over there" comes to the tip of your tongue, do not say it. You may move a little closer to the person in front of you, or make yourself look bigger or smaller so that people are aware of you and no one else will push in, but the person in front of you is already there, so don't make a big scene that makes them feel uncomfortable. Being tolerant is very important but we need to be mindful when we practice tolerance, otherwise it can become selfish by encouraging others to persecute us. We need to find a balance but still we should always be diligent about practicing patience, tolerance, compassion and appreciation.

The text goes on to advise us not to be *sandrog* [fickle]. When someone abandons an old friend for a new friend we call this *sandrog*. Or when someone buys a new cup and never drinks out of their old cup, this is also *sandrog*. Being unstable in this way, always looking for new things, is not very good. We should try to be as stable as possible. Maybe there isn't a word that means exactly *sandrog* in English; if there were it would be similar to advertising. Advertising always appeals to our appetite, always suggests new things, new things, new things, new things. It does not encourage us to be stable at all. Instead it makes us constantly want new things. This is not very good for our progress. It will disperse our efforts and make us greedier. We should really try to remain more stable.

We should also "check ourselves from time to time" to assess our progress. If we do check ourselves in this way, then when we see our progress it will be encouraging and we will know we need to work on our shortcomings. The text then adds that nobody can check up on ourselves better than we can.

The last piece of advice it gives is that we should not expect appreciation. Whatever we achieve in our practice, we should not expect any praise or appreciation for it. In Tibetan we call this *yu*. If I did many things for you and you never showed your appreciation for my help, I might develop *yu* against you. It is not so much resentment as a feeling that we deserve appreciation. A feeling that whoever it was we helped really should at least say thank you. We should not do this. We should not look for gratitude for our practice. If we wish to attain Buddhahood for the benefit of all sentient beings, no matter what we have achieved we do not need gratitude. If people appreciate what we have done that is fine, it is good for them to generate merit in this way. As Mahayana practitioners, however, we should never look for gratitude from others. We should not even be thinking about it, or complaining about its absence. We are working to attain Buddhahood to benefit all sentient beings – we are not working for gratitude. Looking for gratitude is totally contrary to our goals.

This has only been an overview of the seventh point; I have not gone into it in detail but I have covered its essential points thoroughly.

Concluding Verses

When the five dark ages occur,
This is the way to transform them into the path of bodhi.
This is the essence of the amrita of the oral instructions,
Which were handed down from the tradition of the sage
  of Suvarnadvipa.

Having awakened the karma of previous training
And being urged on by my intense dedication,
I disregarded misfortune and slander
And received oral instruction on taming ego-fixation.
Now, even at death, I will have no regrets.

The Seven Points of Mind Training concludes by saying bodhichitta is a simple but very profound practice. It is compared to a lotus. A lotus is the most beautiful, clean flower but it grows in ugly, dirty mud. In the same way bodhichitta can be practiced by anybody, it is the simplest, most efficient and most profound practice. In Shantideva's *Bodhisattvacharyavatara* he describes how the moment before you develop bodhichitta you could be the cruelest person in the whole universe, but the moment after you are a son or daughter of the Buddha. You are transformed in the snap of a finger, from the worst there can be to the best, by the simple wish to "become free like Buddha so you can lead all sentient beings to the freedom of a Buddha."

This simple, sincere decision has the capacity to change the worst into the best. You do not need a crystal-clear pond to grow the most beautiful flower. The transformation of a sentient being from defiled and negative to sacred and positive can take place with the development of bodhichitta, with this simple decision. Many eons ago the Buddha Shakyamuni himself was just an ordinary, everyday beggar with a bowl full of food when he saw the Buddha of that time and became inspired enough to offer his food. He sincerely prayed to become like this Buddha and make all sentient beings like him. This was the beginning of Prince Siddhartha's lineage of enlightenment. Until he attained Buddhahood that seed kept growing and finally it developed into fruit at Bodhgaya under the Bodhi tree more than 2500 years ago. The greatest change comes about with the transformation of attitude. Attitude transformation doesn't cost anything, doesn't take any time, you just have to know because when you know you are no longer ignorant.

I am very happy that I have been able to share a little bit of Atisha Dipamkara's teachings on the practice of bodhisattvas that he received from his master and which is continued in our lineage. I sincerely hope and pray that it will be beneficial to you.

BUDDHA NATURE
Calligraphy by
Tai Situ Rinpoche

Chapter 6

MEDITATION

Now I will be explaining meditation, the Four Noble Truths and the five skandhas. These three topics are connected; parts of one cover parts of the others. I will do my best to give a brief explanation without leaving anything out. I pray that Buddha blesses us so that everything is understood clearly and I don't waste time by repeating things.

Dharma practice is three-fold: we learn, we physically and orally do things and we meditate. At first learning is important but it can only take us to a certain level. It would be the same if we were studying medicine. There would be much to learn about disease, prevention, herbs, medicine and treatments, but unless we applied this knowledge we could not even cure a common cold. To make learning meaningful it has to be implemented.

This is explained very clearly in the *Bodhisattvacharyavatara* where Shantideva says, "What invalid in need of medicine ignored his doctor's words and gained his health?" If the patient does not follow the advice of the doctor how will they recover? If they want to become well they need to take medicine, do certain things and refrain from others. Just knowing everything about their illness is not going to help them. Having twenty kilos of medicine next to their pillow is not going to help them. If they do not want to die from the illness they need to take the medicine, follow the doctor's advice. Implementing the teachings, meditation practice, is important in the same way.

Generally speaking there are two parts to the implementation of the dharma: the first is physical and oral implementation, the second is mental implementation. Physical and oral activities obviously incorporate mental activity but many other activities are specifically mental. If we were only to focus on verbal and physical activity we would need to avoid negative physical activities and engage in positive activities, overcome negative words and engage in positive words like prayers and mantras. But even if we did all of these things with the right motivation, we would have to do them for a very long time to get anywhere. How many times would we have to do good things? How long would we have to pray? How long would we have to avoid doing bad things? If we wish to achieve realizations by physical and verbal actions we will have to pray, and pray, and pray, and pray. We will have to do good, and good, and good. We will have to overcome negativity again, and again, and again, and again. It could go on forever.

Following this approach we habituate ourselves to doing good things and refraining from bad things. Saying prayers, for example, becomes habitual. I especially notice this when I have dinner with friends who do not have much to do with the dharma. If we are eating in a very quiet restaurant and the service people are very courteous, everybody in the restaurant looks over at the other monks and myself when we start habitually saying our prayers. They want to know what is going on. It is a good habit but it can make you self-conscious. I keep waiting for everybody else in the restaurant to explode into laughter. Also, if you habitually start saying OM MANI PEME HUNG in every quiet moment it can make it very difficult to go and watch an opera or listen to a symphony. When the music is quiet you are supposed to listen to the notes, or notice the space in between the notes. If you start habitually saying OM MANI PEME HUNG though, you may waste the $100 or $200 you spent on the ticket by "spoiling" the experience of listening between the notes.

Despite spoiling the opera these are actually all good habits to have. Praying is very important, we should pray. Saying mantras is very important, we should say mantras. It is very important to avoid doing bad things and try to do good things – we should give ten rupees to people with no hands, we should offer 100,000 lamps to the Buddha – but all of these actions are external. Meditation is internal. Without inward development we will not achieve final liberation very quickly. Through performing positive, external deeds it may eventually happen but it will take a very long, long time.

I heard a story once from the time when Tibet had a wild west. Our country, Tibet, is a great country. Everybody there is Buddhist by birth but even up until fifty years ago we had a wild west where bandits would ambush caravans to rob them of their goods. The difference is that even the bandits were religious. The head of one group of bandits was an old man who had a prayer wheel and said OM MANI PEME HUNG. He was in charge of maybe 100 bandits on horses all armed to the teeth but while his watchmen looked out for the caravan they were going to rob, he sat there spinning his prayer wheel and saying OM MANI PEME HUNG. Eventually, when his men told him the caravan was coming, he would put his prayer wheel into his chuba, his prayer beads around his neck and instruct his men. Often he got them to charge together first so they would be more forceful and disperse when they had robbed the caravan so the caravan's guards could not find them. He explained that if the guards thought two bandits had gone one way, three another and five yet another then they would not know who to chase after and this would make capturing them difficult.

It was very good that he said prayers and had devotion, there was nothing wrong with that, it was just his livelihood, his profession, his specialty that was a bit problematic. After he had finished robbing the caravans I am sure he pulled out his prayer wheel and started saying OM MANI PEME HUNG again.

Prayer is good, but prayer without meditation can become a bit like a bandit's prayer. I am sure this smart, brave, patient, battle-hardened man could have understood the real meaning of dharma if he had turned his mind to it, but instead he saw prayer as a cultural habit. He and people like him have some of the qualities necessary to become enlightened. In order to be able to wait for ages in the middle of nowhere for the caravans to come they needed patience. These bandits would wait in these places for months without needing any entertainment, eating the same dried meat and tsampa every day or hunting for meat, just to steal the nicely packed goods from India, China, or Russia. If people like them turned their minds to dharma they would make it. What they are doing is negative, but it has a positive side also; they are dedicated, daring, make decisions and stick to them. They are not at all wishy-washy.

These caravan trains were still in operation until not so long ago actually, early last century. When my teacher was a child his uncle was a great master in my monastery. One day a nicely dressed man showed up and asked him to be his guru, asked him to teach him meditation so he could do a retreat. He did not have any money but he was nicely dressed, a perfect, macho Khampa man. He had not been a bandit. He had been a trader. Still during those times traders also had to carry weapons; the bandits were waiting for them and they had to be vigilant. One day this trader took his gun hunting and shot a deer that happened to be pregnant. After shooting the deer he followed the trail of her dripping blood. He found her with her intestines caught on a bush. She had been shot in the stomach and while she was trying to run away her stomach had caught on and wrapped around a bush. Her fawns had been born but were barely alive. Even in this state she tried to run away when the trader approached.

When he saw her he realized what he had done. He immediately broke his gun, left his caravan with its fifty salesmen, porters and about 100 mules and ran away to Palpung Monastery. Here he met with Kalu Rinpoche's guru, my uncle's teacher, Lama Norbu, and asked to be taught. He was nicely dressed because he was a trader but he had nothing because he had not gone back to get his money. He gave up everything.

As a businessman he had no religious education. The only thing Lama was able to teach him, the only thing he understood, was OM MANI PEME HUNG and how to meditate on Chenrezig. He took that as his practice and lived in caves where people bought him food. He became known as the yogi Chupur Lama (The Lama who flies across water). His cave was next to the Yangtze River, in Tibet we call it the *Dri chu*, the river from Dri, or the golden river because there is so much gold in its sand. In this area the Yangtze River is deep and has a strong current. Mountains rise steeply from its banks on both sides and as one mountain faces east and the other faces west the sun will only shine on one side at a time. In the morning it would fall on one side of the river and in the afternoon on the other. This yogi would fly from one side of the river to the other depending on where the sun was shining. A caravan highway passed this spot, not a car or truck highway but a caravan highway. People passing by on this caravan highway would see him on one side in the morning and on the other side in the afternoon and there was no way he could have walked from one side to the other.

The cave he lived in was very hard to get to so when he heard people singing OM MANI PEME HUNG as they passed he would teach them by singing back to them. They would add a nice stone to the pile of stones on the highway near his cave and say OM MANI PEME HUNG. So many people stopped to be blessed by his singing and add a rock to this pile that it became enormous.

He stayed in this place until he disappeared. No one ever found his body. For many years people had seen him on one side of the river in the morning and the other side in the afternoon, but eventually he just disappeared.

There is another story of someone practicing like this. I don't know if he started out as a bandit or a trader, but he left his livelihood in a similar way. He became known as the white bird Lama, charung Lama. A *charung* is a Tibetan bird that is like a pheasant. It has a white body with a black tail and is indigenous in my area. This Lama also meditated on the mountainside all the time. He had no clothes. He had not taken his clothes off but as he meditated the rain, water and sun had worn them away. Instead the charung birds would come and sit on his head, his shoulders and his lap. They became his clothes and he became their nest. These birds protected him. When people went near him the birds would fly away and the visitors would see a naked man. When they left the birds would come back and sit on him again.

These two stories happened at about the same time, at the beginning of last century. They are real accounts, not legends. They happened because these two people decided to look inwards. Sometimes it takes a dramatic tragedy to realize we need to look inwards, but I pray that through the teachings of the lineage we will not need to face such a situation in order to wake up.

Meditation, looking inwards, is by definition using your mind to recognize the true potential of your mind. This is not something that can happen externally, it happens internally. Meditation has many aspects but generally it can be described as the three yanas: Hinayana, Mahayana and Vajrayana. These three yanas are really Shamatha and Vipashyana meditation, they are just Shamatha and Vipashyana of different levels. In the Hinayana, there are Shamatha and Vipashyana. In the Mahayana there are Shamatha and Vipashyana, and this is also true of the Vajrayana. They may not always be described by these two words but the principles are the same.

In the Mahayana, in relation to the prajna paramita, we firstly focus on the emptiness of everything, which is Shamatha, and then on its clarity, which is Vipashyana. In the Vajrayana we talk about first settling and then manifesting; again this refers to Shamatha and Vipashyana. In these ways Shamatha and Vipashyana are really the definition of meditation. Even very profound meditations such as Mahamudra, which is a direct meditation on the nature of mind, or Dzogchen, which is a direct meditation on *rigpa*, are still Vipashyana. They are, however, the most profound, highest forms of Vipashyana and in order to achieve them you need a profound Shamatha as a base.

Shamatha

Through a particular technique such as concentration on the breath or concentrating on a sacred object such as a Buddha statue or visualization, Shamatha meditation enables us to reach a calm abiding state. Everything but the object we are focusing on dissolves. Any other thoughts that come up become secondary. It is very easy to become absorbed like this when you read a book, for example. If you are focused on each sentence – how clear it is, how lovely – you become absorbed in the book and the rest of the world disappears. This is of course when you are reading a book without stress. If you are reading a book in a relaxed way, sentence by sentence, then that is Shamatha. If we read like this the meaning of each word comes to us clearly. From the beginning to the end of the book, page by page, we understand the meaning – this is like Vipashyana. It is a very simple example, but it explains Shamatha and Vipashyana in a simple way.

In meditation, through breathing or other techniques, we can reach this calmly abiding state. Then we can maintain it with clear awareness. It is not like somebody will hit us over the head with a hammer and stop our thoughts that way. We will not have so many thoughts, but there will be clarity. When we are calm and clear, thoughts come and go. Old thoughts fade away and new thoughts arise, just like breathing they come and go.

The calm abiding itself is Shamatha and maintaining awareness of this state is Vipashyana. Our mind is not efficient when it is not calm, when there is no Shamatha. It is like a candle; if the wind is blowing a candle flame it will not burn clearly or brightly. When the wind isn't blowing on a candle it becomes clear and bright. Our mind is the same, when it is calm its efficiency multiples many times. When our mind is not calm it becomes discursive and neurotic. We build our own torture chamber. We create problems for ourselves where there are none. We do not do this intentionally, though: we only do it because our minds are not calm or clear.

One text describes this process by saying sentient beings in samsara are like silk worms building cocoons they will be cooked alive in. Silk worms build their cocoons so efficiently that when people pick them up by the hundreds and put them in boiling water they cannot escape and are cooked alive. This is what we do also. We create our own cocoons of hatred, jealousy, pride and all kind of things and then we are cooked in the suffering of samsara. When we die inside one cocoon, we build another one – again and again and again. Shamatha makes us realize this and stop building any more cocoons. We can at least try to make freedom available for ourselves. We can try to become free, but when we do we are not motivated by greed, jealousy, or fear. Instead we are motivated by genuine compassion and devotion. We are seeking freedom for the sake of all the other sentient beings who keep building their own cocoons of suffering. In this way the mind with Shamatha is efficient and the mind without it is less efficient.

Many texts describe a path where the meditator first develops Shamatha and then does Vipashyana practices. One such text is Atisha Dipamkara's *Changchub Lam chi Drönme, The Precious Lamp of the Path to Liberation.* In this text Atisha Dipankara says that if we do not overcome the causes and conditions of defilements, we will never achieve a truly calm abiding state, even if we were to meditate for 1000 years. He acknowledges that Shamatha is important but says that if we truly want our mind to abide calmly we need to cut down on the causes and conditions for its discursiveness.

If we do not eliminate these causes and conditions and just do Shamatha meditation, we can calm our minds down temporarily but it will be like stress management. We will not reach a truly calm state of mind. We will develop calm and something will undo it, we will develop calm again and something will undo it. I will give you an example. It may sound a little hypocritical for me to give this example as I am overweight, but anyway it is like someone eating a lot of junk food, getting fat, going on a strict diet, getting thin and then eating a lot of junk food again. It is like getting fat then thin, then fat then thin.

I am not very worried about being overweight, it is sometimes a little hard on my knees and my heart, but apart from that I generally feel well grounded, substantial. It would take a very big hurricane to lift me. I don't have to worry about holding onto anything. But fifteen years ago or so I was in Hawaii for about three months. While I was there someone would take me for a jog along the beach every morning. This person would come and get me in the car and take me to the beach. At the beach we would do a little warm up and then jog for about three kilometers. The first day we did not even jog for one kilometer, but by the end of my stay I could jog for five or six kilometers. Then after that I would go to one of the five star hotels on the beach and eat eggs Benedict. Eggs Benedict is eggs with cheese and white bread, everything that makes you fat. I would also have coffee with real cream. Then I would go home and the people I was staying with would be waiting for me with breakfast and I would eat that too! It was fifteen years ago and it feels like yesterday. I was doing exactly the same thing as I was just describing – do, undo, do, undo.

There is nothing wrong with doing Shamatha practice to relieve stress, to develop peace of mind. These are good things to do. But to reach the true state of Shamatha you need to deal with your defilements also. Our defilements are like a fire and the negative things we do are fuel for this fire. If we cut down on the fuel the strength of the fire will also decrease. In the same way our anger, jealousy, greed, attachment and pride are fueled by the negative things we do, like the ten non-virtues. If we cut down on these negative activities, and engage in positive activities like the ten virtues,[31] then our daily Shamatha practice will truly progress.

It is like taking three-kilometer walks and also eating healthy food, not eating two breakfasts, lunch, dinner and snacks in between. It is like cutting down on snacks and only eating eggs Benedict once a week. I liked the name eggs Benedict because in France they call a blessing a "benediction" and the idea of "blessed eggs" struck me. Then I saw it in the menu and thought I should try it once. It was so good that after that I did not look at the menu, I just said, "Eggs Benedict please." I don't even know if "Benedict" and "benediction" have the same meaning or spelling but it sounded to me as if the eggs were blessed. Or the chicken was blessed; still we robbed the chicken of its eggs and that isn't very nice, is it?

In order to develop Shamatha that will not degenerate, Atisha Dipankara instructs us as beginners to practice in a certain way. Many other teachings also describe this practice. I think all of us can consider ourselves beginners at this point. We may not be beginning beginners, but we are beginners. Even if we are not beginners it is safer to assume that we are. If we are not beginners and we begin again this will not be a problem, but if we are beginners and we jump ahead that will not be helpful. We may get many things wrong. In India we have traffic signs that say, "Better late than never." I don't see as many of them around these days but there used to be quite a lot of them. They mean that it is better to drive slowly and arrive at your destination a little late than it is to drive fast and never arrive. This gives you a good excuse to be late. Starting meditation is the same, it is better to go over things you have done in the past than to miss something out completely. There is nothing wrong with saying, "I take refuge in the Buddha, dharma and sangha," 100 times, sincerely, every day. Each time we say it, its meaning will become deeper and deeper, more and more profound. After all we can only say it perfectly when we become a Buddha. Until we become a Buddha, each time we say it will have more meaning, be deeper, more profound.

As beginners, according to Atisha Dipankara and many other great teachers, we first need an environment conducive to meditation. This means having a nice, calm environment at home, in which we can practice Shamatha meditation, is important. The second thing we need is to be as content with what we have as possible. This does not mean we should not have any ambitions, interests or hobbies, it just means we should cut down on these things and use our time wisely. Human beings do not live more than 100 years, and by the time we reach eighty or ninety we really need to spend time resting. You could keep practicing until you reached 110, if you lived that long, but it would be in a very settled, quiet sort of way. We need to have learnt and practiced everything before this time so we can continue with it then. This means cutting down on our greed for things.

The next thing it advises us to do is to cut down on unnecessary activity. I personally try to be as efficient as possible in this regard. I look at things in terms of what I want, what I have and what I need. These are three very simple ideas: what I want, what I have and what I need. What I want is a lot, but if I really look at what I need, it is not that much. When I look at what I have, though, there are certain things I have more of than I need and certain things I have less of than I need. Through these three groupings I can then work out how to deal with what I don't have and transform any extras I have into something useful. I cannot say by any means that I have renounced everything. I eat breakfast, I eat lunch, I eat dinner and I like to eat good food. I don't like eating bad food because then I get sick, have to go to the doctor and get well, which takes a lot of time, energy and money. I like to drive in a comfortable car. I don't like driving in a car that you can only drive for one hour before you have to rest for two. You can see that I am not living like Milarepa, but I do follow this principle of looking at what I need, what I want, and what I have. Separating things into these three groups helps me very much.

Of course everything I come up with has been influenced by my gurus, but this idea is not from a teaching. It is my own way of dealing with life not based on any particular text. I don't want to contaminate the lineage by inserting this idea into it. I am just sharing my human experience, my technique for life. I can't say I am always successful at it; sometimes I succeed and sometimes I fail, but I do my best. It helps me cut down on unnecessary activities. I want to do so many things. I have so many ideas. I used to have even more but slowly, slowly I have cut down on trying to implement these ideas. Some of them aren't even any of my business. Some are my business but someone else is already taking care of them, so I do not need to do them as well. Other things are my duty and no one else is doing them, so these I really have to do.

The next thing that is helpful for developing Shamatha is to avoid negative companions. Remember, I said at the beginning that this advice was aimed at beginners. Beginners should avoid negative companions. Bad company means people with bad habits – reckless, ruthless, non-compassionate, neurotic people. We should pray for them and we should dedicate our merit to them, but if we do other things for them we may become too involved in their problems and get dragged away. Dealing with them should be like feeding a tiger; we should open the door, put the meat down, shut the door and run away. If we feed a tiger like this the tiger does not go hungry and we still have our hand.

In the beginning we are by definition beginners, we are not that mature, grounded, or developed. This means people can influence us. If we are weak and try to help an alcoholic or drug addict we may become an alcoholic or drug addict ourselves. The drug addict may say, "Don't be stupid. This is nothing, just a few leaves, like roses. You sniff roses don't you? Sniff this, it will make you feel good and relaxed." If you are trying to help this person you will keep trying to be polite to them and eventually may try something, or pretend to. Then they may chastise you for pretending, so you may actually try it yourself and find out you like it. Eventually you may even buy your own drugs and become addicted.

This can happen to weak people. Of course once we are mature, stable and confident then we can go and help people like this. We can help them to become better people, maybe even social workers. Gangsters would actually be very good social workers, they know so many people and how to deal with them. Reformed gangsters would make the best social workers, they have so much energy. When we are ready we should try and make these kinds of things happen, but if we start trying to reform gangsters before we are ready we may end up becoming one. This advice about not associating with difficult people is actually very wise.

When you are mature enough to transform those you interact with, this is a different situation, but your intention and actions should still be positive. The combination of intention and action goes deep. We can have a positive intention and perform a negative action, or we can have a negative intention and perform a positive action. As beginners both our actions and intention should be positive. For the beginner the ends do not justify the means. Once you are mature, however, in the same way as you can transform your interactions with negative friends, the ends may justify the means. If the intention is good and the final result will definitely be good, then those who are mature can employ what look like negative actions. To do this properly we need to be clear and know what will happen, otherwise the end does not justify the means.

It takes a long time for us to develop to this level. One example of the ends justifying the means comes from the stories of the Buddha Shakyamuni's past lives. In one of these past lives he was a sailor on a merchant ship and his name was *Tepön Nying-tob-chän*, "the courageous sailor." There were about 400 or 500 people on this ship, they had collected many precious things from across the ocean and were returning home on a ship filled with treasure. It had been a long voyage and they were getting close to home when one of the men on board stole most of the goods, put them in a lifeboat and started drilling a hole in the hull of the boat. His name was *Mi Nag Dung-thung-chän*, "the bad person with a spear." I think he used a short spear to drill the hole in the boat's hull. His plan was for the ship to sink and kill everybody on board while he escaped in the lifeboat with the treasure.

The Buddha-to-be had clairvoyance and saw what was going to happen. He thought to himself, "If I don't stop this person, he will become the murderer of 400 or 500 people. If I try to stop him and he kills me and still drills the hole this will not help either." Thinking all this through he finally decided to kill this one person to save the lives of 400 or 500 and stop this man from becoming a killer. The would-be-mass murderer had already started to drill through the ship's hull, but perhaps because the wood was too thick he had not finished. The Buddha-to-be first fought with this person and when he could not stop him he finally killed him. This action is still considered to be the action of a bodhisattva because it was not at all selfish. It was performed to save the 400 or 500 people from dying and the man himself from becoming a killer. The karmic result of this killing was for the Buddha-to-be to go to hell but he accepted this in order to help the would-be-killer and his victims.

Even with this selfless motivation his karma was not excused, but he sacrificed himself anyway.

This story from one of the Buddha Shakyamuni's previous lives shows that only in the most extreme, profound, selfless situations do the ends justify the means. I don't know about you, but I think it will take me many lifetimes to reach a state where I can behave like that. Until we reach that stage, while we are still beginners, the ends never justify the means. Our means, our actions and intentions, should both be positive. If we are in a situation where it looks as though we should do something negative in order to attain a positive result, we need to pause and think very carefully. Only when both the action and the intention are positive should we go for it.

This is the last piece of advice on how not to fuel the fire of neurosis or defilement, and how this helps us become successful in Shamatha meditation. Now we should look at the actual practice of Shamatha in more detail. The essence of our mind is the same as the Buddha's – perfect and limitless – but we do not discuss this in the development of Shamatha, because at the moment our minds' capacities are very small. I cannot see clearly beyond a certain distance so I need glasses. If I do not wear my glasses I cannot make out the facial details of people in front of me. I can see them roughly, but I cannot see their mouths or eyes – they look like modern art. My capacities are limited in this way. I can only hear certain sounds over a certain distance. I cannot taste anything until I put it in my mouth. I cannot perceive anything that is unperceivable; I can only perceive that which I have dualistic reference points for. It is only when I have a reference point for something, an experience of it, some knowledge about it that I can perceive it. I cannot perceive anything beyond this. I can't imagine what I can't imagine, but that does not mean that what I cannot imagine does not exist. I don't know the past, I don't know the future and I don't even know everything about the present. I only know a fraction of the present moment superficially. Do you know everything about the present?

In this way our limitless potential does not manifest very much right now, but as our Shamatha practice progresses our capacity will broaden. Our perception increases like the perimeter of an upturned pyramid: at its base it is very small but moving towards the top it increases more and more.

The development of Shamatha progresses from the desire realm, through the different stages of the form and formless realms, until it reaches the Shamatha – calm abiding – state of total cessation. Right now our bodies are in the desire realm. Human beings are in the desire realm, as are many gods. There are even gods at quite high levels who are still in the desire realm. Above the desire realm, within the god realm, there are also the form and formless realms. Practitioners of Shamatha develop the mental states of the form and formless realms, even up to their highest levels, while they still have a desire realm form. As the realization of Buddhahood is above and beyond even the highest of these states, we should put the conquest of these levels of mind to one side and focus on Buddhahood.

Something we do need to focus on, a most important aspect of Shamatha meditation, is physical posture. Our correct physical posture is usually described by seven points that are called, "The Seven Postures of the Buddha *Namba Nangdze*, Vairochana."[32] To these seven points we should also add another important focus of attention – breathing. This makes eight different physical aspects of Shamatha practice: the seven points of posture and breathing.

The mind also has four things it specifically focuses on, four things it observes. These are called the four *mikpa* in Tibetan. These are crucial because merely being in the correct physical posture does not make a Shamatha practice complete: observing the state of the mind is very important. The first of these four states is the "all-pervading observation." Being all-pervading, like the sky or space, it includes everything. Cultivating this focus means the practitioner of Shamatha should have a basic outlook that pervades everything.

The second object of observation is "the observation that purifies." In Tibetan it is called the *chepa namjong*: *chepa* means reasoning or observation and *namjong* means purification. This means, for example, properly examining the objects we find desirous. If we are attached to money, power, antiques, people, fame or fortune then we should look carefully to see whether these objects have the qualities we think they do. Let's examine antiques properly. If you value antiques so much I can give you the most incredible antique – a handful of clay. It is natural, nobody made it, but it is billions and billions of years old. It is the oldest antique you will ever find, yet it has no great monetary value.

Another thing we are really attached to is our body. It is okay to take care of our body, to make ourselves look pleasant and presentable, but we should also remember that they are only flesh, nerves, blood, skin, bone, hair, marrow and so on. If we don't remember what lies underneath their nice, clean exterior we will become neurotic about their care. We will develop attachment to them and as a result have desire and greed, which are not healthy. If we know the truth about our bodies we may still have desire and attachment but at least it will be clear and honest.

Through examining the way things are we will not become neurotic about money, people or power either. Insight into reality will tame our anger, jealousy, attachment, pride and greed. With insight our interactions with things will become sensible. We will be able to do away with the illusions we have about illusions. Experiencing one illusion is enough. If we have illusions about the illusions we experience then we can go on to develop illusions about these illusions also. We will relate to things through a double or triple illusion, and in this way get buried deeper and deeper in samsara. While we are experiencing one illusion – for example, the appearance of phenomena – we can still enjoy ourselves, but when we have illusions about this illusion we will become neurotic, we will become buried deeper and deeper in samsara. In this way the "observation that purifies" is very important.

When you have developed an understanding of the illusory nature of things at the highest level you can start practicing like Milarepa, with no attachment whatsoever, even to food and water. I cannot encourage you to practice like this though, because I cannot practice like this. I would like to encourage you to practice like this, but it would be strange for me to encourage you to do something that I am not doing myself. Unless you are fully committed to practicing in this way it is not easy. When you are committed it is easy. When you are committed you will behave like the trader who shot the deer. You will say, "Oh my god, what have I done?" Actually he would not have said that, he would have said, "Oh my Buddha, what terrible thing have I done?" Then you will break your gun, run away and leave everything behind.

The trader probably left behind a big mess; the people he was with would not have known what happened to him and his leaving could have created problems for people later also. Still I don't think he thought of this, he made a clear-cut decision, free from attachment to anything. His decision was as clean as cutting butter with an axe; attached to nothing, he was gone. If we make a decision like this we can practice like this, but without a decision like this we cannot.

The third object of observation is things we should know, the *ke bä mikpa,* the "object of the wise." There are many things we should know about but some of the most important things to know about are the twelve links of interdependent origination,[33] the Prajnaparamita and the five skandhas. I have already explained the Prajnaparamita roughly and I will explain the five skandhas in the next session. Knowing these things is very important.

The fourth object is the *nyönmong namjong ki mikpa,* "the object that completely abandons the afflictions." This refers to when the practice of Shamatha itself is purification. That is when we are doing the basic practice and for example focus on the Four Noble Truths and their sixteen details.[34] By practicing and understanding these thoroughly there is no way we will not achieve a calm abiding state of mind.

So these are the four objects of observation. The first is all-pervading, the second is a little bit of analysis, the third is being knowledgeable, and the fourth is purification. Each of these four are important, they are all pieces of the Shamatha practice puzzle.

Also try and remember that the point of this talk was to discuss meditation. It was not about merchants, or hunters becoming enlightened, or bandits saying prayers, it was about meditation. Sometimes when a teaching is interspersed with these tales we can forget what it was about.

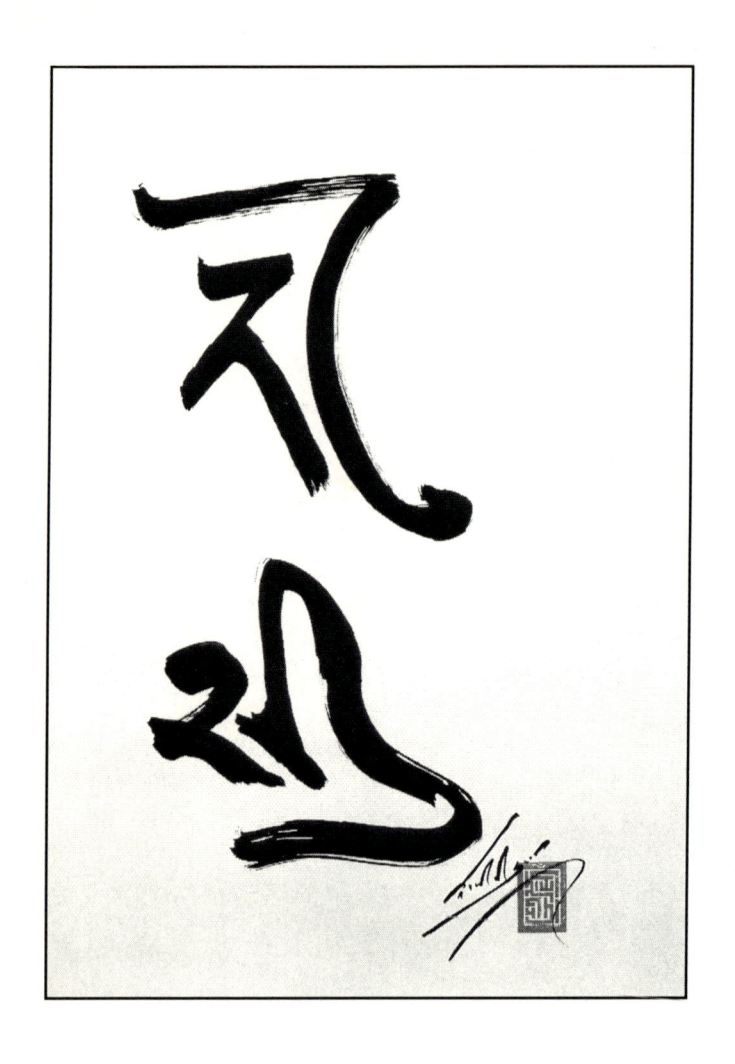

EMPTINESS
*Calligraphy by
Tai Situ Rinpoche*

Chapter 7

THE FIVE SKANDHAS

IN THE PREVIOUS SESSION WE came to the conclusion that all meditation is either Shamatha or Vipashyana and that these two have different levels, some less advanced and others more advanced. We learnt that basic morals are an important part of Shamatha practice and that without them we cannot progress. We also briefly looked at the progression of Shamatha meditation when we have a human form. Even in the human form we can develop form and formless realm mental states through Shamatha meditation. We then went over the importance of physical posture and the four mental objects of observation. Among these four objects the third, "objects of the wise," included "knowing the five skandhas." This is a very wide subject, it covers a lot, but it is relatively easy to understand.

The first skandha is form. "Form" refers to the physical and depends on one element, space. Space enables form to be. Apart from space there are four other elements in form. Sometimes we speak of five elements – including space – and sometimes we speak of four elements – excluding space. As space has no form, however, we should say that form is composed of only four elements.

Space is a mystery. A tiny seed is surrounded by a lot of space, but when it grows into a giant tree that covers perhaps 300 square feet; a lot of this space is consumed. Where does it go? Then when the tree is burnt and turns to ash the space comes back. It is a mystery; it is there, then it is not. Space is like the mind. If it was not there we would be in big trouble, but where is it? Where does it go and where does it come from? When we place something somewhere, what happens to the displaced space? Does it move? What happened to the space that used to surround the seed when it grows into a tree? It is a mystery. It is also the closest metaphor we have to technically describing limitlessness and non-duality. The mind is described by the image of space many times, but it is not space. The best image we can use to understand the mind is the mind itself. There is nothing else that acts as a perfect symbol for mind.

Apart from space there are four other elements that act as the basis of form: earth, water, fire and air. These four are called the *ju-zug-zhi*, the four causal forms. *Ju* means cause, *zug* means form and *zhi* means four.

The next way to look at the form skandha is in terms of the *dre-zug chu-chig*, the eleven resultant forms. *Dre* means fruition, *zug* again means form, and *chu-chig* means eleven. The first five of these eleven are the five senses: sight, sound, smell, taste and physical feeling. In Tibetan these are called the *wang-po nga*, the five faculties. It is much easier for us to recognize the bases for these senses than it is to recognize the senses themselves. Our sight's sense vessel is the eye, the retina, the water ball and so on. Our sound's sense vessel is easy to recognize also, it is our ears with their conch shells and drum sets. Our nose is the vessel for our sense of smell; it has two holes and hair in it. Our taste vessel is this muscle we call a tongue with lots of taste buds on top of it. Our vessel for tactile sensations is our body with one head, two legs, two hands and a middle trunk. These are very simple to recognize, we call them the *wong ten*, the senses' bases, but they are not the *wong po*, the senses themselves.

The senses themselves are specific, subtle, light-like forms. The sense of sight is shaped like a flower, is blue and is located in the eye. The sense of smell is like two thin needles made out of copper. The sense of hearing consists of two forms the same shape as the twisted, wooden screw-shaped creatures that grow underneath the bark of some trees. In ancient India they would take the bark off these trees in order to write on it and they would see these creatures. The sense of taste actually consists of two half-moons on the sides of our tongues. This is why we can only taste something if we put it to the two sides of our tongue and not when we put it right in the middle of our tongue. Our sense of feeling is all over our body, but only when our body parts are attached. If I were to cut off my finger or my whole hand then I would not experience feeling in this finger or hand. Tactile sensation pervades our body but it has this special characteristic. All of these senses are extremely subtle, light-like forms. The organs with which they are associated are the vessels for the senses.

The next five of the eleven resultant forms are the objects of the senses, the *dön nga*. The objects of the sense of sight for example are color, light, darkness and other shades. These forms can also have details; they can be few or many, triangular, square, round, half-moon, horizontal or vertical. These forms are basic, but many combinations of them are possible. There are two types of sound, the sounds of nature and the sound of being. There are, for example, the sounds of insects, people moving around, waterfalls and the wind. There are also two types of smells, natural and man-made. Natural smells include sandalwood, roses, earth, mud, fresh water, etc. Man-made smells come in bottles; people prefer one smell over another, and the more difficult they are to make, the more expensive they become. Things we taste are also natural or man-made. Fruit we eat of the tree is natural, food that is cooked for us is man-made. We cannot find anything growing on a tree that tastes like cooked food. The last of the senses is that of touch, and the last of the sense objects is that which we touch. These are basically divided into our experience of touching the four elements – fire, water, air and earth – but we can also add detail to these experiences by describing them as pleasant or unpleasant, comfortable or uncomfortable and so on.

These are the basic divisions of the first ten of the eleven resultant forms. If we were to combine different elements of these divisions they would obviously become a lot more detailed.

According to the Abhidharma Kosha, the *Ngönpa dzö*, the last of the eleven resultant forms are those that you cannot see, the *Nam rig min zug*. A very simple way to describe this is to take the example of vows. We cannot see vows, we cannot see their lineage that comes from the Buddha through the guru to us, but we receive it physically. Our body and speech are blessed by the vows, we receive them and have them, but we cannot see them. When we take, uphold and cherish these sacred vows, they live on, they are there at all times. Even when we are not doing anything they are developing and growing. They continue as long as the form they are attached to does. That is to say until we die. Having precepts in this life does not mean I will have them in my future life. I will have to take them again. They cease to exist as soon as there is no longer a suitable vessel for them to exist in or when they are broken. They are like a light that exists as long as its electric plug is in the socket but as soon as you unplug it the light goes off.

These forms cannot be perceived by our sense of sight but they are forms and they continue to exist as long as the physical form they are attached to does. They are similar to the senses in that they are subtle physical form that we cannot perceive with our eyes.

This is the way the eleventh resultant form is described by the Abhidharma Kosha, but in another text called the Abhidharma Samacchaya, the *Ngönpa Kuntu*, the eleventh resultant form is described as the *Chöje chebä zug*, the abstract objects of mental consciousness. There are five types of abstract objects of mental consciousness. The first type is the deducted forms, the *düpa lä gyurpä zug*. These are the objects that appear to the mind like compounded phenomena and so forth. These include things like the shortest moment of time and the smallest objects that the mind can perceive, but which we cannot see even with the aid of the biggest microscopes or the cyclotrons that physicists use to break down the smallest particles into even smaller parts. Only our mind can perceive these smallest objects, because beyond our mental conception of them they do not really exist.

This is the same for the shortest moment of time. Right now we define the smallest moment of time as the time it takes for the fastest moving thing traveling the farthest distance to pass through the smallest particle. But what is that fastest thing? At the moment we think light is the fastest thing but I am not sure this is true. There may be things that travel faster than light which we do not know about yet, and because of all this factoring these ideas only appear to the mind. Still they are form. Still they are there. If they were not here this table, this body would not be here. This table and this body are also only perceived by the mind.

The second type of subtle form is occasionally visible form, *Ngönpar kab yöbä zug*. This form is so clear that it cannot be obscured by anything. This is, for example, the light that enables me to see my hand through glass. In this way light is form that penetrates glass and therefore enables us to see through it. The brighter the light, the thicker and darker the glass it can penetrate. This is how we take x-rays, by using very bright lights. It is not only light that does this, however, there are other subtle forms that are not obstructed either.

The third type of subtle form is the same as the subtle form described in the Abhidharma Kosha, that is, the subtle form of vows or precepts, the *Yangdagpar langba le jung wä zug*.

The fourth subtle form is that which is forged, the *Kuntagpä sug*. These are not real, but they are form. This type of form includes, for example, a magician pulling a rabbit out of his hat, or when we dream that a whole country of people are celebrating New Year's Eve with firecrackers and dancing. These experiences are not real like a table we lean on, they are dreams or dreamlike, but they are form. We see them, we touch them.

The last of the five abstract objects are the visions people experience when their practice progresses, the *Wangjorwä zug* or mastered forms. Maybe when your practice progresses you will have visions like these, maybe you will see a deity or a bodhisattva. These will be another kind of form. I find the Beatles song "Let it Be" very moving when it says, "in times of trouble, Mother Mary comes to me, speaking words of wisdom." I don't know if they are describing a time when the Mother Mary really came to them, or it is a song written by or about somebody else and they are just singing it. What they are describing, however, is a vision achieved through a spiritual journey, and these visions are included as one subtle object of form, one *Chöje chebä zug*, by the Abhidharma Samacchaya, the *Ngönpa Kuntu*.

There are seven main Abhidharma texts and many commentaries on them. The Abhidharma Kosha is one commentary and the Abhidharma Samacchaya is another. They describe the eleventh form in these different ways. As an overview of the form skandha we can say that there are four main causal forms – earth, water, fire, air – and eleven forms that result from these four.

The next skandha is *tsorwa* in Tibetan. This is translated many times as feeling but it is more like "sensing" something. "Form" describes things themselves but a *tsorwa* is our sense of that thing; whether it is hot or cold, nice or not nice. When someone says something nice to us, we experience a nice *tsorwa*; when they say something not so nice we experience a hurt *tsorwa*. The sensing skandha is generally speaking the experience of three things; *dewa*, *dungma* and *tangnyom*. *Dewa* means comfort, joy and happiness. *Dungma* means pain and suffering, it is the opposite of *dewa*. *Tangnyom* is neutrality.

Within these general groups we can detail many different experiences. I do not want to go into too much detail regarding these, but we can discuss them a little. To begin with we have the nice, not so nice and neutral experiences of the eyes, the ears the nose, the tongue, the body and the mind, which add up to eighteen different experiences. These eighteen different experiences can also be summarized into two types of experience: mental and physical. Physical tsorwa include the experiences of nice, not nice and neutrality by all the sense organs – the tongue, the eye, the ear, the nose and the body. Mental tsorwa are the mind's experiences of nice, not nice and neutrality. These are called the *lu tsor*, physical sensation, and *sem tsor*, mental sensation in Tibetan.

We can also collect all of these experiences into those that are chaotic, *zang zing chen*, and those that are not chaotic, *zang zing me ba*. A sensation is chaotic or not depending on whether it involves too much attachment or not, whether it is a cause for the suffering of samsara or not. Those that do involve too much attachment and are a cause for the suffering of samsara are called chaotic. When these experiences are not accompanied by attachment, clinging, rejection and so on they are not chaotic. I would say most of our sensations are chaotic. When we eat nice food or food that is too salty, sweet, cold or hot we experience a chaotic sensation that is based on our dualistic attachment. A non-chaotic sensation would not be influenced by any of these. When we consider this it becomes a little bit difficult for any of us to proclaim ourselves free of chaotic sensations.

Sometimes, though, we may become so engrossed in our dinner conversation, so engrossed with the chaos – the *zang zing* – of our conversation, that the experience of our food is not chaotic. We may not even know what we have eaten. We may end up with an empty plate and not know what we ate because the subject of our dinner conversation was so provocative, so interesting, so occupying. Our experience of the conversation was chaotic – was *zang zing chen* – but our experience of the food was not. We did not have any attachment to the food while we were eating it.

The feeling or sensation skandha can also be described as those experiences that are *zhenpa tenpa* [feelings that stimulate attachment] and those that are *ngönjung tenpa* [feelings that express our experience]. For all beings in samsara, feelings stimulate grasping and attachment; our experience of forms – sound, smell and so on – stimulate our attachment, our desire. This is *zhenpa tenpa*.

Ngönjung tenpa is different. These experiences are accompanied by knowing. The person experiencing them knows the harm that attachment brings, knows the baselessness of our reality and is therefore able to overcome any attachment they may have to the sense object that is generating their experience. An example of this kind of insight is the way Buddha Shakyamuni lived on a few grains of rice and a few drops of water for six years on the banks of the

Neranjara River. He did not eat and drink these things because of desire; he ate and drank them to stay alive. He did not want to torture himself either, he knew what it would take to keep himself alive and that is all that he wanted. He wanted to live so he could practice and reach Buddhahood. He acted on his experiences but without attachment, without clinging, without desire, without defilement. These are *ngönjung tenpa*, feelings that truly express our experience, but they are still feelings.

This group of feelings, the *ngönjung tenpa*, also includes those that arise from meditation or visions. If I were to do an Avalokiteshvara Bodhisattva practice for ten years and then, all of a sudden, Avalokiteshvara Bodhisattva was to appear in front of me I would be delighted, moved and feel blessed. These are all feelings but they are not worldly, dualistic feelings. If I had worldly, dualistic feelings I would never experience a vision like that. The feelings that come from a vision like this are necessarily sacred, pure and non-dualistic. These feelings that truly express our experience are also non-chaotic, they are *zang zing me ba*. Perhaps "feeling" is the right word to translate "tsorwa."

The next skandha is *dushe*. This is often translated as "perception." Again I am not one hundred percent sure this is the correct word to use in translation, but we shall find out as we discuss it. A "*dushe*" is the recognition that "this is this" and "that is that." An example of this is when my eye – the vessel – and my eye sense contact the physical form of a marigold flower and I have the *dushe* that, "This is a nice, new marigold."

There are six basic types of *dushe*: those related to the eyes, ears, nose, tongue, body and mind. Each of these can be explained in infinite detail: the eyes, for example, can trigger a perception of white, red, blue, green, black, yellow or a combination of any of these main colors. They could also bring on a perception of shape as well as color. In some ways these perceptions are just like feelings, but where a feeling is just a pleasant, unpleasant or neutral reaction to something, perceptions know what that something is. They consciously perceive that "this is this" and "that is that."

The basic six divisions of the skandha of perception are those that arise from the six perceptions, but we can divide them into other groups also. There are natural direct perceptions *ton la tse mä dzin pa* and processed, added perceptions *tanye la tse mä dzin pa*. An example of a natural, direct perception is when a dog sees a flower, for example. It sees a flower that has a nice or not so nice smell. It sees a flower that it likes or one that makes it sneeze, walk around, rub up against it a little and then keep walking. This group also includes our general perception of blue, green, red, etc.

Processed perceptions, perceptions where we add something, are perceptions like, "This is the kind of orchid that lives for six months. It is expensive. It costs 2000 US dollars." Or, "This other orchid will only cost ten dollars." Or, "This is a marigold mala, it will only cost ten rupees." These perceptions are not natural. Dogs, cats and birds don't have as many of these. They have a few but not many. A dog may, for example, encounter certain types of dog biscuits that they like and others they do not. But they have nowhere near as many of these processed perceptions as we do.

Another example of a processed perception is the different ways we perceive a shirt with a designer crocodile label, one with another label and one with no label. Even though they may be exactly the same quality we will see one as expensive, one as okay and one as cheap. We will see the expensive one as a shirt we should wear and the inexpensive shirt as something we should not wear. Or maybe we will see them the other way around. Maybe we will think that we should not wear the expensive shirt because we are a guru and that would be bad PR. People make jokes about gurus with gold watches and expensive cars so we have to be careful.

Another way of categorizing perceptions is into six types. The first of these are the *tsenche kyi dushe*, the perceptions with signs. These are the perceptions we do not have names for. Those we have, for example, when we go to a country that is completely foreign to us and encounter signs in a language we do not know. The signs may say, "The restaurant is this way" and "The bathroom is that way," but if we cannot read the signs we may go into the bathroom for a meal. When our perception is a *tsenche kyi dushe*, a perception with signs, we perceive something but do not know anything about the thing we perceive. Another example of this kind of perception would be the first time someone comes into a Tibetan Buddhist temple. They see all the paintings and mandalas, hear all the horns and music, but do not know what is happening. Perhaps they might think it is praying, but they might think it is an orchestral rehearsal, modern art or therapy.

Perceptions without signs, *tsenme dushe*, are interesting because they can be either very advanced or very dull perceptions. If I just space out, this is a perception without signs, but it is also a perception without signs when we attain holy, sacred, advanced states of being. In these attachment-free states we have no perceptions either. This means that spacing out and achieving these high states, in themselves, are similar. The difference is that when we finish spacing out our defilements will return but when we have realized a perception-free state we will only progress further from that point.

The third type of perceptions in this division are the *gya chung wä dushe*, the limited perceptions. The fourth are the *gya che wä dushe*, the greater perceptions. The fifth type are the *tse me bä dushe*, the limitless perceptions, and the sixth type are the *chi yang me bä dushe*, the perceptions of nothing whatsoever. These different types of perceptions relate to the progress of Shamatha I talked about earlier. At the beginning of our Shamatha practice we are limited by our physical capacities as humans on planet Earth. As human beings on planet Earth we are in the desire realm. The physical reality of the body we inhabit limits our perception. This limited perception is the third type of perception.

As our mind has a greater capacity than the vessel that hosts it, however, we can transcend this limited capacity. This means that we do not have to stop at the highest state of mind compatible with our physical reality, we can progress beyond it. The state of mind beyond this is the fourth type of perception, the greater perception. This state of mind is at the same level as the minds of the gods in the form realm. The form realm is a higher realm than the desire realm and has seventeen levels. Within the desire realm we have human beings and some gods. There are six different levels or abodes of desire realm gods: the *Gyäl-chen Rig-zhi* or the Heaven of the Four Great Kings, the *Sumchu-tsa-sum* or the Heaven of the Thirty-Three (this has thirty-three different levels), the *Tab-drel* or the Heaven with No Combat, *Ganden* or Tushita the Joyous Heaven, *Trulga* or the Heaven of Enjoying Emanations, and the *Zhen-trul Wang-che* or the Land of Controlling Others' Emanations.

As our Shamatha mediation progresses, our state progresses beyond the limitations of our physical body and through these levels. This means that when we are doing Shamatha practice well we may start by feeling like a perfect human, then progress to feeling like a desire realm god, but we do not have to stop there, we can progress even beyond this state to the form realm. When we do this our perceptions become "greater perceptions."

There are four main meditative states, four main levels of samadhi, in the form realm. The first of these is called the first concentration, the *samten tangbo*. This first concentration has three different sections: the *tsang ba* or Brahma level, the *tsangba dun na dun* or the in front of Brahma level and the *tsang chen* or great Brahma level. The second concentration, the *samten nyiba*, also has three sections: the *ö chung* or little light level, the *tseme ö* or limitless light level, and the *ö sel* or radiant light level.

This form realm, the realm of light, is also where we believe some humans originally came from. In the Abhidharma it describes how they made some mistakes, lost their light and slowly fell down to Earth. After this they started eating and slowly became human. In this way humans are okay but not as great as their ancestors. Other human beings, we Tibetans for example, did not come from this realm. We came from the union of the *drak sinmo* – a powerful female spirit – and the *bi-u chungchub semba* – the bodhisattva monkey. These two parented six kids who started the *mi'u dung drug,* "the six bone lineages of little humans." *Mi'u* means "little humans." I guess if you compare humans to the other things in our world we are little. These six lineages represent ignorance or pig-headedness, attachment and greed, aggression, jealousy, and pride.

This is how we believe humans evolved. We do not believe they all evolved in the same way. Some descended from the heaven of the clear light gods, ate what we call the "cream of the earth" and lost their light. After this they began to develop organs with which they could take in and dispose of food, and in doing so became humans. Other humans came into existence from the union of a spirit and a monkey. We also believe that humans can come into existence in other ways.

The third concentration, the *samten sum,* also has three levels: the *ge chung* or small virtue level, the *tsä me ge* or limitless virtue level and the *ge gyä* or great virtue level. The fourth concentration, the *samten zhi,* has eight levels. The first three levels are: the *drin me ö* or cloudless level, the *sö nam kye* or born from merit level and the *dre bu che ba* or great result level. It also includes the five pure gods' abodes, the *nä tsang mä lha*: *mi che wa* or not great, *mi dung wa* or without pain, *gyanom nang wa* or excellent appearance, *shin tu thong wa* or great perception and *ög min* or below none.

When we develop levels of consciousness equal to gods in these realms, this is known as the *dushe chenpo,* the greater perception.

Still subtler levels of consciousness are to be found in the formless realm. There are four levels of gods in the formless realm. The first level is called *namkah taye* or limitless as space. The second is the *namshe taye* or limitless as consciousness. The perception that equals these states is called the *tseme bä dushe,* the limitless perception, the fifth of the six types of perceptions in this categorization.

The sixth of the perceptions, the *chiyang mebä dushe,* the perception of nothing whatsoever, is equal to the highest Shamatha states. These states are not Buddhahood, though, they are still in samsara. The gods abide in the highest realm, and the highest god realms are in the formless realm. Within the four levels of the formless realm the third highest realm is called the *chi yang me bä,* nothing at all. There is nothing limited, solid, dualistic, destroyable or touchable there. There is nothing except mind itself, it is pure mind. Not enlightenment, but pure mind. The limitations and limitlessness develop in this way.

As human beings, we are able to start off as we are now, become calm and stable, then as our Shamatha meditation progresses, to develop the highest mental states our human capacity allows. Our mind, however, can progress past this and we can reach the same mental states as those enjoyed by the desire realm gods, then the form realm gods and then the formless realm gods. Yet this is all still in samsara. The highest state we can reach while we are still human is the third level of the formless realm, the *chi yang me bä*, the nothing at all state. The fourth level of the formless realm is a continuation on from the third. It is called the *dushe me dushe me min,* the perception that is neither discriminating nor non-discriminating. As human beings we cannot achieve this highest level of existence. This means that as we progress through Shamatha states, as human beings, we have to stop at the third level, the state of *chi yang me bä*, nothing at all. We can go a step even higher than this though and achieve the first of the bodhisattva levels. This realization is higher than the highest of the god realms.

These six types or aspects of perception are another way of looking at perception. I have explained them to you because as your Shamatha progresses you will experience these states on your cushion. What happens off your cushion is another story. If you were to do Shamatha meditation for two hours every day for the next ten or twenty years you might reach these states. Whether you are able to maintain them off your cushion is something else. We should not be meditating in order to become meditation experts, however. We do not want to become a form or formless realm god: our ultimate aim is to reach Buddhahood.[35] Knowledge of these states is important, but in order to stop you developing misgivings or misunderstandings it is important that I emphasize our motivation for meditation.

The fourth skandha is the *duche phungbo,* the skandha of formations. It includes everything that is not in the other four skandhas. This skandha, this aggregate, is generally divided into two parts: fifty-one mental formations and twenty-four conditions that are not exactly mental. It is slightly irregular for a mental aggregate to have elements that are not mental, but they are included within this aggregate, this skandha.

The first fifty-one mental aggregates include memories of things we are well acquainted with and the ignorance that comes about from not knowing. I will not go into these in detail. If you are interested in them you will be able to find their descriptions in other books, especially those dealing with the Abhidharma (see appendix on page 288 for list). Some of them even have charts explaining how the fifty-one different types of mental aggregates fit together. When our mind encounters an object through our eyes, ears, nose, tongue or body, the mental skandha develops out of this.

As I said, in the other section of this skandha, this aggregate, are the *duche* or formations that are not mental formations. This group is usually translated as either the "non-associated compositional factors" or the "non-concurrent formations." It includes those things that we cannot call consciousness but cannot call inanimate objects either. There are twenty-four of them and they include, for example, numbers. Numbers are neither mental nor physical. One and one is two. Two plus one is three. Two times three is six. But none of these are mind or physical entities. If I have six things in front of me that is physical, and when I perceive that there are six of them that is mental, but the number "six" itself is neither.

Another example of this is ownership. If somebody bought something it belongs to them; if I were to take it from them that would be stealing. If on the other hand they were to say, "Have this," and I took it, that would not be stealing. There is no difference in the physical action I am performing, but there is a difference in the situation. You cannot find it when you look for it but it is there. If I take a diet coke that is not given to me, a diet coke that belongs to somebody else, I become a thief and have the karma of stealing. If, on the other hand, somebody wanted to accumulate merit by giving me a diet coke, and I received it, I would not become a thief. I would become the recipient of a diet coke and have to digest not only the diet coke but the karma of receiving offerings.

Digesting a diet coke is easy compared to digesting the karma of receiving an offering of a diet coke. In order to digest this karma I have to earn it. I have to deserve it. I have to be genuine about receiving it. The person is giving genuinely but I also have to receive it properly. In one of his songs, Milarepa said, "I am not afraid of anything more than other people's offerings." He said they are like drinking boiling lava: if you don't have the stomach for it all your virtue will be destroyed and you will end up in hell.

This grouping of non-associated compositional factors also includes order. That is, for example, how a shoot and later a flower will grow after you put a seed in the ground. There is an order to these things, they will not happen backwards. The seed, shoot and flower may be tangible but the order is not. Nor is it mind, but it is there. There are twenty-four different things like this that are included within the *duche phungbo*, the skandha of formations. They are included within this skandha because our consciousness is aware of them. I know that I cannot take things that do not belong to me without stealing. I know they do not belong to me and that I have to pay money for them. We cannot pinpoint exactly what makes this so, but it is there. This type of thing is described as *den ba ma yin bä duche*, non-associated compositional factors. They are *duche*, but they are not mind or form.

The last of the five skandhas is the *nampar shebä phungbo*, the skandha of consciousness. This has a relative and ultimate aspect. People tell me they have seen films in which artificially made humans take over the planet. I tell them that if these artificially made beings have consciousness then they are sentient beings too. If they only have working senses that enable them to react to light, messages and input, they are not sentient beings. My mobile phone is not a sentient being. It tells me somebody is ringing, lets me know who it is, lets me hear their voice, respond to them, store messages, and it even lets me know when I have made a mistake dialing a number. It has all these functions but it is not a sentient being because it does not have consciousness.

I don't know that many people consider these differences. Many people do not accept consciousness, so they do not see us as being any different from machines. I went to a conference here in Delhi a while ago, and there was a wonderful couple there. The woman was working very hard to help nuns and establish bhikshuni ordination. Her husband was a scientist and not a Buddhist. I didn't know that. He gave a speech, and then she gave a speech. I was very impressed with their speeches and what they were doing. Then later when I talked about Buddha-nature he stood up and made a point of saying that he did not believe in any of what I was saying. He said we are all made out of molecules and nothing else. This made me realize that many people, like that wonderful gentlemen, believe we are just naturally grown robots. That natural development has turned us into advanced, organic computer chips. Up to a certain point this is true. The "certain point" being whether we have consciousness or not.

Consciousness is the ability to know beyond what we see, to find ultimate meaning, the ultimate source or essence of what we see. Reality is multi-layered. The room we are in right now is the Gurumoha room of the Indian Habitat Center in Delhi. You have all come from Taiwan, America, Malaysia, Europe, Tibet, other parts of India and other parts of Delhi to be here. This is one reality. There are, without question, other beings having other experiences within this space also. For another being there may be nothing here. For yet other beings something unbelievable may be happening here. For them it may be the middle of an ice age, or a volcanic age. Maybe there is even a big bang happening, or it is the center of a black hole. In this way reality is multi-layered and consciousness is that which has the ability to comprehend this.

There are six consciousnesses.[36] Here we are not talking about the senses but the consciousnesses associated with these senses; the eye, ear, nose, tongue, body, and mind consciousness. The king of these consciousnesses is the mind; the rest are only ministers. Consciousness is described as *chö nam kyi ton kyi ngo-o so-sor rang rigba che ba*. *Chö* is dharma. Here it does not only mean a Sutra, Tantra or text: it means everything that is perceivable, everything that is capable of being an object of mind. In Buddhist philosophy we describe objects of sight as form, objects of hearing as sound and objects of the mind as dharma. The next syllable in this sentence, the *nam*, indicates that it is plural phenomena not a phenomenon. *Ton* means "meaning." *Ton kyi ngo-o* means the nature or essence of the meaning. *So-sor* means clearly, definitely, not mixed up. *Rang* means individually and *rigba che ba* means that which makes you understand, realize or know. So a consciousness is "that which makes you clearly understand the essential meaning of individual phenomena."

This also shows how the machines that scientists create in movies do not have consciousness, because when they go haywire there is always one smart guy, or boy, that can tap, tap, tap on a computer and make them all fall into a heap. Then they can bulldoze them into a corner because they do not work. If they had consciousness this would not happen, they would find a way to fight back.

The circumstances, the conditions that bring these consciousnesses about are of course the senses. They are the tools through which one is able to see form, hear sounds and so on. We are then able to process these experiences further, however, and develop a clearer, deeper and finally ultimate understanding of them.

These are the six general consciousnesses – from eye consciousness to mind consciousness. For the sake of completeness we should discuss two more. The next, the seventh, is the *nyönmongpä yi*, the afflicted consciousness. *Nyönmongpa* means defilement, and *yi* means mind. This is the part of consciousness that perceives myself as me. It also perceives that I am better, more important, more deserving than others, this idea is always there, as if everybody owes us something. Another aspect of the afflicted consciousness is ignorance. Perceiving ourselves as an "I" is ignorance, holding onto this "I" tightly is another form of ignorance. The example I use to explain this grasping is a hungry monkey. If a monkey has not eaten for many days and then manages to get a mango it will hold onto that mango with everything it has. While it is biting the top of it, it will hold the rest of it with its hands, its feet and its tail. We hold on to our "I" with the same kind of attachment. This grasping, these defilements continue constantly. This negative aspect of the skandha of consciousness we call the afflicted consciousness, the *nyönmongpä yi*.

The last of the eight consciousnesses is the *kunshi namba sheba*, the consciousness that is the foundation of all.[37] All five skandhas, and the individual details of their parts, are perceived by consciousness. The foundation consciousness is nothing more, and nothing less, than this perception. Foundation consciousnesses are all the same, whether they be the consciousness of the most compassionate or evil being. The evil person will perceive something, think that perception through and take action that he or she will profit from without regarding the way this will affect others. The kind and compassionate person will perceive in the same way, will see the same thing, but he or she will find a way to use this information in the most positive way. They will use this knowledge from their perception to benefit others regardless of any loss they may encounter. The way they use the perception is different but the perception, the foundation consciousness, is the same.

The foundation consciousness is the last of the eight consciousnesses, and consciousness is the last of the five skandhas. All phenomena within the many layers of reality are contained within these five skandhas – form, feeling, perception, formations and consciousness. There are variations in the skandhas sentient beings have, though. Some sentient beings, for example, do not have eye consciousness because they have no light. The formless gods do not have taste, smell and other things like this, because they are irrelevant for them.

Before we began talking about the skandhas we were discussing the four observed objects in Shamatha practice. The third of these was the *ke bä mikpa*, objects of the wise or knowledgeable observations, and the five skandhas are important objects of knowledgeable observation.

In the next session we will go through the last of the four observed objects, *nyönmong namjong ki mikpa*, the object that completely abandons the afflictions. The teachings emphasize a particular way to completely abandon the afflictions. This method is, in general, the sixteen aspects or stages of the Four Noble Truths, Lord Buddha's first teaching.

After we have completed this we will talk about Shamatha and Vipashyana in Theravada, Mahayana and Vajrayana. In Tibetan Vipashyana is called, "*Lhaktong.*" *Lhak* means extra, profound, and *tong* means seeing. It is my hope that you will not leave here seeing things in the same way you did when you arrived. Maybe it will only have been a baby step in the right direction, but that will at least mean you are one step closer to profundity, completeness, health and being more beneficial.

Chapter 8

THE FOUR NOBLE TRUTHS

I HAVE BEEN TALKING ABOUT meditation, specifically Shinay/Shamatha meditation. Out of the four observations of this meditation (the all-pervading observation, the observation that purifies, the object of the wise and the object that completely abandons the afflictions) we still have to cover the last. This fourth observation is the core of the practice, the way it is implemented. In Tibetan it is called the *nyönmong namjong ki mikpa*. *Mikpa* means "observation" or the specific focus of a stage of practice. *Nyönmong* means defilement and *[nam] jong* means purification. The two words together refer to the purification of defilements. This is an enormous subject, but I am going to explain it through the Lord Buddha's first teaching, the Four Noble Truths. Lord Buddha gave this teaching in Varanasi seven weeks after his enlightenment, to his first five human disciples, although other beings also came to participate.

The Four Noble Truths are the truth of suffering, the truth of the cause of suffering, the truth of the cessation of suffering and its causes, and the truth of the path that achieves this. The Buddha described these four truths in sixteen stages; each truth has four features or details, and four times four is sixteen. These sixteen features are further described in two ways: according to their descriptions, *tsen nyi* in Tibetan; and according to the definitive meaning of their terms, *nge stig*. A description of fire, for example, is "hot and burning," and its "definitive meaning" would be an exact explanation of what the word "fire" meant.

The first truth, the truth of suffering, has four features: impermanence or *mitakpa*, suffering or *dugngelwa*, emptiness or *tongpa*, and selflessness or *dagmeba*. The first of these is impermanence, *mitakpa*. According to its description this means that every composed thing is impermanent because it is bound to separate into its constituents. It is impossible for something that is composed to remain forever. If you put up a building today, you will need to maintain it, and in the end, without question, it will fall down anyway. Anyone born today will definitely die. We will definitely lose everyone we now know. Anything that is composed has an impermanent nature. This is a fact and the first feature of the first truth.

The next feature is suffering, *dugngelwa*. We suffer because everything we cherish is by its nature impermanent. When we lose our friends we are sad. When we lose money we suffer. We may do our best to keep ourselves healthy but we are going to get sick and when we do we suffer. We may also worry about keeping the things we have. In this way everything impermanent has suffering as its nature and this suffering is the second feature of the truth of suffering.

Its third feature is emptiness – suffering is empty, *tongpa*. As we learnt earlier, the idea of having something, owning something or not owning something is all perception. It is an effective perception but really just an illusion. Everything that is suffering is actually related to everything else in that it does not exist independently and therefore is empty. The last aspect is selflessness, *dagmeba*. Everything that is empty is selfless. In this way impermanence leads to suffering, which leads to emptiness, which leads to selflessness. This is the presentation of these four features according to their descriptions.

Then we need to go through these four things again from the point of view of the definitive meaning of these terms. From this point of view all composed things – all the things that happen around us, within us and outside of us – are impermanent because they depend on circumstances. The conditions are such that the temperature outside is cold and the temperature in this room and my car is hot. Therefore, for example, the circumstances have come together for me to get a cold. When the conditions are there the composed things that depend on them are there. When they are not there the things that depend on them are also absent.

This situation then causes suffering because there is always discomfort. You could buy the most comfortable, most expensive, powerful, fastest, shiny car – perhaps a brand new, red Ferrari – but it will cause you constant discomfort from the moment you get it. You will have to tiptoe around it and drive it very carefully in case somebody scratches it, touches it or bumps into it. Or you might get a gadget that changes the temperature in your room at the press of a button, but then you will have to hold on to its remote control at all times in case it gets a bit too cold or a bit too hot. You may have 200 channels on your television – National Geographic, Discovery Channel, local news, international news – and you may watch it from bed with four pillows behind you or maybe you could get a "couch potato chair" that acts as a bed on your bed but you will still have to constantly hold on to the remote control. You will still have to go backwards and forwards between one channel and another. An advertisement will come on in the middle of your movie and you will have to flick through all the other channels. It is constantly uncomfortable. We think we need more entertainment – more this, more that, more samsara – but these things do not really make us comfortable. They actually cause us more discomfort.

We can never create the pure land of Sukhavati, the land of great bliss, here in samsara. It is impossible. Even if we had a machine to take care of everything we need, even if we had nothing to do, we would not be happy. In fact, we would be just like a pig in a pig farm. If even our toothbrush were to come out by itself and clean our teeth for us we would become so frustrated. It would be the most uncomfortable feeling. Samsara is like this, it is discomfort, and this suffering is what is being referred to here.

We should also look at emptiness from the perspective of its definitive meaning. Emptiness refers to the fact that the thing we call "I" is actually not there and when we say something is "mine," when we think something belongs to us, it is just an illusion. Of course my text is mine as opposed to yours and if you were to take it that would be stealing, but it is not really there. It is only molecules and atoms, and even they can be divided again and again into the smallest objects or the smallest amount of time, things we can never find. We may then ask how we can own something that is not really there. The answer is that it is superficially there. It is superficially mine, but in essence it is not. In this way emptiness refers to the objects that I say are "mine," including my body and the rest of the five skandhas. They are all empty. This emptiness is the antidote to being attached to things I call "mine."

The last of these four, selflessness, is an antidote for thoughts of "me." This "selflessness" is also emptiness – our essence has no limitations of dualistic reality. Nobody can pull us out of our body and say, "This is you here." When we die we leave behind a corpse and nobody can catch what leaves – it is selfless, it is limitless. It cannot be put in prison, it cannot be burned in hell, it cannot be enshrined in heaven, it is above and beyond any kind of dualistic reality – but without question it is there. I am speaking, you are listening and because of this you will have ignorance, knowledge or wisdom. There is no question this process exists but it exists in a limitless, non-dualistic manner. Its nature is limitless and non-dualistic. This last point then is the antidote to "me." The third point – emptiness – was the antidote to "mine" and this point overcomes "me." These four features, from these two perspectives, cover the truth of suffering.

The Buddha taught the next truth, the truth of the origin of suffering, in four steps: the cause or *ju*, the source or that which makes things happen or the *kunjung*, that which gives birth to things or the *rabche*, and conditions or *chen*. The cause, the *ju*, is both the defilement and the karma that created the defilement. It plants the seed for forthcoming existents. This simply means that actions we perform by following our defilements are the cause for the manifestation of samsara.

The second feature of this truth is *kunjung*: *kun* means "all," *jung* means "coming from." Therefore it means the "source of everything," where everything comes from. Sentient beings like us accumulate tendencies, what we call *bakchag* in Tibetan. Then we create karma by following these tendencies and this creates all the outer and inner realities of the six realms. These tendencies can be similar. For example, all of us have similar tendencies or imprints that have led us to create similar karma which, in turn, has created our human realm birth and similar – but not the same – experiences. Each of us has different hobbies and interests and we can tell this just by looking at each other – the clothes we wear, our long or short hairstyles. I like short hair because the Buddha said it was good and it is easy to look after. I don't have to worry about it. Others among us like this or that other style. Some of us like to have more hair on our head and less on our face, others like to wear more facial hair and less on top. Sometimes people even do this by choice! Some of us have black hair, some pink or a mixture of colors. All of this shows how our experiences, and we ourselves are similar but not the same. This similarity is the second feature of the second noble truth.

The third feature is *rabche*, production. It refers to the way we manifest as individuals even though we may be born in the same community, race or environment. The Buddha used the word *rabche* to describe how specific causes and conditions cause this individualism to manifest.

The last, the fourth feature of this second noble truth, is the condition. *Chen* means condition. Right now I have a human form and I am in the human realm. In my next life I may be in this or another realm but I will definitely be in a different body. The thing that causes me to have a different body in my next life is a condition.

All four of these features are actually aspects of karma, but the Buddha divided them into four different sections so we could understand each of them one by one. The first, the cause, is like a seed. The second, the source of all, refers to the way ten thousand sunflower seeds will bloom as sunflowers, all alike. The third, production, describes how each sunflower is individual; how some have bigger leaves and some have smaller leaves, some have a bigger core and some have a smaller core. It is like the sunflowers Vincent Van Gogh painted. He painted fields of sunflowers that all looked the same, but he also painted individual sunflowers in pots, each with a different character. A few of the sunflowers have leaves missing. Others are fresh. The fourth, condition, refers to the way one sunflower, through its seed, gives rise to the next sunflower. This is the way these four features of the second noble truth are taught from their descriptions.

Now we should look at the same four things in terms of their definitive meaning. From this perspective the cause is like a seed. The source, the *kunjung*, is like the reason for the seed to sprout. After all, a seed will remain a seed if something doesn't make it grow. The *rabche*, production, describes how everything is connected. I am connected to the same things as you are. I am a human being on planet Earth and so are you. We have the same eyes, ears, noses, tongues and hands, and with these we perceive things in a similar way. We can all touch this table, I can touch it and you can all touch it. There are other things, however, that we are not connected to. In this very space other realms, other realities, exist, but as we are not connected to them we cannot experience them. Some people can see ghosts, gods and auras. They have slightly different eyes to us and connections to these things. I do not have this kind of perception. Forget about auras: I cannot even see people clearly without my glasses!

The fourth feature, condition or *chen*, is described as that which causes things to manifest. Right now, for example, I am a human being. As a human being a piece of bone means nothing to me. I may well throw it away. Other things though, like money, gold and fresh food mean a lot to me. If I were to die and be born as a dog, a bone would mean a lot more to me than a large diamond. A diamond doesn't smell or taste like anything so as a dog it would not mean that much to me. A big piece of gold would mean nothing to me, or a pile of money. I might even rip up a million dollars, because it is fun to tear things up, but my bone, you know, that would be too precious to lose. If anybody went near it I would bite him or her. It would not be a problem if they took my diamond, but not my bone. The condition, the *chen*, is what makes this happen. It is what makes us change from what we are now into something else just by dying and being born somewhere. These four features then, from these two perspectives, complete the description of the second noble truth

The third noble truth is the truth of cessation. This is also taught through its four features: *gogba* or cessation, *zhiwa* or peace, *chanompa* or precious, and *ngejung* or truly becoming. As with the other truths each of these features is taught according to their descriptions and the definitive meaning of their terms. If we look at the way they are described, "cessation" refers to the cessation of suffering. The cause of all suffering is defilements. The immediate cause of all suffering is karma, of course, but karma's cause is defilements. When we are free from suffering it ceases to exist for us. When we reach arhathood we have zero defilements, zero karma and zero suffering.

The second feature is peace. At the moment, because we are influenced by the skandhas we do not experience any peace. My body, feelings and perceptions do not allow me any peace. Having this body means I have to take a shower every morning, then eat breakfast and lunch. It means I will get cold and have to move somewhere warmer. It means I will get hot and have to move somewhere cooler. This skandha will not allow me any peace. External forms also stop me from experiencing peace. I cannot walk through many external forms. I may have to turn left, then right to get around a wall for example. I may want everything to happen for me right here, right now, but it will not. I have to work at it. I have to arrange things, have meetings and lots of discussions. My head has to spin a lot before finally maybe two, three or ten percent of what I want to happen happens. Or maybe something else that I did not want to happen will happen. In this way the skandhas do not let us have any peace.

When we overcome the causes and conditions, the influence the skandhas have on us and our involvement in them, we are at peace. Arhathood is peace. As arhats we are not influenced by the skandhas. Sometimes people misunderstand this and think that arhats have supernatural powers. An arhat's body cannot be burnt by fire and cannot be bothered by poison, but this is not a supernatural power or magic. It is liberation, true liberation. Magic is not the same thing as a miracle. To perform magic you need to know a technique or alchemy. Miracles show the secret of reality, they are not tricks. I guess magic is not "trickery" either. Someone has a lineage of magic, they know how to do something, they perform it and other people are interested in what they have done because they do not know how the trick is performed. We may not know how to pull ten small rabbits out of a hat, so we are impressed when somebody else does it.

A miracle is different. Miracles happen when we reach beyond dualism, when we have worked out all of our karma. When the five skandhas and the elements do not affect us in a dualistic way, everything is possible. One time the Buddha put his staff in the ground and it grew into an enormous tree that covered five hundred *bagtse* [about 5000 kilometers] and was filled with all kinds of wish-fulfilling fruits and beautifully fragrant flowers. Everybody who encountered it enjoyed it, but he had not performed magic, he had performed a miracle. We can do this when we have overcome karma, cause and result as well as their base, the defilements. Then we will have no suffering whatsoever and be at peace. When there is no more suffering there is peace.

The third feature of this third noble truth *chanomba* – which means precious, noble, or divine – refers to the purity that exists when there are no more defilements.

The last of the features is *ngejung*, truly becoming. This means that our achievements will not be corrupted or contaminated once we reach this stage. It is not reversible. The truth of cessation is not a temporary state. It is not as if we have done a good meditation, reached a peaceful state that resembles the state of an arhat, then when we stop our meditation and do our day-to-day things we end up back at square one. It lasts forever. We can only progress further from this state. We can never slide backwards from it. This is why it is called definite or true becoming. These features show us how the cessation described in the third noble truth is arhathood.

Now we should look at these four features from the point of view of their definitive meaning. From this perspective, when the defilements and their outcome – karma, cause and result – are worked out that is cessation. There is also peace, because there is freedom from that which is composed. Remember, when we were going through the truth of suffering, we learnt that everything that is composed must fall apart, that it is impermanent. Well this is that's total opposite. Peace – the cessation of an arhat – is not the result of composition. It is peace because it is a true, non-dualistic realization.

It is also precious because the ultimate essence of everything is perfect and good. Ultimately, of course, there is no good or bad but the ultimate is closer to good than bad. Often it is easier for people to do bad things than good things because their karma and environment manifest negative things. Yet for other people their karma and environment make it easier for them to do good things. Even if these two sorts of people were in the same room, the same environment, one sort would find it easier to manifest good karma and the other sort would find it easier to manifest bad karma. For some of you to have faith is easier than doubting. For some of you to doubt is easier than to have faith. These are all manifestations of our karma. It is the same for our environment. As I mentioned already, there is an old Tibetan saying that the king crying in the palace and the beggar crying under the tree shed the same tears.

This feature, preciousness, points out that although an individual's karma and environment may manifest differently, the essence of everything is good. If you say something good or bad, both their essences are good. Still we need to do good things. It is not as though someone has decided what is good and what is bad. There is no committee or powerful force making these decisions. It is just the way things are. Stealing, for example, is bad because people do not want to lose what is precious to them. Giving is good because people want things they do not have. It makes them happy. Still, giving alcoholics bottles of vodka is bad because it harms them. Giving is good but we need to be a little sophisticated about what we give. Perhaps taking away their Vodka and replacing it with a lighter drink like beer would help. It is still a bad thing to do but it is better they drink beer than a stronger drink that may kill them. Instead of killing them beer will just make them a little fat. Then perhaps we can slowly, slowly help them overcome their bad habits.

Giving and so on are naturally good things to do but their ultimate essence is beyond good. Just realizing what is good and bad is not Buddhahood. Buddhahood is the realization of the essence of everything, the transformation of everything. Here, however, as we are discussing the Four Noble Truths, we are talking about the realization of an arhat, not Buddhahood, and this realization can be described as virtuous, good and precious.

The last feature is "truly becoming." It is a calmly abiding state of mind whose clarity is beyond this calmness. The only thing beyond this state is Buddhahood. In this context we cannot say that Buddhahood is something you "reach." It is more like the total manifestation of primordial wisdom. Again, as we are describing the Four Noble Truths here, and this teaching leads us to the state of an arhat, we can say that the phrase "truly becoming" describes a "state" that we reach.

The last noble truth is the truth of the path. This was also taught in four stages: the path or *lam*, awareness or *rigpa*, cultivation or *drubpa*, and "making true becoming certain" or *ngejin*. This last feature leads to "truly becoming," the fourth feature of the path of cessation. The truth of the path leads to the truth of cessation. They are just not taught in this order. *Ngejin* leads to *ngejung*. We teach it upside down and therefore have to explain it more. Many times I have tried to explain this and people have just looked at me blankly. It is not only their fault that they do not understand it, though: I may not explain it very clearly either.

Again the truth of the path has two aspects – its description and its definitive meaning: we will start with its description. From this perspective, the path feature of the fourth noble truth is the journey of practicing dharma. This journey is the search for ultimate truth that leads us to not only an understanding of ultimate truth but also a realization of it. The path means the way we walk.

Rigpa, the second feature, is probably "awareness," but I am only using this as a working translation, as there is a lot more to *rigpa* than just awareness. It is the practice of Shamatha and Vipashyana, but particularly Shamatha, which creates awareness. You can only have awareness if your mind is stable and clear. When your awareness is not calm and clear it will not be accurate or adequate. This means that Shamatha awareness is an antidote for ignorance. We talk about the effects of karma, but without defilements we would not have any karma. When we follow our defilements, karma happens. But again these defilements do not mean much without ignorance because all the defilements – such as attachment, anger, jealousy and pride – all come from ignorance.

There are many kinds of ignorance. The ignorance we are talking about here is the ignorance of our essence. When we do not recognize our very essence, we perceive ourselves as "me," and as long as that happens everything else will be "other." As long as everything else is "other" we are bound to have attachment, greed, hatred and jealousy. If we separate things into self and other we will perceive things as "mine" and not "yours." Or they will be "yours that I want to buy" or "yours that I cannot have even though I have been working hard for ten years to get it and therefore am jealous." We may even hate someone because they stop "us" from getting things done the way we want them done, because they stop "us" from fulfilling "our" dreams. These things are bound to happen once we separate ourselves from everything else. *Rigpa* recognizes the truth and overcomes the ignorance – the *marigpa* – that looks at things in this way.

The third feature is *drupa*. *Drupa* means practice, cultivation and implementation. At the moment we perceive everything so solidly. Our practice is to overcome this illusion so that we can see the true essence of everything, including ourselves. We practice the dharma to recognize and realize the truth, the essence of ourselves and everything else. We practice compassion, for example, because we know that nobody likes to suffer. This is a simple fact and living according to it is compassion. We practice devotion when we realize that we can become a Buddha. We realize that whatever it was that made Prince Siddartha a Buddha we also possess, therefore we want to become like him. As I mentioned, devotion is wishing to become like someone. I may respect my computer teacher but I am highly unlikely to be devoted to him or her, because I am highly unlikely to want to become exactly like them. I am devoted to the Buddhas, the bodhisattvas, Tara, Avalokiteshvara and Manjushri because I would like to become like them. Working to achieve this is the practice, the cultivation, the *drupa*.

The last feature of the truth of the path is *ngejin*, "making true becoming certain." This refers to how following a dualistic path – practicing meditation, saying sacred prayers, practicing generosity – becomes non-dualistic. The bodhisattva Shantideva gave a simple metaphor for this. He said you do not need to carpet the whole world to protect your feet; covering your feet with shoes will have the same effect. In the same way, if we recognize that in essence both ourselves and others are nirvana: the path that Buddha showed us will lead us to it. Again I am saying "nirvana" in this context instead of "Buddhahood" because we are discussing the Four Noble Truths. In this way practice is *ngejin* – making true becoming certain – and it leads to *ngejung* – true becoming.

When we look at the same four features from the perspective of their definitive meaning, the path is the journey, the way to travel. Awareness, *rigpa*, is clarity and knowledge. It is not ignorance. It is not *marigpa*. Cultivation, *drupa*, is pure, proper cultivation. *Ngejin*, making true becoming certain, describes what happens when we cultivate ourselves like this. It describes the process by which we become pure.

These are the Four Noble Truths, which each have four features that are, in turn, taught in two ways – from the perspective of their descriptions and their definitive meanings. This means we can learn about this first teaching of the Lord Buddha in thirty-two ways.

This then completes our discussion of the four objects of Shamatha meditation. We have learnt quite a bit about Shamatha meditation, but we need to know right from the beginning that it will not be successful unless we lead a moral, ethical life. If we don't live a moral and ethical life then the only effects of Shamatha practice will be a little more comfort and efficiency. That is about it. We have to overcome our defilements and they are fueled by immorality. An action is defined as either "immoral" or "moral" depending on whether it feeds the defilements or not. If it does it is immoral and if it purifies and transforms them it is moral. Things do not become moral or immoral because rules have been made up for convenience. They become one or the other for this simple reason.

This basically sums up Shamatha meditation, but before we go onto Vipashyana I would like to share four metaphors of Shamatha practice that come from an important Mahamudra teaching. Shamatha is not just a Theravadan practice. There are Theravadan, Mahayana and Vajrayana Shamathas. In one Mahamudra teaching, Shamatha practice is compared to a river's journey to the ocean. At the beginning the mind is like a waterfall in a rough mountainous area: churned up, confused, the stones and other things it passes over make it ferocious. Bits of it flow one way, other bits flow in other ways and all the bubbles coming up create a loud noise. This is like the mind of a beginner meditation practitioner. It is like our mind. Then, when our Shamatha practice progresses a little, it becomes more like a river passing through a very deep gorge. At this stage the river is still very powerful but it is moving smoothly and does not make as much noise. It is nowhere near as tumultuous. Then as we progress even further our mind becomes like a river spread out across a plane; the water is not concentrated into a narrow gorge so it is not as dangerous or fast. It moves very slowly. At the last stage of Shamatha meditation our mind becomes like the ocean, vast and deep. This final state of mind is described as like a lamp, a candle, unaffected by the wind. These are just examples, however; in reality there is much more to these states.

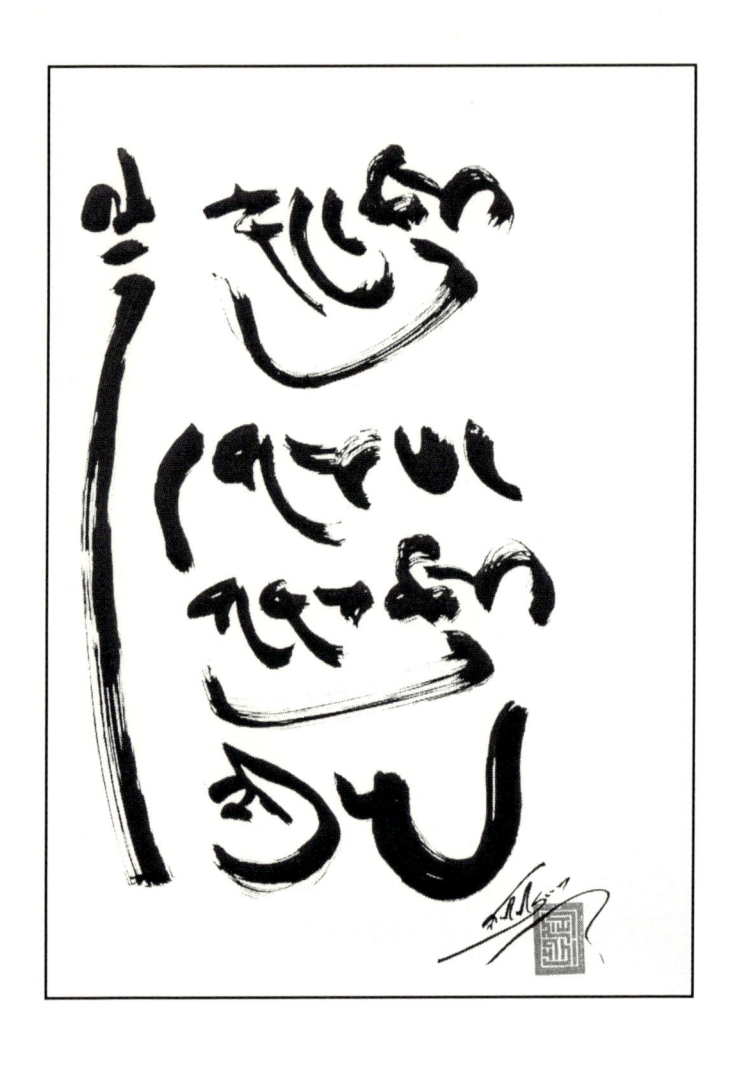

TRUE NATURE IS THE PURE ESSENCE OF ALL MANIFESTATION
Calligraphy by
Tai Situ Rinpoche

Chapter 9

VIPASHYANA (INSIGHT) MEDITATION

I WILL BEGIN NOW WITH A LOOK at Vipashyana meditation and then go on to briefly describe Mahayana and Vajrayana meditation. So you can understand the difference between Shamatha and Vipashyana I will give you an example of both. Say you were very quietly and respectfully reading your favorite text, let's say it is the *Heart Sutra*, and perhaps you had a light offering and incense burning next to you. If you have received the transmission of the *Heart Sutra* and were reading it calmly, if you knew the meaning of every word because it has been explained to you, that is Shamatha. If you understand its meaning very clearly, however, and if you were able to observe your mind as you went through the text, then that would be Vipashyana in Sanskrit, or *Lhaktong* in Tibetan.

These two, Shamatha and Vipashyana, can also be described by the metaphor of a lamp. Shamatha is like a lamp undisturbed by the wind and Vipashyana is like the light it generates. Shamatha creates a calm abiding state of mind and Vipashyana is this calmly abiding mind joined with awareness. As Shamatha and Vipashyana are both Sanskrit/Pali words I should perhaps explain the different ways different lineages define them. Sometimes what I call Shamatha is called Vipashyana, and what I call Vipashyana is called Shamatha. When I use the word Shamatha I am referring to what is called *Shinay* in Tibetan. When I say Vipashyana I am referring to what is called *Lhaktong* in Tibetan.

Our texts describe quite a few different levels of Vipashyana. There are actually endless levels of Vipashyana just as there are endless levels of Shamatha, but we will only go through four of them: *jikten kyi Lhaktong* or samsaric Vipashyana, Theravadan Vipashyana, Mahayana Vipashyana and Vajrayana Vipashyana.

Samsaric Vipashyana refers to states in which it is very difficult for a person to do bad things; almost automatically they do positive things. For people who have this insight, to steal, lie and do unbecoming things is difficult, it does not occur naturally. Being generous, patient and tolerant on the other hand is easier and more natural for them. This insight is an outcome of their Shamatha, but it is samsaric, worldly. The word *jikten* means "worldly."

Theravadan Vipashyana is recognizing and realizing the essence of the Four Noble Truths at all times. We have just gone through the Four Noble Truths so you should know what they are. When we are able to live according to them, understand them, be aware of them, see, hear and smell from their perspective, we have reached the Vipashyana of the Theravada.

Mahayana Vipashyana is being able to see emptiness, the ultimate bodhichitta, and the interdependent manifestation of everything. When we are able to experience – see, hear, taste and smell – everything through this perspective then we have achieved Mahayana Vipashyana. Vajrayana Vipashyana is recognizing and realizing the limitlessness of everything's essence. It is recognizing the sacredness of everything.

These may all seem very easy to understand when we go through them one by one, but to actually realize these views takes a lot of practice. I do not know how you all do your practice, but if it is anything like the way I practice then it is going to take hundreds of lifetimes to reach these states. I practice every day but there are many other things that I have to do so all I can do is try to keep these things in mind. You could all see me look at my notes when I was teaching on the Four Noble Truths, for example. When I am teaching on the twelve links of interdependent origination, emptiness and other topics I also have to look at my books. This is clear proof that I am very far away from achieving any of these realizations. I still have the potential to reach these states though, as does everybody else, so we are all okay. We are absolutely okay.

Actually, I want to explain to you why we are all okay. We are all okay because we have what we have right now. Each of us has lots of problem for sure, but that is all on the surface. If we look under that surface, all of us are doing very well. We are quite okay. Being okay is a result of our past life karma. I do not believe we have done something unimaginable or unbelievable in the past to get where we are now. We have all done okay so we are all okay. We have not done anything unimaginable and unbelievable and therefore we are not unimaginable and unbelievable. If we do our best to live this life happily, positively, morally, ethically and follow the dharma we will improve. If we do our best in our day-to-day life, in our day-to-day practice, and don't let ourselves get carried away by anything that happens to us – whether it is a wonderful or terrible thing – and keep going we will improve.

We shouldn't get carried away. We shouldn't get lost when things happen to us. Getting lost in good things is as bad as getting lost in bad things. We should not get lost in anything. We should always be aware and mindful. We should always follow the path no matter whether we are taking baby steps, elephant steps or kangaroo steps. Kangaroo steps are pretty big. Elephants cannot jump because their knees bend backward not forward, but Kangaroos can. Anyway, whether our steps are big or small we will get there. Our destiny is nothing more and nothing less than our potential, and our ultimate potential is no less and no more than Prince Siddhartha's. Whatever he was able to attain, we will attain. Do not worry too much about your life. Enjoy it. Just do not be too indulgent. Practice diligence but do not let your practice become a burden for you. That is not very good karma. You may find yourself thinking, "Oh no, I have to do my practice. I have to do this hard work. I don't like it but I have taken vows so I have to do it." This is very negative. Do not let it happen. Instead practice comfortably, happily, joyfully with honor and gratitude. It may be bad karma for me to speak like this but if it helps you to understand more clearly then that is okay.

When we look at Milarepa his life story looks uncomfortable and unpleasant, but I tell you it was not. He enjoyed it. He was honored to be like that and if we are honored to be like that then we should do it. If we would hate to live like that then we are not ready to be Milarepa. Instead we can try and remember that we are human beings, not kangaroos. If I try to jump like a kangaroo I may end up a small way away with at best a broken leg, perhaps a broken neck. Instead I should try to remember that I am a human being, and as a human being I should try to walk.

If we keep walking, eventually there will come a time when we are so inspired that we have no choice but to go for it. I think other religions call this a "vocation." I am not sure if this word can be applied to Buddhism, but it is something similar. We will behave just like the trader who broke his gun, left everything and went for it without a second thought. Until then we cannot pretend we are like this and forge ahead being naive and biting off more than we can chew. It does not help us. I think slow and steady is better for most of us, most of the time. The thing that helps me remember this, that keeps me going personally, is remembering that I have Buddha-nature. Remembering that I am okay. I hope it helps you also.

Now to return to Vipashyana meditation. Once you have a very good grounding in Shamatha, you can start to practice Vipashyana. One text says that, "Shamatha is the beautiful tree on which the flowers of Vipashyana thrive." In order to practice Vipashyana we look into reality, we look into ourselves, our minds or a particular defilement or obstacle. Vipashyana has two aspects: *che gom*, analytical meditation, and *jog gom*, placement meditation. Working things out intellectually and analytically is called *che gom*: *gom* means meditation and *che* means analysis, thinking things through.

We also need to do *jog gom*, placement meditation. In placement meditation we do not analyze anything, we are just aware and rest in this awareness. When I say "resting," I do not mean resting like a baby who is about to fall asleep. I mean resting in a calmly abiding state that has full awareness. This is *jog gom*.

As Vipashyana practitioners we will progress through three Vipashyana states: *Lhaktong jetunba*, temporary Vipashyana; *Lhaktong tsen nyiba*, definitive Vipashyana; and *zhilhag sungjug*, the union of Shamatha and Vipashyana. The first of these, temporary Vipashyana, includes mental states such as those in which we see emptiness and impermanence very clearly while maintaining a Shamatha state. As this Vipashyana is temporary, however, we are only able to maintain this insight while the right conditions and an environment conducive to meditation are present. We can develop this state only to lose it and to get it back we will need to practice again.

Lhaktong tsen nyiba, definitive Vipashyana, is much more stable than this. It is a mental state in which, having progressed further with our practice, we have reached a truly calm abiding state. All of the signs that this state has been reached will be evident; our defilements and discursiveness will be effortlessly stopped. Temporary Vipashyana is achieved with lots of effort, lots of preparation. When we practice we will only achieve this state at first, then we will be able to abide in it for longer and longer periods of time, until finally we are able to enter into a calmly abiding state without effort. This is definitive Vipashyana. When we have developed this state we can say that Vipashyana is manifesting in our mind stream rather than us having to put effort into developing it.

These days, when people get upset, angry or neurotic, many people will say this is just "human nature." But this is not true. Human nature is actually Buddha. It is just so automatic and natural for us to have attachment, jealousy, pride and anger that people consider these emotions human nature. When we develop definitive Vipashyana, however, it becomes natural for us to abide in a good mental state instead.

The third Vipashyana state is the union of Shamatha and Vipashyana. In this highest and most profound state we see everything clearly. We do not separate things. We see everything as it is – an inseparable union of emptiness and clarity. This is the inseparable union of Shamatha and Vipashyana.

Most of this description of Shamatha and Vipashyana has come from the Theravadan vehicle. I should let you know though that even what I say about the Theravada will be according to the Mahamudra lineage. Everything that comes out of my mouth as dharma will always accord with the Mahamudra lineage because I learned dharma from Mahamudra masters. Even if I try to talk about the Theravada it will not be from a purely Theravadan perspective.

I could also discuss in detail the Mahayana and Vajrayana practice of Vipashyana, but we do not have a lot of time so I will try to simplify them for you. In the Mahayana the most important first step is taking the bodhisattva vows. The moral precepts you keep in these vows are similar to those of the Theravada but they are based on bodhichitta rather than whether the actions themselves are good or bad. These actions are performed via the sincere, pure motivation of bodhichitta, but the capacity of this bodhichitta will vary. The person performing the actions may have the bodhichitta of a beginner, the bodhichitta of a quite advanced practitioner or the bodhichitta of a highly evolved, mature bodhisattva. The bodhichitta will transform, it will not stay the same. It grows in the same way a person does. In the beginning it is like a child, then it becomes like a teenager, then an adult, then it may go through a mid-life crisis before finally becoming old but not senile. Old people have a different perception of things than the young. They may think in the same way but they have more depth, experience – let's say clarity – in their perception

In order to practice the particular practices of a bodhisattva, we first need the base of Shamatha and Vipashyana, but what really becomes our central focus is ultimate bodhichitta. Ultimate bodhichitta is different from relative bodhichitta. Relative bodhichitta is the thought, "I wish to become a Buddha to help all sentient beings attain Buddhahood." This thought is dualistic. In thinking it we have an objective wish. It is sacred, holy and profound, but it is dualistic. Ultimate bodhichitta is the same as ultimate emptiness. Ultimate emptiness is also different from relative emptiness in that it is non-dual. Relative emptiness is an analytical conclusion that everything is neither truly existent nor substantial. Ultimate emptiness, on the other hand, is the limitlessness of everything's true essence. Ultimate emptiness refers to the lack of subject and object, dualistic limitations. It is beyond this. In this way the ultimate emptiness, *töntam tong* in Tibetan, and the ultimate bodhichitta, *töntam changchubsem* in Tibetan, are exactly the same thing.

Having this focus means that as beings on this path practice Shamatha and Vipashyana – or any other bodhisattva practice such as Tonglen – the method of relative bodhichitta reveals the wisdom of ultimate bodhichitta. They work towards recognizing their *rig[s]*, their Buddha-nature. That is to say, they have to recognize that their nature and the Buddha's nature are exactly the same. This Tibetan word *rig[s]* has a different spelling to the "*rig*" in the word *rigpa*. It has an extra "s" on the end of it, although it is pronounced the same. *Rigpa* means awareness, intelligence and clarity. *Rig[s]* means the incorruptible quality that is the essence of the mind.

First recognizing this nature, then overcoming the obstacles and obscurations to realizing it, through implementing the proper conditions and circumstances, is the practice. If we were to fast-forward the million or so lifetimes it may take us to recognize our Buddha-nature, we would see ourselves going from one realm to another, one solar system to another, one pure land to another, doing this and that and all kinds of things, but the point of it all would be to recognize our Buddha-nature. We may look very, very busy but we would be busy trying to overcome the obstacles to recognizing our essence. We would be busy trying to cultivate the necessary conditions to recognize our essence. This is what Mahayana practices are. These practices can also be summarized into the ten paramitas and the eight-fold noble path. The eight-fold noble path is not exclusive to the Mahayana, but it is clearly emphasized in it. These paramitas and this eight-fold path describe the details of how to go about solving obstacles and developing positive conditions, good karma and wisdom. They are the practices of a bodhisattva.

The beginning of a bodhisattva's practice is quite simply that we should have a limitless intention. When I say a limitless intention I don't mean we should have many thoughts, I mean our perception should be limitless. If we are small-minded we will not really practice the Mahayana successfully. When we say, "May all sentient beings be free from suffering," for example, we are not just wishing that all humans have enough to eat. It includes this but also many other things. We are wishing that all beings, including humans, be free from all aspects of suffering, including hunger. We do not only think about the poor, sick and powerless but also the rich, healthy and powerful because they are also suffering. Suffering does not only mean not having something or experiencing pain, it includes all the aspects of suffering we went through in our discussion of the truth of suffering.

Nor should our aspiration just focus on humans. We should think about animals, those in hell – every single sentient being from heaven to hell. Saying "May all sentient beings be free from suffering" refers to all sentient beings from heaven to hell. It is also important to make sure we are not only focusing on ourselves. We should not be asking, "Why me?" We should be asking, "Why not me?" In this way we will have a bodhisattva's perception – a limitless, totally impartial perception.

Something simple that may be helpful for you to remember are the three different perceptions that bodhisattvas have: *semchen la migba*, the perception observing sentient beings; *chö la migba*, the perception observing phenomena; and *migba meba migba*, objectless perception. With the first kind of perception, the bodhisattva's limitless thought is directed towards all sentient beings who have a limitless potential but do not realize this, and are therefore suffering in samsara just like us. The second perception, *chö la migpa*, is the realization that the ego, attachment and all these things are really baseless and illusory. Bodhisattvas with this perception still have the obstacle of subject and object duality, though. They might not have attachment like us but they still have the obscuration of subject-object dualism. Their limitless thought is that all reality is just an illusion. How we understand this illusion to exist accords with our capacity, something we went through with the second of the Four Noble Truths.

This reality that we see in front of us is indeed a reality, but it is relative reality. It is indeed a truth, but it is relative truth. Reality has many layers. I think I am "I," but billions of me's live inside of me.

None of us is just me, I am not just the Tai Situ. Millions and millions of sentient beings reside inside this physical thing I call "me." Each of them has their own perception of themselves and goes about their business, looking for food, getting sick, eating each other, helping each other. Sometimes animals do help each other. If you watch horses you will see them scratching each other's backs. All sentient beings do all sorts of things like this everywhere. This is a physical reality that we should not have any doubts about.

Reality is very real, complex and complicated, but at the same time a simple, big dream. The dream I am experiencing now will end when I die. It is no different to the dream I dream until I wake up. The only difference is that other people can see me sleeping in a bed but they cannot see me sleeping in my waking life. They even tell me that I do not snore, but I don't know about that. Maybe I am asleep, snoring and dreaming that a hundred elephants are chasing me through the jungle, until eventually after some time they become my friends. Maybe this dream feels very real. Maybe I will get scared, attached, angry, jealous, stupid, make mistakes in this dream. I have heard it said that dreams have no colors, but this has to be wrong. I see many colors in my dreams.

Apart from people watching us, the only difference between these short dreams and dying is that when we die we wake up in a different place. The short dreams come from our memories and experiences. We cannot dream anything that has nothing to do with us. This is also true of our waking life. It is the result of our past lives' karma. It has been created by our physical and verbal actions that follow our mental defilements. They are the causes and conditions for this long dream. When our body dies, our mind continues on just as it has up until today. It cannot die. Because of this I find the word "re-birth" misleading. We are not "re-born" any more than today is "re-yesterday." Today is not re-yesterday. Tomorrow is not re-today. Monday is not re-Sunday. February is not re-January. There is no "re" about these or our continuum so leave the "re" alone. Through our lives there is no repetition. There is only continuity. We die and are born then we die and are born. It all happens continuously.

Perceiving ourselves and all phenomena in this way is the *chö la migpa*, the perception observing phenomena. It is not just the individual being that is perceived in this way but all phenomena. Then this perception is again developed into the *migba meba migba*, objectless perception. Here the bodhisattva asks how long they need to be dualistically compassionate, diligent and generous. After contemplating this they stop trying to be compassionate and become the embodiment of compassion. They stop trying to be devoted and become the embodiment of devotion. Or the embodiment of loving-kindness and all the limitless intentions they initially tried to develop. Becoming the embodiment of all these things is called "objectless perception." They do not focus on sentient beings. Instead they realize their essence and by realizing their essence they become the essence of everything. This objectless perception starts on the first bodhisattva level. There is much, much more I could say about these, but I will not go into it more here.

Another important aspect of Mahayana Vipashyana is the eight characteristics that define a Prajnaparamita text as a "Mother" text, which I have already explained. You will remember that when we discussed the Prajnaparamita I mentioned that out of the seventeen Prajnaparamita texts six are called "Mother" texts and the rest are called "Daughter" texts, depending on whether they have eight characteristics or not. I also explained that even one chapter out of one text is called a "Mother" text in its own right because it has these eight characteristics – omniscience, knowledge of the path, knowledge of the foundation, complete implementation, implementation that reaches towards the top, the gradual implementation, the momentary application and the dharmakaya.

Within this topic of Mahayana Vipashyana meditation it is also important we note the difference between meditation and post-meditation. This distinction is related to the difference between Shamatha and Vipashyana, in that Shamatha only refers to the meditative state and Vipashyana can also refer to the post-meditation state. That is to say you can do Shamatha and Vipashyana meditations, you can develop *Lhaktong jesutunba* or *Lhaktong drabowa*, both of which mean temporary Vipashyana, in meditation, but if you have developed true Vipashyana, *Lhaktong tsen nyiba*, you will also experience it post-meditation. There are different ways we can describe this post-meditation state, but I would like to do it in terms of the three main Madhyamaka, or Middle-way, schools: *Uma rangjuba* or the Middle-way Autonomist School, the *Uma teljurwa* or the Consequentialist School, and the *Shentong* or Empty of Other School.

The meditation of those who meditate according to the *Uma rangjuba*, the Middle-way Autonomist School, perceives the non-existence of everything in the same way as we can look at the middle of the sky. When you focus on the middle of the sky there is actually nothing to focus on. You can see the middle of the sky, you can focus on the middle of the sky, you can rest looking at the middle of the sky but there is no actual "thing" there. You can see it, you can keep looking at it, but you cannot see anything there. It is like looking at something that cannot be looked at.

The only difference between this meditation and the meditation of those who meditate according to the *Uma teljurwa*, the Consequentialist School, is that this school perceives the space and the mind perceiving the space as one, inseparable. In this meditation I may be looking at an empty space but that empty space, which is nothing, and my mind, which is everything, are not separate.

The meditation of those who meditate according to the *Shentong*, Empty of Other School, is similar again, but they not only meditate on the inseparability of the mind and the space it is perceiving, but also on how it is clear, luminous, ultimately profound, incorruptible, unimaginable, ineffable and the essence of everything. There isn't any limitation on what can be produced by this essence. Everything can arise from it.

The post-meditative states of those who meditate according to the *Uma rangjuba* or Middle-way Autonomist School and the *Uma teljurwa* or Consequentialist School will be alike in that they will accumulate merit and practice morality while realizing that everything is just an interdependent manifestation. Still, as long as they regard themselves as "I," they should be very careful and mindful of what they do. It does not matter whether everything is emptiness or not. As long as they call themselves "I," as long as they get angry, happy or jealous, their behavior matters. They should follow a moral path, they should practice the other disciplines, but deep inside they should remember that everything is just like the middle of the sky.

A Shentong practitioner's post-meditative state will also be similar except that a truly accomplished Shentong practitioner will experience post-meditation as a manifestation of the limitless essence of the Buddha. For them everything happening around them is no different to a Buddha's pure land. This is how it should be, but for Shentong practitioners like me it is not the case. This is not a pure land for me! When I meditate, when I practice, I believe this view, but when I have to deal with things I do not like I do not experience things as a pure land. When I have to throw things away that I do not want to throw away, or when I have to talk about things I do not want to talk about – again and again – it does not seem like a pure land to me. These seem very much like external experiences to me. I am a Shentong practitioner but I do not have that kind of post-meditation accomplishment.

Although I have been describing Mahayana Vipashyana, this view should also be included within Vajrayana Vipashyana, because Shentong is very much a Vajrayana view. In content it is close to the Mahamudra or Maha Ati – Dzogchen – view. It would be incorrect to describe it as a purely Mahayana view. In it the views of Sutra and Tantra are mixed together. The end of one thing and the beginning of another are always mixed. When you look at a rainbow you cannot pick out exactly where the red ends and the yellow begins, or the blue ends and the green begins, because they merge into each other. In the same way you cannot distinguish Mahayana and Vajrayana practices. In fact, the essence of all three yanas, Theravada, Mahayana and Vajrayana, is the Mahamudra. Even the essence of a high Tantra like Kalachakra or Guhyasamaja is the Mahamudra.

There is also much more I could say about the practice of Mahayana Vipashyana, but I will leave it now and briefly describe the Vajrayana. If we compare the Theravadan and Mahayana traditions' teachings with those of the Vajrayana it is like comparing a nice, small garden with the Amazon jungle. Looking at the scope of the Vajrayana – the plethora of Tantras, mantras and practices – is like looking at the Amazon jungle. And it will keep increasing because the dharmakaya and sambhogakaya of a Buddha never cease manifesting. The nirmanakaya, the emanation body of the Buddha manifested on Earth 2500 years ago, but the other two aspects continuously manifest. They cannot cease manifesting. In the Vajrayana the Buddha is limitless, so therefore the Buddha's manifestations are limitless.

Within this enormous array of Vajrayana Tantras we find some that are called *kama* and some that are called *terma*. There are a fixed number of *kamas* because they were translated from Sanskrit into Tibetan, but *termas* can manifest even today. *Ter* means "treasure" in Tibetan and this name indicates that they can be discovered just like treasure. These discovered texts are very sacred and holy but when we examine new *terma* we should do so with a magnifying glass. We should also make sure we have salt, pepper and sugar to mix them with just to make sure they "cook" right. We have to be sure that they are true manifestations of Lord Buddha's teaching. Any Mr So-and-so or Mrs So-and-so can show up with three volumes of text and say they are a *terma*. In the Vajrayana the Lord Buddha's teachings do indeed manifest limitlessly, but as it is hard to know whether *termas* are real or not we usually stick to the Tantras we already have. In this way we may be a little skeptical, but we are not naive. In the Vajrayana we treasure lineage, we try to uphold the lineage and perhaps this could be an obstacle to practicing new *termas*. But as I mentioned earlier, in India we have a saying, "It is better to arrive late then never." That is to say it is better to be safe and follow existing practices rather than jumping into new practices because we think they are interesting.

Even taking into account this skepticism, the Vajrayana perception of the dharma is quite vast. No matter how skeptical and careful we are, we still cannot overlook the limitless ability and quality of the Buddha. The Buddha can manifest through anything, so as a Vajrayana practitioner I cannot be adamant that "the dharma I practice is the only pure, sacred lineage of the Buddha that leads to enlightenment." I cannot say whether other practices will lead to enlightenment or not. If we look at the teachings of Tilopa and

Naropa, for example, we see that they taught through music and many other things. There is even a story of a lady who used winemaking to reach enlightenment. Now, in general, making wine is considered a "wrong livelihood." When you make wine and sell it to people they get drunk and have health and family problems. It is a very bad job, but this master was able to transform it into a practice and became enlightened. In a similar way, if we do anything ultimately, correctly and profoundly, then its essence is the same as everything else.

From this point of view, if I did not know anything about their background or lineage, it would even be impossible for me to say that a very skilled musician definitely did not have realization. I am not omniscient, so I could not say whether they had realizations or not. Instead, I just enjoy their music and then go back to my practice. In this way the Vajrayana outlook is very broad, and when we do Vajrayana practices we should also try and keep our outlook very broad.

As I also mentioned, there is a lot of similarity between Shamatha/Vipashyana and the two stages of Vajrayana practice, *che rim*, the visualization stage, and *dzog rim*, the completion stage. Visualization practice is similar to Shamatha, and the dissolution or completion stage of Vajrayana practices is like Vipashyana. They are not the same but there is definitely room for comparison. In my lineage we have fourteen main Tantras that were brought to Tibet from India by Marpa Lotsawa more than 1000 years ago. He went to India three times and spent in total twenty-one years there. Sixteen years and seven months of this time he was with his teachers, receiving transmissions and practicing. The rest of the time he was traveling to and from Tibet and searching for his teachers. His main deity was Hevajra and his main guru was Naropa, although he had many other gurus and deities. In this way Marpa Lotsawa attained realization.

What are these deities? What do they mean? When the Buddha manifested to highly evolved bodhisattvas he manifested in the form of a deity. Sometimes this deity was a single male or female form, but most of the time it was both a male and female form in union. When the Buddha manifests as both male and female deities in union, it is not two people. We should not misunderstand and think that the Buddha is in union with somebody else. When we see images like Kalachakra and consort, they are the Buddha in sambhogakaya form instead of nirmanakaya form. This form of the Buddha is something we can only see in paintings and statues at this stage.

Before these teachings came to Tibet these images were secret, they were not displayed in public. About a century or so ago they were made public for blessing and practice, but as you need to complete their basic preliminary practices and so on, their actual practice is still quite rare. Viewing these images, however, has become commonplace. Before this time the only people allowed to see these images were their practitioners, those who had taken their initiations and received their transmissions. A lot of changes have even taken place since I was a child. I would not have been allowed to read the book I now use as a daily practice book then, not until I received the initiations and transmissions associated with it. Nowadays we can get these kinds of books anywhere, they have all been translated.

I personally do not think these changes are that damaging. They just mean that we have to explain things that traditionally it was not considered appropriate to explain. This even applies to the vows of monks and nuns. Traditionally, unless you were going to become a monk or a nun you did not know anything about these vows. These days, though, many people who do not want to become a monk or a nun now want these vows explained to them. This was even more true for tantric practices. Unless you were going to do a practice you would not have even seen its mandala or its statues. You would not have been allowed to read the texts or be taught the details of the practice. I think there are benefits to these things being public, though, because given all the bad PR that Tantra has had, if we keep everything secret people will think there is really something bad going on. If we are open about tantric practices, they will realize there is nothing bad happening. I tell you, there is nothing bad in them.

As for tantric meditation, Shamatha and Vipashyana are its base, but another important aspect is its visualizations. The visualizations can involve seeing yourself as the deity and your surroundings as the environment of a deity, what we call their mandala. The exact nature of this visualization depends on which level of Tantra you are practicing. In Kriya Tantra, for example, you visualize the deity above you. In Yoga Tantra you and the deity are visualized equally, like twins. In Anuttarayoga Tantra you are the deity. In this way the visualization develops in steps.

When you practice Kriya Tantra you should also be vegetarian and keep yourself very clean. At this stage this is very important, but when you reach the Anuttarayoga Tantra stage these things are not considered important. This stage of practice is meant for people who are beyond the basic duality of cleanliness and dirtiness, so staying clean becomes irrelevant. If you are truly in the Anuttarayoga state then these things are irrelevant. You will be above and beyond them. What we tend to do, however, is practice Anuttarayoga and still try to keep clean. Again it comes back to the saying, "It is better to arrive late than not at all."

In our three-year retreats we still symbolically observe these distinctions, however. One stage of this retreat focuses on the main deity, Vajravarahi, for about six months. During this time those in retreat do not wash, cut their fingernails or shave their hair or beards. It makes for quite a scene. They are in retreat so nobody is allowed to see them, but as I have to go in sometimes to teach, I get to see them. Sometimes I do not recognize them. They look like an entirely different person. It is interesting, though, that as soon as the Vajrayogini stage of the retreat is over almost all of them shave, cut their hair and wash themselves, because they cannot stand to be so dirty. For most of them it is really just a symbolic way of observing the distinctions. Beyond that we do not tend to make many distinctions. We practice Anuttarayoga but try to keep up the habits of a Kriya Tantra practitioner.

That is, of course, except for becoming vegetarians. Ninety-nine percent of Tibetans eat meat. Not because we are practicing Anuttarayoga Tantra but because of our habits and environment. We come from a very high land and like the Mongolians our staple foods come from animals. These habits still exist, even in exile. Perhaps in a few generations these habits will have disappeared. I know that since I came to India as a child the eating habits of Tibetans have changed enormously. This was only forty years ago so maybe in another forty or eighty years the Tibetans will be pure vegetarians like Brahmans. It is possible because India's climate makes it much, much healthier to be a vegetarian. Vegetables are a lot easier to digest and Indian vegetarian cooking, especially in the south, is exquisite.

I tried to be a vegetarian personally. Twenty-something years ago I went on a trip to Malaysia. It was my second or third trip out of India and people kept asking me questions about eating meat. In those days I was in my late twenties and I was much more egotistical. Or perhaps I am just egotistical in a different way these days. Anyway, at this stage when people asked me how Buddhists could eat meat I would turn bright red. There was also so much wonderful vegetarian food there that I thought I would try to be vegetarian. They even had things that looked and tasted like meat: vegetarian chicken, fish, beef and shrimps. I did not dare take a vow to be vegetarian in case I could not keep it but I did try. I had been happily vegetarian for twenty days, or three weeks or something when I had to do a ceremony in a bright, big hall. I think it was a crown ceremony. When I stood up from doing it I felt so light I almost fell off the throne I was sitting on. I think I was unconscious for a split second. Everything looked really small, like I was looking at it through water. Then everything tingled and I was okay again. I was normal.

I don't think anybody noticed. They probably thought I was just doing a standing meditation or something. I told some people about it and they seemed to think that it happened because I had been eating meat my whole life and then I stopped eating it all of a sudden. Maybe, but I do not really know.

Anyway, now I think that roughly completes our discussion of meditation.

MAHAMUDRA

Calligraphy by

Tai Situ Rinpoche

Chapter 10

MAHAMUDRA[38]

PERHAPS THE BEST WAY TO describe Mahamudra is to say that every religion or ideology of every ancient or modern society comes from people's minds. They are nothing more or less than this. As a Buddhist, of course I respect Buddha more than anyone else, but Buddhahood was realized or discovered by Prince Siddhartha, who was a human being. I cannot think of any other religion that was not realized, heard or inspired by a human being either. Even if a religion started when something fell down from the sky, that thing still had to be discovered by a human. This means that all of these religions and ideologies have everything to do with our minds. Everything outside of us also has everything to do with our minds, with what is inside of us. I can only see what is in front of me. I cannot see what is not. I know that I can see the same things that other people around me can see, but my perception of these things still comes from within. Our eyes are the binoculars of our mind and our ears are its headphones. Everything we experience is totally centered around our mind. The moment that our mind leaves our body it is not our body any more. It used to be our body, but it is not our body any more.

Our relatives and friends may think it looks like us and feel emotionally attached to our old body. They may even wrap it up, make a mummy out of it or something like that, but it is not us. We have gone. We may have become an amoeba, a mosquito, another human being or maybe even a monkey in the Himalayas. We could have taken birth as anything, because it is the mind that makes us who we are. In this way everything is centered around, and based on, the mind.

Mind is a very complicated subject for philosophers and intellectuals. For scientists it is even more difficult. Scientists will never find out about mind. No matter how hard they try they will never find it. I can guarantee you this. I will put money on it and my bet will be valid for the next 10,000 years. They will never find anything out about the mind because there is nothing to find. Trying to find out about the mind is like to trying to find the center of space. You can never find the center of space. You could travel for countless light years east and you would not find it. Then you could travel for that long west and you would still not find it. You could go up, down and in every direction forever but you would not find the center of space. Eventually you would have no choice but to give up and in that minute you would find the center. It is where you are. There is no other center. The center of space from my perspective is right here. Our center of space is planet Earth. This is not the case for other beings in other places but it is our reality.

From a New Age, popular, politically correct point of view the Mahamudra transcends religion. I respectfully call this view "eccentricism": when you add "ism" to eccentric it becomes "eccentricism." There is some truth to this assertion of theirs, but "eccentricism" does not suit me. Or maybe it suits me so much that I do not think it suits me. The reason they can say Mahamudra transcends religion is that from Mahamudra's ultimate point of view there is no good and bad. Relatively, however, there are reasons for things to be good or bad. There is room for this. If it was the other way around – if ultimately there was good and bad but relatively there was not – we would be in trouble. If this were the case, what kind of society would we have to live in? It would perhaps be like the kind of society that we are moving towards today. These days it is as if there is ultimate good and bad but relative indifference – the survival of the fittest. The fastest, fittest and most aggressive win. It would be better if we could start looking at things the other way around.

The View

In order to explain the basic philosophical view of the Mahamudra, I would like to share with you some poetry I was inspired by my guru's teachings to write a long, long time ago. I was very inspired when I was learning from my guru. This poem is related to the lineage of course, but these are my words not the words of a great, enlightened master. When I wrote them I was quite young and freshly blessed by my guru's wisdom and compassion.

What moves and what does not move, what is visible and
   what is not visible,
All interrelate with space
Space neither moves, nor stays still,
Is neither visible nor invisible.

This is how I understood the external view of Mahamudra philosophy. The next verse tells how I understood its internal view.

Knowing or not knowing, realizing or not realizing
Interdependent space and mind are never separated,
Mind is light in space – never bound never released,
Beyond obscuration and clarification – beyond all limits.

This is the base Mahamudra, the *netsul*, "the way it is." There are internal and external *netsuls*. From this point of view, anything we look at is not separate from the things we can and cannot see. Anything we think is not separate from that which is understandable and that which is not understandable. There is nothing that is not primordially connected. Everything is primordially united beyond the concepts of far and near. Things can be billions of miles away but they are still united. This is, let us say, a simplistic way to describe the internal and external view of the Mahamudra.

Eternalists and nihilists, who are habitually at each other's throats, often misunderstand this view. Not understanding, the eternalists look at the Mahamudra view and call it nihilism. Not understanding, the nihilists look at the Mahamudra view and call it eternalism. The Mahamudra view does not say we want to realize nothingness, that Buddhahood is the realization of nothingness. We understand emptiness as being beyond everything. Actually, it is quite the opposite of nothingness. It is everything-ness.

Nor is the primordial essence permanent or impermanent. If someone held me up at gunpoint and ordered me to say whether it was impermanent or permanent, I would rather say it was permanent, but this is not necessarily correct. I would only say this under duress. What I would comfortably say is that understanding Mahamudra philosophy means understanding the unity of the universal, transcendent and relative truths.

The Meditation

After the view the next step is to look at the process of Mahamudra practice. For me Mahamudra practice is not exactly like joining a religion, fulfilling its rituals and duties and making sure you are part of the group. After all, the Buddha Shakyamuni was able to become the best Buddhist – a Buddha – without any of these institutions. For me what he did was Mahamudra practice. Before him three other great beings also attained Buddhahood in this way, on this Earth, in this age. They were able to do this because of the principles that are clearly described in the Mahamudra view. I have no problem calling myself a Buddhist. I have no problem calling myself a Tibetan Buddhist. As difficult as they are, as complicated as they are, I am more than honored to shoulder my Buddhist responsibilities. Every day they become more and more confusing, more and more complicated. It is like swimming in the Pacific Ocean; I don't know where I am and I don't know where I am going, but I know I am surrounded by water and that I am still alive, so I have to keep kicking for as long as I can. I do not think it is just me who has this experience these days though. I think most religious people experience this sensation to some degree. Of course I am honored to live like this and happy about it, but at the same time I cannot take it more seriously than it is. Buddhism is Buddhism and that's all. Nothing more, nothing less. It is what it is.

I understand this, I think, through the Mahamudra lineage that was transmitted to me by my gurus. Otherwise I would be a proud, pacifist, revolutionary Buddhist. Not a fundamentalist but someone who counted every new member in their group and worried about losing any of them. I could be like this, but I am not, because I do not think this is important. What I do consider important are the aspirations I try to fulfill. To me there is nothing more than this in our lineage, and nothing less. I am part of a living tradition, a living lineage, so I have to do what I have to do in order to keep it alive. If I was not part of this lineage I could do whatever I wanted. My father passed away a long time ago, and after he passed away it was okay to bury him: while he was alive, though, I had to do everything in my capacity to keep him alive. I have the same approach to our lineage: while it is alive we must do whatever it takes to protect it from things that could kill it. So that is what I think we are doing, keeping the living lineage alive by protecting it from all that can cause its death and providing whatever it takes to keep it alive.

When I say, "whatever it takes" I am only talking about that which accords with its purpose. The dharma is for the freedom, happiness and liberation of all sentient beings. Whatever you do for the sake of the dharma has to come within this boundary. It must be beneficial, helpful and make sentient beings' lives better. Within this boundary we need to do whatever it takes to keep the lineage alive. A dead lineage is a topic for archeological research institutes to study. They can research what the Buddha said, compare books from different places, tell us what they thought he meant and receive a PhD – wonderful – but that is it. Fortunately things are not this bad yet. We have not reached this stage and therefore we have an important duty to keep the lineage alive. From the Mahamudra point of view, however, this duty is not more than what it is and not less than what it is.

Practicing Mahamudra is dealing with ourselves. A basic tool for dealing with ourselves is to be mindful and aware. This is a basic Buddhist tool but I think it is also part of every religion. In Christianity, for example, they have the Ten Commandments. Having Ten Commandments makes this teaching easy to remember; you remember the first commandment then the second, third and so on, this keeps you mindful of them. In Mahamudra this awareness is key. It is the foundation of all these practices, and because of this I wrote a verse describing it. The first line is:

The wandering mind looks at the still mind.

It seems very strange to me now that when my teacher taught me this as a teenager I was able to understand it. I used to fly kites, I was a very good kite flyer in those days, but I never liked kites with tails. When kites do not have a tale they just go. Kites with tales are not exactly square, and as they are a bit crooked they fly crazily, wildly and you have to control them. When my guru explained the idea I describe in this line to me, I understood it because it was just like flying a kite; standing still on the ground I was like the mind that did not wander, and the kite was like the wandering mind. When I flew the kite I pulled this way, that way, up and down, but I made sure I did not fall off the roof I was standing on to fly my kite. The kite responded to me; if I wanted it to go right it went right, if I wanted it to go left it went left, if I wanted it to make a loop it made a loop, and if I wanted it to cut other people's kites it did. If you make a loop around other people's kites you can actually hijack them you know.

This is similar to observing the nature of your mind. You observe the nature of the wandering mind, which is thought, unstable thinking. Through doing this you come to observe the nature of the mind that is beyond moving and not moving. This is the definition of awareness. After many years of practice, when we are able to achieve this, we move on to the practice described in the next line.

The still mind looks at the still mind.

This looking is similar to somebody cutting our kite's string; it is as if we have lost our kite and 2000 meters of our best string. They have got us, there is no kite left. There is only the still mind looking at itself. When this happens the practitioner experiences the next two lines.

Realizing your primordial nature,
Wandering transforms into wisdom.

This describes a state in which you do not have to meditate. It is like being fifty and no longer needing to fly kites. In the beginning we establish our awareness. At this stage our reference is within and our method is without. External methods take external objects as focuses for meditation – the breath, Buddha images, prayers, visualizations – and they are used to look at the internal essence. Once this has been achieved and we see, hear and feel the internal essence, we will be able to maintain awareness of it naturally. At this stage whatever happens, even the arousal of thoughts and emotions, will be the embodiment of wisdom. This has not happened to me yet, and it will take many more years or lifetimes of effort for it to happen, but I understand how this process works, I have felt it, through the instructions and presence of my guru.

I was with my guru, His Holiness the 16th Gyalwa Karmapa, for nine years solid. You would think that after nine years of seeing somebody every day they would become like your buddy. He never did. Because my previous incarnation was his guru he always treated me well, with honor and respect. He never beat me, or shouted at me, he was not ten feet tall, so there was really no reason to be afraid of him. But interacting with him was like being in the presence of a lion. I think this was because of his ever-present awareness. He was like a big, healthy, strong lion that understood me, took care of me and taught me with kindness and compassion. Everything was also very quiet around him even though he had an aviary full of birds, ten little dogs, a huge white dog, Siamese cats and a green peacock from Java. It was just like being in the depths of the ocean. I think this quietness also came from his ever-present, primordial wisdom. It had to have.

I think I was describing my guru in the fourth line of this verse. I think I was describing how the wandering mind becomes transformed into ever-present, primordial wisdom. The next verse's first two sentences are:

Criticism and suspicion are caused by hope and fear.
Greed comes from fear, hope and criticism.

This describes criticism and suspicion. It describes thinking things sound too good to be true. It is like when people tell me I am their guru and I am wonderful. I may say, "Okay, okay," but something inside does not feel right. This disturbance comes about because of hopes and fears. Hope is always connected to fear; we will have as much fear as we have hope. This also happens in reverse. Hope comes about through greed, fear, doubt, suspicion and criticism. When we are critical we might be criticized. When we find out about this connection, once we realize that these two things only come about because of each other, then they cease to be. They are not there by themselves. Therefore, the third and the fourth sentences say,

They only manifest interdependently,
There is nothing to fear, there is nothing to long for.

Hope and fear only exist because of each other, they only exist interdependently. Personally I find this very, very comforting. When I remember this, again and again, it is like being tired, going to bed, resting and recovering. Having this practice, knowing this, means we can relax, rejuvenate and then hopefully be able to follow the footsteps of our guru. Before we become a lion maybe we can become a nice puppy.

The next four sentences describe meditation itself. I meant them for everybody. Here I was not only describing my guru or myself, just meditation as I understood it.

Wherever you are right now, is both the end and center of space.

You have to find the end of space. You have to find the middle of space. But you don't have to build a rocket or use sophisticated equipment to get there. You do not have to spend time and energy to get there. You can sit right here and know you are at the end and in the middle of space simultaneously.

Whatever you look at, listen to, taste, smell or think is
Mahamudra.

It cannot be anything else. We cannot find anything that has nothing to do with ultimate truth. Everything has everything to do with ultimate truth.

The third sentence is:

Don't hold it, don't release it, leave it as it is.

Don't restrain it. Don't restrict it. Don't free it, open it or release it. Leave it as it is. Now the last sentence of this verse says:

All varieties have one taste – free from arising perceptions.

That is to say that if we are able to practice the first three sentences, then everything has the same taste. Tibetans, for example value butter and tea. These days most people value certain pieces of paper that have numbers ending in zeroes on them – the more zeroes the better. Dogs value bones. Cats value rotten fish. Kite flyers value good string and paper – not plastic – kites. All of this happens because we decide to make something out of these things, we perceive them as something special. One person may be crazy about diamonds, but another person will be crazy about emeralds, and yet another person will love crystals. One person will try to defend and another will try to conquer. All of these are just ideas that we have decided to make a big deal of. Perceiving everything with one taste means we see beyond this. It means we perceive everything's equal-ness. Ten kilograms of gold and ten kilograms of mud ultimately have the same value, but we only consider the ten kilograms of gold to be precious. Nobody would make the effort to carry around ten kilograms of mud. This is our reality, but a dog would quite happily choose a bone over a three-kilogram diamond; it would not even sniff at the diamond.

When we recognize this truth everything will fall into place. Everything will manifest exactly as it is, which at that stage will be paradise. When this perception manifests we are the Buddha and this is our paradise. If you believe in God you can think of this as becoming God in his or her paradise. Until we develop this perception, we live on the ground floor, God lives on the top floor and there is no ascending staircase. There are people wearing nice clothes who have permission to go upstairs and talk to God on our behalf, but if we do not have this specially tailored outfit – the special cut, the certain design and color – we will not be allowed past the first gate. For the Tibetans this means wearing yellow, for the Christians white – the Pontiff wears white – and for Hindus saffron.

THE ACTION

The next few sentences move on from meditation to action, to our regular activities.

Naturally pure and clean, the lotus grows in the mud.

You can be in the middle of samsara's ocean of suffering, but if you have no attachment to it you are like a beautiful lotus glowing in a pond of mud. The lotus is not just pure despite its environment, it is also externally clean. It is not like, for example, a faultless, pure diamond that is covered in dust and dirt. This metaphor refers to renunciation, which is the most important thing in Buddhism. When

I wrote this poem I was about to become a Bhikshu, so I was trying very hard to understand renunciation. It was the sixties. I happened to be in India at the time and not in the west, but because of the influence of the time I had some trouble understanding renunciation properly. The feeling of the time was to view renunciation as abandonment. Prince Siddhartha looked in on his wife and son in their chamber in the middle of the night, saw them sleeping, closed the door and ran away. This view was not only present in the sixties; even the other day somebody asked me if Milarepa was a good son. After all, this person said, he left his mother and sister. I was influenced by this way of thinking, but through my guru's teachings deep in my heart I understood what renunciation was.

Renunciation does not mean that you turn against people. It means you renounce your clinging and attachment to them. You become just like a pure, beautiful lotus in a smelly, muddy pond, a lotus that by its presence also makes the muddy pond beautiful. Prince Siddhartha renounced his kingdom, he renounced everything, but he did not turn against his queen or his son. Instead he renounced everything for his queen, his son, his kingdom, humanity and all sentient beings. After his faithful chariot driver showed him what happened in the world – how people got sick, old and died – he renounced his attachment to the worldly glory he had enjoyed for so many years. Until this time his father and his father's court had protected him from seeing or even hearing about suffering. This meant that when he saw them he wanted to do something about them and it was because of this that he left the palace. It was because of this that he renounced attachment. He did not renounce his queen, son and kingdom. He renounced his attachment to his queen, son and kingdom. This is how I understood renunciation and what I expressed in these four sentences.

Another important part of Mahamudra practice is doing things for others, even before we become Buddhas. This means doing however much we can for others right now, but from the Mahamudra point of view it does not mean doing things for others in a dualistic way. It does not mean that when we see injustice we should grab the person perpetrating it, shake him or her up, knock them out and then put them in a safe place or argue with others. We should try to work for others in a different way.

Serve others out of respect for their potential,

When we see an unfortunate being suffering, true Mahamudra compassion should arise. We should recognize that he or she is a Buddha who does not know that he or she is a Buddha, and is therefore suffering. If we recognize this, it means that whatever we do for him or her we will do out of service to an unenlightened Buddha. In this way we will have great respect for the subject of our compassion, and our compassion will be nourished by and derived from devotion. The more devotion we have for the Buddha, the more compassion we will have for sentient beings. We will know the ultimate essence of Buddhas and sentient beings. In the same way that this is both the center of space and the end of it, this sentient being is an unenlightened Buddha.

Provide what you can for the benefit of the recipient,

For me, this is an important idea. Many times we give to people because we want to feel good about giving. I feel good when I can help others, so therefore I want to help them. There is nothing wrong with feeling good about helping people, but it should not be the reason we do it. If it so happens that we feel good by helping others, that is okay, but it should not be our primary motivation.

We often talk about "merit." I grew up in a society where people always talk about merit, so I have no problem with this idea. It is not even something I got confused about in the sixties, even though a lot of other people did. They thought it sounded like boarding school, that somehow your merit was going to be counted, tallied in a book or kept on file, and it would affect your graduation marks, or which college you went to. It is not like that. It is better to perform good deeds for the betterment of others without any vested interest, even the expectation of a gift of merit. It is better to give without expecting something to happen as a result of that giving. You will accrue merit, it will happen; it just should not be your main reason for acting. If you sit in the sun long enough you will get tanned, if you sit in the sun too long you will get burned. The last sentence in this verse says,

> We reach the ultimate service when the server and the
> recipient become one.

This is the paramita of giving, when the giver and the recipient become one. In a paramita there is no dualism. How I understand this is that after practicing Mahamudra, after doing the meditations and the day-to-day activities, eventually everything comes together. This state is the paramita. There are many levels of paramita but in Mahamudra we talk about a "one pointed level." On the one pointed level you have truly recognized your Buddha-nature, it is similar to the first level of a bodhisattva.[39] This is the activity of the Mahamudra.

THE FRUITION

The last stage of the Mahamudra is the result, the fruition. This verse that I wrote about the fruition of Mahamudra was definitely influenced by the sixties. It is very "deep" but I would like to share it with you anyway.

> The great, primordial dharma space
> Is filled with limitless wisdom
> Like the always pure space
> Filled with countless galaxies of stars.

Although they are not really very deep, for me these four sentences describe the sambhogakaya and the nirmanakaya. Space is part of the mandala and so are we. When we realize the dharmakaya, the space around us becomes the sambhogakaya and the nirmanakaya; the sambhogakaya manifests for highly realized beings and the nirmanakaya manifests for ordinary beings. A dog living 2500 years ago in Bodhgaya would have seen the nirmanakaya of the Buddha walking around, not the dharmakaya. When Buddha's first five disciples sat on their knees and received his first teaching on the Four Noble Truths what they saw was the nirmanakaya, but when the bodhisattvas Manjushri and Avalokiteshvara received teachings on bodhichitta they saw him in his sambhogakaya form. When the King of Shambhala saw Prince Siddhartha in the form of three mandalas – with the Kalachakra mandala in the middle – he also saw the sambhogakaya of the Buddha. Nobody saw the dharmakaya because this level is beyond seeing and not seeing.

I hope these words that I wrote long ago are beneficial for you. I think they contain the fresh blessings of my guru.

CONCLUSION

I would like to end where I started by sharing two more verses from the text, *Ground, Path and Fruition*, which I wrote a long time ago. The first four are:

The ultimate is beyond description,
But we use relative ideas to describe it,
Therefore the descriptions are not completely accurate
And our view needs to continually evolve.

As the ultimate is beyond description and we can only use relative concepts to describe it, they are never going to be one hundred percent correct. It is impossible to describe the ultimate relatively. Instead what we need to do is constantly review what we know, learn more and upgrade our understanding. The words we use to access it are never going to be a hundred percent correct but we are able to improve our understanding because of one thing, the living lineage. The dharma we encounter today has been alive since the time of the Buddha. It has continued in an unbroken lineage through the devotion of the disciples and the compassion and wisdom of the masters. This guarantees our upgrade. It guarantees that our progressive transformation will be successful. If it was not here we would have to wait until the next Buddha attained enlightenment to learn the dharma.

The last four sentences read:

As you climb the stairs of this house
You reach towards liberation.
With each step your view, meditation and action progress,
As this happens your realizations will also progress.

This is what I believe. This is what my masters taught me and this is exactly what I hope will happen to you. As you climb each step on the staircase to liberation, your view, meditation, activity and actions will also progress. As this progresses so will your realizations. The progress will be continuous.

Dedication

It is my sincere wish that the merit all of you have created by coming to these teachings will not be wasted. You have come from many different parts of the world, many different parts of the city, to listen to me teach; some of you requested these teachings and some of you even organized them. I wanted to end with this verse because I hope that this is what will come from these teachings. I hope from these teachings we will climb the steps of the house to liberation, to Buddhahood, and that our view, meditation and action will progress on the way.

As you know, everything that I have said was passed on to me in one way or another by my great masters. Some of them have passed away and some are still alive. It is because of their teachings that I am able to share these words of dharma with all of you. If you gained anything positive from these teachings it is due to them. If there were any mistakes or shortcomings they were mine. I sincerely pray that I did not contaminate the lineage with my own interpretations. I always try not to do this. I always try to make it clear when something is my own thought as opposed to the lineage I am trying to pass down to you. In these teachings I hope I made it clear that seeing things as what I have, what I want and what I need was my idea, it did not come from the lineage. Apart from that everything I said comes from my lineage, one way or another. And I would like to confess any contamination I may have brought into the lineage. I did not do it intentionally.

There is another prayer that we have in our lineage.

The child of the garuda and the lion,
Will be greater than their parents.

In the Mahamudra lineage, the disciples are said to be greater than their masters. They are like garudas and snow lions. The garuda chicks grow up to be mightier than their parents. The snow lion cubs becomes more powerful than their parents. Likewise, I sincerely hope that you can attain Buddhahood before I do and then I can become one of your disciples.

I would like to dedicate the merit we have accumulated here to all my great masters, including His Holiness the Dalai Lama and His Holiness the Karmapa. May they live for a long time and may their dharma activities benefit all sentient beings. May my masters who are not alive right now incarnate soon and continue the activities of their predecessors. And may there be peace, prosperity and happiness in the Arya Bhumi, India. I came here when I was almost six and it is my second home. May there also be peace and harmony in my own country. As you all know, we Tibetans are fortunate enough to be sandwiched between two great civilizations, India and China. It is almost as if we have two pillars supporting us. India is the land of our gurus and China has been the land of our patrons and supporters. May all of our neighboring countries have peace and harmony.

May there also be peace and harmony in the entire world. There are so many things happening right now in the world: fighting, earthquakes, famine and all kinds of frightening, incurable diseases. May the Buddhas bless all of us to purify this kind of karma. May humanity realize that we are all the same, equal in our basic needs. Nobody likes to suffer, everybody likes to be happy. I used to do a lot of work for peace. At that time I did not know much about this kind of work and people who were more experienced than me would come up to me and say, "Is world peace really possible?"

I would honestly reply, "Why not?"

They would look at me with very big eyes, thinking I knew a secret. So I would say to them, "Why not? Do you know anybody on Earth who likes to suffer?"

They would reply, "No."

Then I would say, "Do you know anybody on this Earth who does not want to be happy?"

"No," they would say.

"That," I would tell them, "is how I know it will happen."

If everybody wants to be happy, if nobody wants to suffer, then peace is more than possible. Now I am a little bit more knowledgeable and it seems to me that we need to make continuous effort. We need to engage in what I have decided to call "active peace." It means constantly trying to fix this and that here and there so we can remain at peace.

As a religious person, I try to do this from a religious point of view. I do my best to let all my fellow religious people know that although what we believe in is slightly different, we are all following a path that leads to one ultimate destination. There cannot be two, three or four ultimate destinations. Having this belief means I respect every religion. As a religious person, though, I try to stay out of politics, economics and these kinds of things. I try to leave these things to other people. I have more knowledge about these things than I used to have, but they are still none of my business and I should not make them any of my business. My business is religion. I am involved in Buddhism. It is what I practice, how I pray, what I try to do my best at. In this way I hope to contribute. In our own ways each of us can contribute to the betterment of humanity.

Mahamudra

by

His Eminence Tai Situ Rinpoche

The View

What moves and what does not move, what is visible and
what is not visible,
All interrelate with space
Space neither moves, nor stays still,
Is neither visible nor invisible.

Knowing or not knowing, realizing or not realizing
Interdependent space and mind are never separated,
Mind is light in space – never bound never released,
Beyond obscuration and clarification – beyond all limits.

The Meditation

The wandering mind looks at the still mind.
The still mind looks at the still mind.
Realizing your primordial nature,
Wandering transforms into wisdom.

Criticism and suspicion are caused by hope and fear.
Greed comes from fear, hope and criticism.
They only manifest interdependently,
There is nothing to fear, there is nothing to long for.

Wherever you are right now, is both the end and center of space.
Whatever you look at, listen to, taste, smell or think is Mahamudra.
Don't hold it, don't release it, leave it as it is.
All varieties have one taste – free from arising perceptions.

The Action

Naturally pure and clean, the lotus grows in the mud.
Serve others out of respect for their potential,
Provide what you can for the benefit of the recipient,
We reach the ultimate service when the server and the recipient become one.

The Fruition

The great, primordial dharma space
Is filled with limitless wisdom
Like the always pure space
Filled with countless galaxies of stars.

The Buddhist Schools

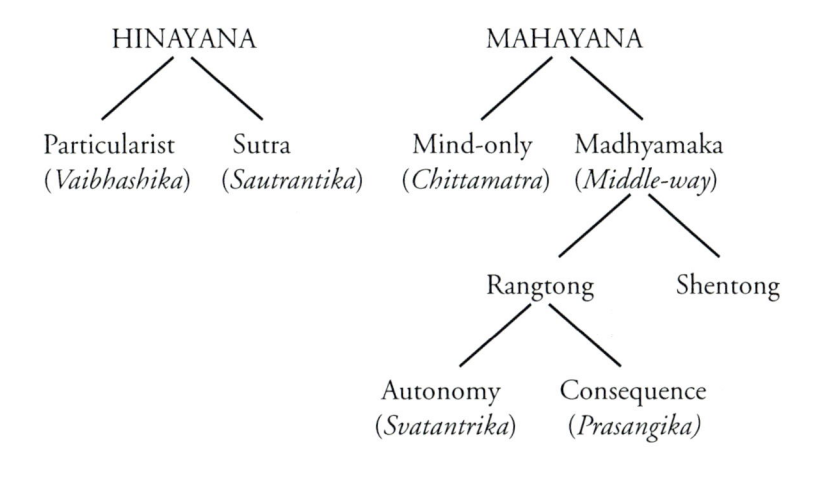

```
        HINAYANA                          MAHAYANA
        /      \                          /        \
Particularist   Sutra              Mind-only      Madhyamaka
(Vaibhashika)   (Sautrantika)      (Chittamatra)  (Middle-way)
                                                   /        \
                                               Rangtong    Shentong
                                               /     \
                                          Autonomy   Consequence
                                        (Svatantrika) (Prasangika)
```

The reader can refer to the glossary of terms for further information on these terms.

The Six Realms of Samsara

Name	As pictured in thangkas	Obstacle
HIGHER REALMS		
God (Skt. *deva*)	The celestial paradises are shown	Pride
Demi-god (Skt. *asura*)	Demi-gods are involved in conflict with the gods.	Jealousy
REALM EASIEST TO ATTAIN ENLIGHTENMENT		
Human realm	Human beings in their houses practicing the dharma	The five disturbing emotions
LOWER REALMS		
Animal realm	Animals on earth	Ignorance
Hungry ghost (Skt. *preta*)	Beings with large bellies and very small mouths and necks	Desire
Hell beings	Beings being tortured in hot and cold realms	Anger

The Five Paths

1. Path of Accumulation	**Practice** four mindfulnesses, recognize the four marks of existence (impermanence, absence of a self, suffering and peace). **Practice** four renunciations **Practice** four concentrative absorptions (strong interest, perserverance, attentiveness, and investigation)
2. Path of Application	**Practice** five controlling powers (confidence, sustained effort, mindfulness, samadhi, and prajna). These powers become "unshakable" at the end of this path.
3. Path of Insight/seeing	**Attain** the first bodhisattva level of perceiving emptiness. **Develop** true awareness of the Four Noble Truths and their 16 aspects. **Develop** seven factors of enlightenment (memory, investigation of meaning and values, effort, joy, refinement and serenity, samadhi, and equanimity).
4. Path of Cultivation (Meditation)	**One** goes through the 2nd to 10th bodhisattva levels. **One** practices the eight-fold Noble Path (right view, right intention, right speech, right action, right livelihood, right effort, right mindfulness, and right meditation).
5. Path of Fulfillment	**This** is Buddhahood.

The Bodhisattva Levels

1. The Joyous One
(rab tu dga' ba)

Emphasis on generosity
(sbyin pa)

2. The Stainless One
(dri ma med pa)

Emphasis on discipline
(tsultrim)

3. The Illuminating One
('od byed pa)

Emphasis on patience
(bzod pa)

4. The Flaming One
('od 'phro ba)

Emphasis on exertion
(bzod pa)

5. The One Difficult to Conquer
(shin tu sbyang dka' ba)

Emphasis on meditation
samadhi

6. The Manifest One
(mngon du gyur ba)

Emphasis on wisdom
(sherab)

7. The Far Going one
(ring du song pa)

Emphasis on skillful activity
(thabs la mkhas pa).

8. The Unshakable One
(mi gyo ba)

Emphasis on future projection
(smob lam)

9. The One of Good Discrimination
(legs pa'i blo gros)

Emphasis on efficacy
(stobs)

10. Cloud of Dharma
(chos kyi sprin)

Attaining enlightened wisdom
(yeshe)

Transformation of Conciousness into Wisdom

Organ	Consciousness	Wisdom	Kayas
Eye Ear Nose Tongue Body	1. Eye consciousness 2. Ear consciousness 3. Nose consciousness 4. Tongue consciousness 5. Body consciousnes	All-accomplishing wisdom	Nirmanakaya
Mind	6A. Non-conceptual mind consciousness		
	6B. Conceptual mind consciousness	Dharmadhatu wisdom	Svabhavikakaya
	7A. Immediate mind consciousness	Discriminating wisdom	Sambhogakaya
	7B. Afflicted mind consciousness	Wisdom of equanimity	
	8. Alaya consciousness	Mirror-like wisdom	Dharmakaya

Fifty-One Mental Factors

In the *Abhidharma Kosha* of Vasubandhu, fifty-one types of mind states or mental factors are distinguished. In the main they are categorized by their relationship to the main delusions of attachment, anger and ignorance, (see below) and their relevance to mind training. Note that the English terms used are approximate and often have connotations not contained in the Buddhist definitions. Although the list below may appear to be a dull list of definitions, its careful study can explain much of the Buddhist attitude towards the mind. This list is not supposed to be a complete description of all possible mental states though. It merely describes the most important states in relation to spiritual practice.

The Five Omnipresent (Ever-Recurring) Mental Factors
1. **Feeling** (the second aggregate).
2. **Recognition** / discrimination / distinguishing awareness (the third aggregate).
3. **Intention** / mental impulse – The idea that, "I will ..."
4. **Concentration** / attention / mental application – focused grasping of an object of awareness.
5. **Contact** – as an object connects with the mind. This may be pleasurable, painful or neutral as experienced by the aggregate of feeling.

The Five Determinative Mental Factors
6. **Resolution** / aspiration – the direction of effort to fulfill a desired intention. This is the basis of diligence and enthusiasm.
7. **Interest** / appreciation – holding on to a particular thing and not allowing distraction.
8. **Mindfulness** / Recollection – repeatedly bringing objects back to mind, not forgetting.
9. **Concentration** / *Samadhi* – one-pointed focus on an object. From this basis we can increase intelligence.
10. **Intelligence** / Wisdom – "common-sense intelligence." This fine discrimination examines the characteristics of objects, stops doubt and maintains the root of all wholesome qualities.

The Four Variable (Positive or Negative) Mental Factors

11. **Sleep** – makes the mind unclear, the sense consciousness turn inwards.
12. **Regret** – when regarding a previous action with disdain the mind becomes unhappy. This prevents the mind from being at ease.
13. **General examination** / coarse discernment – depending on intelligence or intention, this factor searches for a rough idea of the mind's object.
14. **Precise analysis** / subtle discernment – depending on intelligence or intention, this factor examines the object in detail.

The Eleven Virtuous Mental Factors

(Note that 18 and 19 are not necessary always virtuous. The first three are also known as the roots of virtue.)

15. **Faith** / confidence / respectful belief – this is a positive attitude towards virtue and objects worthy of respect. Three types of faith are distinguished and the last is preferred.
    a. uncritical faith: faith with no apparent reason.
    b. longing faith: the faith of an emotionally unstable mind.
    c. conviction: faith based on sound reasons.
16. **Sense of Propriety** / self-respect – usually the personal conscience that stops us performing negative actions and encourages the performance of positive actions.
17. **Considerateness** / decency – avoids evil towards others and is the base of unspoiled moral discipline.
18. **Suppleness** / thorough training / flexibility – enables the mind to engage in positive acts at will without being interrupted by mental or physical rigidity.
19. **Equanimity** / clear-minded tranquility – a peaceful mind that is not overpowered by delusions and has no mental dullness or agitation.
20. **Conscientiousness** / carefulness – this makes us avoid negative acts and do good; it is a mental factor with detachment, non-hatred, non-ignorance and enthusiasm.
21. **Renunciation** / detachment – no attachment to cyclic existence and objects.
22. **Non hatred** / imperturbability – no animosity to others or conditions; rejoicing.
23. **Non-bewilderment** / non ignorance / open-mindedness – usually understanding the meaning of things through clear discrimination, never unwilling to learn.
24. **Non violence** / complete harmlessness – compassion without any hatred, pacifism.

25. **Enthusiasm** / diligence – doing positive acts (specifically in terms of mental development and meditation) with delight.

The Six Non-Virtuous Mental Factors
The Six Root Delusions. (A delusion is defined as any secondary mental factor that, when developed, brings about suffering and uneasiness to self or others.)
26. **Ignorance** – not knowing about karma or the meaning and practice of the Three Jewels. This mental factor includes closed-mindedness and a lack of understanding of emptiness.
27. **Attachment** / desire – its definition is "not wanting to be separated from someone or something." It is grasping at the aggregates in cyclic existence that causes birth and the suffering of existence.
28. **Anger** – its definition is, "wanting to be separated from someone or something." It can lead to relentless desire and hurting others. It causes unhappiness.
29. **Pride** – an inflated sense of superiority supported by one's worldly views that includes the disrespect of others.
30. **Doubt** / deluded indecisive wavering – being in two minds about reality that usually leads to negative actions.
31. **Wrong views** / speculative delusions – that are based on emotional afflictions. These are divided into five types: belief in the self as permanent or non-existent (as opposed to the view of emptiness); denying karma; not understanding the value of the Three Jewels; closed-mindedness (my view – which is wrong – is the best); and wrong conduct (that is conduct that does not lead towards liberation).

The Twenty Secondary Non-Virtuous Mental Factors
Those derived from anger are:
32. **Wrath** / hatred – is bought about by increased anger and is a malicious state wishing to cause immediate harm to others.
33. **Vengeance** / malice / resentment – means not forgetting the harm another person has done and seeking to return this harm.
34. **Rage** / spite / outrage – is the intention to use harsh speech in reply to unpleasant words when wrath and malice become unbearable.
35. **Cruelty** / vindictiveness / mercilessness – is devoid of compassion or kindness and seeks to harm others.

Those derived from anger and attachment:
36. **Envy** / jealousy – internal anger caused by attachment; the inability to bear the good fortune of others.
Those derived from attachment:
37. **Greed** / avarice / miserliness – the intense clinging to possessions and their increase.
38. **Vanity** / self-satisfaction – seeing one's good fortune gives one a false sense of confidence; being intoxicated with oneself.
39. **Excitement** / wildness / mental agitation – a distraction towards objects of desire that does not allow the mind's focus to rest on something wholesome; this obstructs single pointed concentration.
Those derived from ignorance:
40. **Concealment** – hiding one's negative qualities when others with good intention refer to them. This causes regret.
41. **Dullness** / muddle-headedness – is caused by fogginess which makes the mind dark/heavy – like when we go to sleep. Coarse dullness is when the object is unclear, subtle dullness is when the object is not intensely clear.
42. **Faithlessness** – no belief in that which is worthy of respect; it can be the idea that virtue is unnecessary, or a mistaken view of virtue; it forms the basis for laziness (43).
43. **Laziness** – being attached to temporary pleasure, not wanting to do virtue at all or only a little; this is the opposite of diligence (25).
44. **Forgetfulness** – this causes us to not remember virtuous acts clearly and induces disturbing distraction – it is not "just forgetting," but a negative tendency.
45. **Inattentiveness** / lack of conscience – "distracted wisdom" after a rough or no analysis, not fully aware of one's conduct, this is careless indifference and moral failings or intentionally seeking mental distraction like daydreaming.
Those derived from attachment and ignorance:
46. **Hypocrisy** / pretension – pretending we have non-existent qualities.
47. **Dishonesty** / smugness – hiding one's faults and not giving clear answers when asked. This stops regret for snobbery and conceit, self–importance and finding faults with others.
Those derived from attachment, anger and ignorance:
48. **Shamelessness** – consciously not avoiding evil, it supports all root and secondary delusions.

49. **Inconsiderateness** – not avoiding evil, being inconsiderate of other's practice, ingratitude.
50. **Unconscientiousness** / carelessness – the three delusions plus laziness; this mental factor includes wanting to act in an unrestrained manner.
51. **Distraction** / mental wandering – the inability to focus on any virtuous object.

Notes

1. The Buddha's teachings occurred in three important phases, known as the three *dharmachakras* or three turnings of the wheel of dharma. The first turning includes the teachings common to all traditions, those of the Four Noble Truths, the Eight-fold Path, selflessness and impermanence, which can lead to liberation from suffering. The second turning expanded on the first, the fruition of its teachings being on the emptiness of all phenomena (the Prajnaparamita teachings) and that universal compassion is Buddhahood. The teachings of the third turning are those on the Buddha potential and its inherent qualities. For a detailed account of the three wheels of dharma see Thrangu Rinpoche's *The Three Vehicles of Buddhist Practice* published by Namo Buddha Publications.

2. These lines refer to the dam pa'i tshul dgu/ dam bä tsool gu, also called "the nine qualities of noble scholars." These nine qualities are described in a book by Khenchen Thrangu Rinpoche called, *The Tibetan Vinaya: Guide to Buddhist Conduct* published by Sri Satguru Publications. In a chapter entitled "Nine Aspects of a Noble Being," Rinpoche describes how the first three – hearing, contemplating and meditating – benefit ourselves. The second three – speech/teaching, debate and composition – benefit others. And the last three – being learned, well-disciplined and compassionate – benefit both self and others.

3. When you talk about guru in the Mahamudra lineage, there is the pure (dharmakaya) aspect of the guru, the distance lineage gurus, and the close lineage gurus. The distance lineage gurus start with the Lord Buddha and extend in a continuous, unbroken succession of enlightened masters and students all the way down to the Karmapa.

We call that the distance lineage because it goes all the way back to the Buddha Shakyamuni.

There is the close lineage of Mahamudra as well. That lineage begins with the Buddha Vajradhara who bestowed Mahamudra teachings on the Bodhisattva Lodro Rinchen, which teachings then come down to Tilopa and Naropa. In the case of the great masters who received Mahamudra lineage transmissions directly from the Buddha Vajradhara, those transmissions happened a long time after Prince Siddhartha's paranirvana. The physical Buddha, the historical Buddha Shakyamuni, Prince Siddhartha, was at the time no longer in physical Prince Siddhartha form. What happened was that first these great masters received the teachings of the Buddha and the Buddha's disciples through "distance lineages," and they practiced them. Through their practice they attained realization. As part of their realization the Buddha manifested to them, not as Prince Siddhartha, but as Buddha Vajradhara. So, Buddha, the sambhogakaya of the Buddha, and the nirmanakaya of the Buddha, which is Prince Siddhartha in our case. The Buddha Vajradhara means all in one – the ever-present Buddha, the timeless Buddha.

Then the Buddha Vajradhara transmitted directly to certain great masters, but only as a result of the realization of the teachings they had already received from their masters, whose teachings started with the historical Buddha. In this way, the Mahamudra lineage and many Vajrayana Buddhist lineages actually have distance lineage as well as close lineage.

4. Rinpoche is referring to the Dege Printing Press in Kham, east Tibet.

5. Generally, a yidam represents Buddha as seen by an ordinary being at some particular stage of their spiritual development, thus serving as a means to approach the goal. An aspirant acquires a yidam by receiving that deity's empowerment, practicing the meditation, reciting the mantra and praying to them. Each aspirant specializes in the group of practices associated with one particular yidam that is chosen with the Lama's help, to suit the aspirant's needs and disposition. The question of yidams and their functions is a complex one. The groupings of yidams as well as the particular siddhi associated with each one vary from text to text. But generally speaking, meditating on the yidams clears away obscurations. This leads to the ability to practice various yogas by which

one's ordinary life, tainted by the five disturbing emotions, are transformed into enlightened being and the five wisdoms.

6. There are four sections of tantra – Kriya, Charya, Yoga and Anuttarayoga – according to the new schools (Kagyu, Sakya and Gelugpa). In the Nyingma or old school there are also the three inner tantras of Maha, Anu and Atiyoga. Mahayoga is the first of the three inner tantras and emphasizes the creation stage. The second, Anuyoga, emphasizes the completion stage and the mandala as it is contained within the vajra body. Atiyoga is the third stage and is the same as Dzogchen.

In general, the Kriya tantra is the first level of the four tantras. Kriya literally means action. The second level is called Charya tantra. Charya means behavior. Yoga tantra is the third and the fourth is called Anuttarayoga, or highest yoga tantra. One way that the differences between the levels are traditionally presented is in terms of the degree to which the practice of the tantra involves external conduct as opposed to internal meditation. In Kriya tantra the emphasis is on the actions (or Kriyas) of ablution and external purity. In addition, no matter what form the meditation takes, there is a sense of considering yourself as inferior and the deity as superior. To clarify the difference we will consider the third level, Yoga tantra, next. It is called Yoga tantra or the tantra of unification because there is an identification with the deity that is so strong – because there is no longer any sense of inferiority or superiority – that the external actions or Kriyas of ablution and so forth are unimportant. The fourth level, Anuttarayoga tantra, is beyond any kind of duality whatsoever between the practitioner and the deity. The second level, Charya tantra, is a combination of the meditative practices of the Yoga tantra with the ritual ablution of Kriya tantra. – *Bardor Tulku Rinpoche*

7. See *The Uttaratantra* by Thrangu Rinpoche, Namo Buddha and Zhyisil Chokyi Ghatsal Publications for a detailed account of these.

8. Marpa passed the lineage to Milarepa who in turn transmitted it to Gampopa. Four of Je Gampopa's disciples founded the four major Kagyu Schools: Babrom Dharma Wangchuk founded the Babrom Kagyu, Pagdru Dorje Gyalpo founded the Pagdru Kagyu, Shang Tsalpa Tsondru Drag founded the Tsalpa Kagyu, and Karmapa Dusum Khyenpa founded the

Kamtsang Kagyu, also known as the Karma Kagyu school. The eight minor Kagyu lineages originated with Pagdru Dorje Gyalpo's eight main disciples. These eight lineages are: Taglung Kagyu, Trophu Kagyu, Drukpa Kagyu, Martsang Kagyu, Yerpa Kagyu, Yazang Kagyu, Shugseb Kagyu and Drikung Kagyu.

9. The additional four foundation or superior preliminaries are unique to Mahamudra practice. They are unlike the Ngondro [preliminary practices], in that they are not practices that need to be done separately. They are four things you need to understand and keep in mind about the environment or circumstances surrounding the practice of meditation. If you understand these four things, which are called the four conditions for practice, then you will greatly enhance your practice of both the Shamatha and the Vipashyana aspects of Mahamudra.

    The four conditions are: the causal condition, revulsion for samsara; the principal condition, reliance upon the guru; the focal condition, direct recognition of the mind's nature; and the immediate condition, the absence of hope or anxiety about one's progress in meditation.

10. For a detailed commentary of the Nyungne practice, see *Rest for the Fortunate* by Bardor Tulku Rinpoche, Rinchen Publications.

11. These are six special yogic practices transmitted from Naropa to Marpa: the subtle heat practice, the illusory body practice, the dream yoga practice, the luminosity practice, the ejection of consciousness practice and the bardo practice.

12. The first recognition of the nature of mind, which is brought about in the student's experience through the intervention of the lama – whether during a teaching, a ritual ceremony, or guided meditation – becomes the basis for the student's subsequent practice of dharma, the purpose of which is to enable the student to become accustomed and habituated to experiencing the world in the manner first pointed out. When, through the practice of the path, the student's experience reaches the ineffable fruition of Buddhahood, he or she is said to have fully realized the nature of mind. – *Lama Tashi Namgyal*

13. When deities manifest as a protector these are generally wrathful expressions of bodhisattvas who have undertaken to assist practitioners

by clearing away disruptive forces through the four kinds of activity: pacifying, enriching, magnetizing and destroying.

14. In the Nyingma lineage they talk about (1) the *chö nyi ngön sum gi nang ba*, the visionary appearance of the direct perception of reality; (2) the *nyam gong phel bä nang ba*, the visionary appearance of ever-increasing contemplative experience; (3) the *rig pa tshä pheb kyi nang ba*, the visionary appearance of reaching the limit of awareness; and (4) the *chö nyi du dzin pa zä pä nang ba*, the visionary appearance of the cessation of clinging to reality.

15. Ignorance is purified into dharmadhatu wisdom represented by Buddha Vairochana, anger is transformed into mirror-like wisdom represented by Akshobya, pride is transformed into the wisdom of equality represented by Ratnasambhava, desire is transformed into discriminating wisdom represented by Amitabha, and jealousy/envy is transformed into all-accomplishing wisdom represented by Amoghasiddhi. See *Transcending Ego* and *The Five Buddha Families* by Thrangu Rinpoche, Namo Buddha Publications and Zhyisil Chokyi Ghatsal Publications.

16. It is usually said to have 25,000 and is called the *'bum 'bring pa*. But in the Kanjur, to which Rinpoche is referring, it is called the "*Tri Nyi*," which means 20,000. It is the same text.

17. See Thrangu Rinpoche's commentary *The Ornament of Clear Realization*, Namo Buddha and Zhyisil Chokyi Ghatsal Publications.

18. The six paramitas are: generosity, moral ethics, patience, diligence, meditative-concentration, and wisdom-awareness. The ten paramitas are the above six and skillful means, aspiration, strength, and primordial wisdom.

19. We do not realize that the nature of our mind is emptiness and consequently fail to recognize it. We then falsely fabricate the notion that a self exists of its own accord and cling to it as a solid entity. At the same time, the mind possesses the aspect of unobstructed lucidity. Failing to recognize the unobstructed clear aspect of the mind, we think other things exist and cling to them as distinct and real. Having generated the assumption that self and other truly exist of their own accord,

attachment and aversion evolve – attachment arising from closeness, aversion arising from a feeling of distance. Attachment brings forth grasping toward what or whom we are attached to and aversion against what or whom we dislike. Dualistic concepts evolving from not recognizing the empty and clear nature of the mind arise from attachment and aversion. We need to cut through clinging to this duality.

Since we cling to the duality of a self and other, we grasp at all experiences and things as concrete and abstract existents. We need to understand that all experiences and things in and around us are a projection of the mind and do not exist unconditionally or naturally. Having understood this point, we realize the clear aspect of the relative truth. – *Jamgon Kongtrul Rinpoche*

20. For a detailed commentary on the five paths and these stages, see Khenchen Thrangu Rinpoche's commentaries on *The Ornament of Clear Realization* and *Jewel Ornament of Liberation*, Namo Buddha and Zhyisil Chokyi Ghatsal Publications.

21. The Madhyamaka or Middle-way school is divided into two major schools by the Tibetans: the Rangtong school, which maintains that everything is empty, and the Shentong school, which maintains that this emptiness is indivisible from luminosity/clarity (Tib. *salwa*) and that this indivisibility of emptiness and luminosity is the Buddha-essence.

22. In terms of resolving the view, the Buddha taught in stages. In accordance with that, various philosophical schools or tenets have come about. There are in particular four major schools. The first is the *Vaibhashika* school or Great-exposition or Particularist school, which is associated with the shravakas. The second is *Sautrantika* or Sutra school. The third is the *Chittamatra* or Mind-only school. The fourth school is known as the *Madhyamaka* or Middle-way school.

The Particularists (Vaibhashika) and Sutra (Sautrantika) schools are Hinayana and the Mind-only and Madhyamaka schools are Mahayana.

The Buddha taught the philosophical view in these stages and if we proceed through these philosophical views we will come to understand that appearances are just mind and that mind itself has no inherent existence.

23. The Mind-only and Shentong Schools both use the three natures or aspects of experience to explain their view: however, there are differences between their presentations of these aspects.

The three natures or three aspects of experience are: the imaginary nature (Skt. *parikalita,* Tib. *kuntag*), the dependent nature (Skt. *paratantra,* Tib. *zhenwang*) and the perfectly existent nature (Skt. *parinispanna,* Tib. *yongdrub*).

In the Mind-only view, the imaginary aspect of experience refers to what our thoughts are thinking about, what our thoughts are projecting. These are just conceptual creations, they have no existence and don't appear anywhere in the world. This includes all the names that we give to things and it is pretty easy to understand.

The dependent aspect of experience refers to all the things that we actually do experience. They are called dependent because they don't have any control over their own existence, they only come into existence when certain causes and conditions come together to produce them.

The perfectly existent nature or aspect refers to the essential nature of the dependent nature. What the essential nature of the dependent nature is, is that it is free of the imaginary aspect. What we do is confuse the dependent aspect and the imaginary aspect as the same thing, leading us to believe that the imaginary aspect really exists. When you look at the dependent aspect, the imaginary aspect does not exist within it at all, and this dependent nature empty of the imaginary is the perfectly existent nature of reality.

If we dissolve our attachment to the imaginary aspect we will see the nature of the dependent aspect, which is the perfectly existent aspect. Perfectly existent means it's really there, it is genuine reality.

The Shentong explain the three natures differently: whatever thoughts are focused on, whatever they imagine exists, are the imaginary nature; the objects of thoughts are imagined. The thoughts themselves are the dependent nature or the dependent aspect because they arise in dependence upon the habitual tendencies in the mind. The true nature of the thoughts is the clear light nature of mind, the perfectly existent nature.

The difference between this view and the Mind-only school's view is that the Mind-only school said that the perfectly existent nature is the dependent aspect empty of the imaginary aspect. Whereas the Shentong says that the perfectly existent nature is empty of both the dependent and the imaginary natures. In the Mind-only School there is still the quality of the dependent nature having some existence whereas in the Shentong view the ultimate perfectly existent nature is empty of both the imaginary and the dependent.

24. The Buddha first taught about the skandhas or aggregates, indicating that a person is a collection of many different parts, that external phenomena are also collections of many different things: they are not single, solid objects. External appearances, then, are just a collection of many very tiny particles that we could call "atoms." As for internal apprehending consciousness, it is a collection of indivisible moments of mind. This is the view of the Particularists or Vaibhashikas, who say that the minute partless particles and irreducible moments of mind are truly existent and it is through a collection of such inseparable particles or a continuum of such irreducible moments of mind that the gross phenomena that we ordinarily apprehend come about. It is only through a continuum that, for instance, something such as a year or a month comes about. There is no large, hard thing that exists in the way in which things ordinarily appear. – *Khenchen Thrangu Rinpoche*

25. The Sutra or Sautrantika School differentiates between 1) what is a mere abstraction, having only general characteristics: objects of our thoughts or abstract images that we can construct conceptually, and 2) what is a specifically characterized thing, something that has its own unique characteristics, an actual thing that appears before us which is there whether we think about it or not. For example, when we think "fire," the fire we're thinking about can't burn anything, it doesn't do anything, it cannot perform the function of burning. What actually does something is the actual thing that is there beyond our names and concepts, to which we give the name fire: it has its own totally unique characteristics unlike anything else. It is a unique object and it is performing the function of being hot and burning whether we think it burns us or not. That's what the Sautrantika school say, that there is an object there which really does exist beyond our concepts about what it is, and that the concepts are mere fabrications that don't really exist. The Sautrantikas also say that external, material phenomena have the nature of being established as particles, which are the cause of appearances.

If you look then at the specifically characterized object itself, it doesn't have any name, it doesn't have any conceptually fabricated characteristics at all. It is its own unique entity, and what that is is completely indescribable and inconceivable. Our own mental experiences are precisely the same. When we feel happy or we feel down then we give it those labels but if you really examine the experience, it's inexpressible. It can't be named or labeled by any conceptual term, and that in the Sautrantika School is evidence of a specifically characterized thing. Therefore the inexpressible, specifically characterized thing truly exists, according to the Sautrantikas.

There are various differences between the Particularist (Vaibhashika) School and the Sutra (Sautrantika) School, but in terms of their view, it is basically the same. Both hold that apparent and gross phenomena are, in fact, merely collections of truly existent partless particles and truly existent irreducible moments of mind. The important point of these views is that ordinarily we apprehend coarse or gross phenomena and these viewpoints show this is a great mistake. If we are able to realize that phenomena are not the massive, solid things that they appear to be, then that is the first step on the staircase towards a more profound understanding. – *Khenchen Thrangu Rinpoche*

26. *Semtsam do zhi*: 1. *The Sutra Unraveling the Intention*, 2. *Travel to Lanka Sutra*, 3. *The Sutra Taught in the Highest Pure Land* "Greatly Adorned," 4. *The Flower Ornament Sutra*.

27. Birth in samsara is described in terms of three realms, the desire realm (this includes the six realms of hells, craving spirits, animals, humans, demigods and gods), the form realm (gods of subtle form), and the formless realm (beings in high meditative states of absorption).

28. Translation of "The Root Text of the Seven Points of Training the Mind" © 1981, 1986 by Chögyam Trungpa; revised translation © 1993 by Diana J. Mukpo and the Nālandā Translation Committee; published in *Training the Mind* by Chögyam Trungpa. © 1993 by Diana J. Mukpo. Reprinted by arrangement with Shambhala Publications, Inc., Boston, www.shambhala.com. For a detailed commentary of these points see also *The Benevolent Mind, A Manual in Mind Training* by Traleg Kyabgon Rinpoche, Zhyisil Chokyi Ghatsal Publications.

29. This is to be born with a free and well-favored situation; the eight

freedoms and ten opportunities (*tal jor*). *Tal* is often translated as "freedom" and *jor* as "endowments," "qualities," "resources" or "opportunities" which constitute a precious human birth in which dharma can be practiced. The eight freedoms are traditionally enumerated as: freedom from birth as a hell-being, a hungry ghost, an animal, a barbarian, a long-lived god, a heretic, a mentally handicapped person or living in a dark age (here meaning when no Buddha has come, in other contexts, according to the teachings on five degenerations we are living in a dark age). Of the ten conjunctions or opportunities, the five personal conjunctions are: having a human body, being born in a land to which the dharma has spread, having all of one's senses intact, not reverting to evil ways and having confidence in the Three Jewels. (Having one's senses impaired to the extent that one's mind cannot function properly in the study and practice of dharma would constitute the loss of one's precious human birth.) The five conjunctions that come by way of others are: that a Buddha has been born in this age, that the Buddha taught the dharma, that the dharma still exists, that there are still followers who have realized the meaning and essence of the teachings of the dharma and there are benevolent sponsors. – *Lama Tashi Namgyal*

30. Remorse and confession are part of the four powers for purifying negative actions. 1: The power of reliance. This means to reassert one's refuge commitment to the Three Jewels and bodhichitta, by reciting the vows. It is the basis for purification. 2: The power of renunciation or abandonment. This means sincerely regretting the downfall or violation we have committed. 3: The power of remedial action. This power is engaging in some specific method in order to repair or counteract the force of our violation. 4: The power of restoration. This means making a commitment to refrain from this deed in the future.

There are three different remedial actions we can apply: the best is to meditate on emptiness, the second best group of techniques are specific practices like the Vajrasattva mantra, and the third best remedial action is to simply base the confession on the recollection of the downfall and confess it using the four powers.

31. The ten non-virtuous actions are: killing, stealing, sexual misconduct, lying, slander, abusive words, idle gossip, covetousness, ill-will and wrong views. Acts are non-virtuous or unwholesome when they result

in undesirable karmic effects. Thus, this list of ten unwholesome acts occurs generally in discussions of the functioning of karma. The first three are actions of body, the next four of speech, and the last three of mind. The ten virtuous actions are the opposites of the above ten non-virtuous actions.

32. These are the main positions of posture for meditation: (1) Straighten the upper body and the spinal column, (2) Look slightly downward into space straight across from the tip of the nose while keeping the chin and neck straight, (3) Straighten the shoulder blades in the manner of a vulture flexing its wings, (4) Keep the lips touching gently, (5) Let the tip of the tongue touch the upper palate, (6) Form the legs into either the lotus (Skt. *padmasana*) or the diamond (Skt. *vajrasana*) posture, and (7) Keep the back of the right hand flat on the left open palm with the inside of the tips of the thumbs gently touching.

33. *Interdependent origination.* The twelve links of causal connections which bind beings to samsaric existence and thus perpetuate suffering: ignorance, karmic formation, consciousness, name and form, the six sense bases, contact, sensation, craving, grasping, becoming, rebirth, old age and death. These twelve links are like an uninterrupted vicious circle, a wheel that spins all sentient beings around and around through the realms of samsara.

    The twelve links of interdependent origination are 1. Ignorance. 2. From ignorance we create the mental formations of the karma of virtue and non-virtue, called "mental formation conditioned by ignorance." 3. This seed of karma, which is carried by the mind, is called "consciousness conditioned by mental formation." 4. The power of that karma forces the mind into the mother's womb, called "name and form conditioned by consciousness." 5. This development gives rise to all the senses of the eye, ear, nose, etc., known as "six sense fields conditioned by name and form." 6. The interaction of the sense organs such as the eye with their corresponding objects and consciousness is "contact conditioned by the six fields." 7. From contact we experience feelings of happiness, suffering and indifference, called "feeling conditioned by contact." 8. When there is feeling and happiness there is attachment called "craving conditioned by feeling." 9. From attachment our craving increases, due to not wanting to be separated from the object of attachment, which is called "grasping conditioned by craving." 10. From grasping, we create more karma and existence by body, speech and mind, called "existence conditioned by grasping." 11. From that karma come the five aggregates (Skt. *skandhas*), which is called "birth conditioned by existence." 12. After birth the aggregates increase, ripen (aging) and cease (death), which is "aging and death conditioned by birth." Ignorance, craving and grasping are the afflictive mental states; mental formation and existence are karma, and the remaining seven are suffering. For a detailed explanation of this see Thrangu Rinpoche's *The Twelve Links of Interdependent Origination*, available from Namo Buddha and Zhyisil Chokyi Ghatsal Publications.

34. The First Noble Truth is the truth of suffering; its four main points or insights are: impermanence, suffering, emptiness and selflessness. The Second Noble Truth is the origination of suffering; the four points here are: cause, source, production and conditions. The Third Noble Truth of cessation's four points are: cessation, peace, preciousness and truly becoming. The Fourth Noble Truth is of the path and its four points are: the path, awareness, cultivation and making true becoming certain. See *The Ornament of Clear Realization* by Thrangu Rinpoche, Zhyisil Chokyi Ghatsal Publications, for a detailed account of these.

35. Those born in the realms of gods do so due to the accumulation of virtue and meditative practice in previous lives. While their present state is one of great happiness, it is temporary and dependent on past actions. Being completely absorbed in their present state of bliss they generally have no time or inclination for dharma. Unlike the human realm where we have moments of satisfaction, in the god realm there is a continual craving and continual gratification of that craving. But once their previous store of virtuous karma is exhausted, they fall into lower states of existence. However, there are many beings in the god realms who are not totally bewildered by their experience of pleasure and do practice the dharma.

36. It may be helpful here to understand the term for "consciousness," which in Sanskrit is *vijnana*, which is a specific type of cognition. It is the term for "cognition," *jnana*, with the prefix *vi*, which means "complete or fully developed." This is a more specific term than cognition and although it may sound like a positive thing to say "fully-developed cognition," in this context it is actually somewhat pejorative because it

refers to cognition that has become developed in the sense of becoming coarsened. This is the type of cognition, or consciousness, that we as ordinary individuals have and which is divided into the eight or six types of consciousnesses. All of these consciousnesses are considered manifestations of the mind's impurity. They are things that arise when a mind does not recognize its own nature. The basic idea of the development of consciousness is that when a mind does not recognize its own nature, its inherent lucidity, which is just a mere cognition or bare awareness, it runs wild. And running wild it becomes coarse or develops into deluded cognition or consciousness, which is characteristic of samsara. Nevertheless, in the midst of all this confusion, the nature of these consciousnesses, the nature of this deluded mind is unchanged.
— *Thrangu Rinpoche*

37. This is the ever-enduring basis of the other consciousnesses constituting mind. The foundation or storehouse consciousness is called the *kunshi* on the relative level. Failing to recognize the innate essence, we experience duality of self and other, and consequently behave positively or negatively by accepting and rejecting confrontations. We consequently develop habitual patterns that subside into and are stored in the storehouse consciousness. Due to those stored habitual patterns, karma ripens as intensified negative habits of body, speech and mind. We understand that the *kunshi* does not lead to bewilderment; rather, the habitual patterns do. When we recognize the ultimate state of the *kunshi* ground consciousness, which is free of habitual patterns, we have realized wisdom. When it is free of all habitual patterns, it is no longer the *kunshi* consciousness but the *kunshi* wisdom, the *jnana-alaya*.

38. This chapter has been added from a separate teaching given by Tai Situ Rinpoche.

39. There are four yogas of Mahamudra; these are the stages of realization within fruition Mahamudra, each representing the fruition of a certain level of meditation practice. These are the yoga of one-pointedness, the yoga of non-conceptuality (simplicity), the yoga of one-flavor (taste) and the yoga of non-meditation.

One-pointedness, the first yoga, is founded upon the practice of calm abiding or tranquility meditation (Shamatha). When we are able to rest in mind's natural evenness one-pointedly, i.e., free of any distractions, wisdom of special insight dawns, which is bliss and clarity. Due to perfected Shamatha practice, we are able to abide in bliss and clarity. At the stage of one-pointedness, mind recognizes itself and one has a glimpse of the ordinary mind or wisdom. Mind recognizes itself for a certain period, depending upon a practitioner's capacity to remain settled in the pure state. As beginners, we claim to be meditating but apply effort. Therefore, our practice is conditioned and we judge. Such fabrications impede the mind from truly recognizing itself. Perfect Shamatha means the mind is pacified enough to recognize itself, pacified enough to experience glimpses of the ordinary mind. One-pointedness is completely unconditioned.

The second yoga of non-conceptuality or simplicity is based upon the ability to rest the mind one-pointedly in its natural state. The timespan gradually increases. During the practice free of any mental fabrications, we win certainty that mind and appearances are inseparable; that a mirror and its reflections are indivisible. At the moment, we separate our mind from outer appearances as objects that we cling to. During simplicity yoga, we experience that all outer objects are a mere projection of the mind. Since this is the case, the experience of non-duality sets in.

In short: simplicity means not differentiating mind and its appearances – subject and object – and realizing that all experiences and phenomena are a projection of the mind, that they are in fact non-differentiate. Having experienced non-dividedness, we practice the third yoga, called "one-taste."

At this stage of inner refinement, we experience the single taste of samsara and nirvana one-pointedly. Presently, we cling to samsara as a state of suffering we aspire to escape from and to nirvana as a state of happiness we wish to reach. During the practice of one-taste, we realize samsara and nirvana are actually non-differentiate while we abide in simplicity, free of any intellectual speculations.

During the final yoga of non-meditation, the realization of non-divided clarity of meditation and of the ultimate sets in, i.e., we are able to observe mind's luminosity during meditation as well as in post-meditation, the union of practice and fruition – mind's clarity is continuously present. – *Jamgon Kongtrul Rinpoche*

There is a correspondence between these four stages of Mahamudra and the five paths of accumulation, application, seeing, meditation and no-more-learning. When we analyze the four stages of Mahamudra, we find three sub-stages in each one, so that in the first one, which is one-pointedness, there are the lesser, the middling and the greater stage. In the next one, freedom from concept (simplicity), there are also a lesser, middling and greater stage, and so on. We have these twelve aspects, sometimes called the twelve yogas of Mahamudra. The first stage of one-pointedness refers mainly to one-pointed tranquillity (Shamatha) meditation. The lesser and middling stages of one-pointedness would be more or less associated with the path of accumulation. The greater stage of one-pointedness would be more associated with the path of application because one is joined to the true meaning. The second Mahamudra stage of freedom from concept (simplicity) is associated with the path of seeing. The stage of beyond concept means that first of all we have developed the power of Shamatha, and then through that tranquillity meditation we develop Vipashyana. Because of the insight of Vipashyana, we realize the true nature, which corresponds to the path of seeing.

The third Mahamudra stage of one-flavor corresponds to the path of cultivation or meditation, and the fourth Mahamudra stage of non-meditation corresponds to the fifth path of no-more-learning. The one-flavor stage corresponds to the second to the seventh bodhisattva levels. The eighth bodhisattva level corresponds to the lesser aspect of non-meditation. The ninth and the tenth bodhisattva levels correspond to the middling aspect of beyond meditation level. Then the state of Buddhahood would be the highest of the twelve sub-sections, the highest point of the non-meditation level.

When we reach the twelfth stage, the highest stage of non-meditation through Mahamudra practice, then the qualities of mind that we achieve are the same as those of Buddhahood, those achieved through the classic, long Mahayana path. But the speech and the physical qualities are not quite the same. This is because when we traverse the ordinary Mahayana path, then for many endless kalpas we are taking birth again and again and generating virtue. This is an extremely powerful thing, even though it is a much longer process. In that long process we accumulate such vast virtue that this will lead, at the end of the ordinary Mahayana path, to the tremendous physical and speech qualities that we associate with the thirty-two and eighty marks of the Buddha. When we go through the very profound and rapid path of Mahayana, we won't necessarily get those. If we look at the life of Jetsun Milarepa or the life of Gampopa, they didn't manifest the thirty-two signs and the eighty marks like the Shakyamuni Buddha did. This is because, for instance with Milarepa, he was born into an ordinary body and quickly perfected the Mahamudra. So the mind quality of realization is exactly the same, but the body and speech qualities that manifest for others are not the same. – *Khenchen Thrangu Rinpoche*

Glossary of Terms

Abhidharma. (Tibetan pronunciation: *chö ngön pa* / Tibetan spelling: *chos mngon pa*) The Buddhist teachings are often divided into the Tripitaka (the three baskets): the sutras (teachings of the Buddha mainly on mental discipline), the Vinaya (teachings on conduct, physical and oral ethics) and the Abhidharma. The Abhidharma is a phenomenological or metaphysical tradition primarily based on commentaries on the Buddhas teachings.

Abhidharmakosha. (Tib. *ngön pa dzö* / *mngon pa mdzod*) An authoritative scripture by Vasubhandu on Buddhist metaphysics according to the Hinayana tradition.

Afflicted consciousness. (Tib. *nyön yi* / *nyon yid*) The seventh consciousness. It has two aspects: the immediate consciousness that monitors the other consciousnesses, making them continuous and the klesha consciousness that is the continuous presence of self grasping. (See *consciousnesses, eight*)

Amitabha. (Tib. *Ö bag me* / *'od dpag med*) One of the five Buddha family deities known as the "Buddha of boundless light." Usually depicted as red.

Amoghasiddhi. (Tib. *Döndrup* / *don grub*) One of the five Buddha family deities whose name means "all-accomplishing one." Usually depicted as green.

Amrita. (Tib. *dut tsi* / *bdud rtsi*) A blessing substance that can cause spiritual and physical healing.

Anuttarayoga tantra. (Tib. *nal jor la na me pay ju* / *rnal 'byor bla na med pa'i rgyud*) In the new transmission of tantras there are four levels of the Vajrayana and Anuttarayoga tantra is the highest of these. It contains the Guhyasamaja, Chakrasamvara, Hevajra and Kalachakra tantras.

Archarya. (Tib. *lo pön* / *slob dpon*) A term used both to describe a spiritual master or preceptor and someone who has completed a course of study similar to a doctorate.

Arhat. (Tib. *dra chom ba/ dgra bcom pa*) A being who is "Free from the four maras." The mara of conflicting emotions, the mara of the deva, the mara of death and the mara of the skandhas. The highest level of the Hinayana path. An arhat is a male and an arhati is a female.

Aryadeva. (Tib. *pagpa lha / 'phags pa lha*) A disciple of Nagarjuna and author of many important commentaries.

Asanga. (Tib. *thok may / thogs med*) A fourth-century Indian philosopher who founded the Chittamatra or Yogachara School and wrote down the five works of Maitreya, which are important Mahayana treatises. He is also the brother of Vasubandhu.

Atisha. (982-1055 C.E.) A Buddhist scholar from Nalanda University in India who came to Tibet at the invitation of the King to overcome the damage to Tibetan Buddhism wrought by Langdarma. He helped found the Kadampa tradition.

Autonomy or Svatantrika School. (Tib. *rang ju / rang rgyud*) The reason this school is called the Autonomy School is that they assert the autonomous existence of valid reasons. It, along with the Prasangika School, is one of the two main divisions of the Middle-way or Madhyamaka School. The Svatantrika itself also has two main sub-sections that both assert conventional reality to be like illusions, but do so either in accordance with the Sutra School or the Mind-only School. Both these sub-sections, and therefore the entire Svatantrika School, assert that ultimate reality is emptiness and free from conceptual fabrication.

Avalokiteshvara. (Tib. *Chenrezig / spyan ras gzigs*) The bodhisattva that embodies the compassion of all the Buddhas. Depicted holding the wish-fulfilling gem between folded hands. One of the eight main bodhisattvas. The mantra associated with this bodhisattva is known as the king of mantras, OM MANI PEME HUNG.

Ayatanas (Tib. *che che / skye mched*). The six inner ayatanas are the five sense-faculties – the eyes, ear, nose, tongue, and the body as a whole – and the mental faculty. The six outer ayatanas are the six objects of the various sense faculties: form, sound, smell, taste, touch and objects of conceptual thinking.

Bhikshu. (Tib. *ge long / dge slong*) A fully ordained monk.

Bodhisattvacharyavatara. (Tib. *chö jug / spyod 'jugs*) A famous text on the bodhisattva's way of life by the great Indian master Shantideva.

Bodhichitta. (Tib. *chang chup chi sem / byang chub kyi sems*) Literally, the mind of enlightenment. There are two kinds of bodhichitta: absolute bodhichitta, which is the completely awakened mind that sees the emptiness of phenomena, and relative bodhichitta, which is the aspiration to practice the six paramitas and free all beings from the suffering of samsara. There are also two kinds of relative bodhichitta: aspirational bodhichitta and action bodhichitta.

Bodhisattva. (Tib. *chang chup sem pa / byang chub sems dpa*) "Heroic mind." Literally a "hero" (*pa*) or "being" (*sattva*) who exhibits the mind of enlightenment. *Bodhi* means blossomed or enlightened. An individual who has committed him or herself to the Mahayana path of compassion and the practice of the six paramitas in order to achieve Buddhahood to free all beings from samsara. These are the heart or mind disciples of the Buddha.

Bodhisattva levels. (Skt. *bhumi*, Tib. *sa*) The levels or stages a bodhisattva goes through to reach enlightenment. These consist of ten levels in the sutra tradition and thirteen in the tantra tradition. The ten are: 1. Overwhelming Joy, 2. Stainless, 3. Radiant, 4. Luminous, 5. Difficult to Practice, 6. Obviously Transcendent , 7. Far Gone, 8. Unshakeable, 9. Excellent Discriminating Wisdom, 10. Cloud of Dharma.

Bodhisattva vow. The vow to attain Buddhahood for the sake of all beings.

Buddha. (Tib. *sang je / sangs rgyas*) An individual who attains – or the realization of – complete enlightenment, such as the historical Shakyamuni Buddha.

Buddha Shakyamuni. (Tib. *shakya tubpa / sha kya thub pa*) The Shakyamuni Buddha, often called the Gautama Buddha. He was the fourth Buddha of this age and lived from approximately 563 to 483 BCE.

Buddha-field. (Tib. *sang gye chi shing / sangs rgyas kyi zhing*) 1) One of the realms of the five Buddha families, in either their sambhogakaya or nirmanakaya forms. 2) Pure personal experience.

Buddhahood. (Tib. *Sang gye chi ko pang/ sangs rgyas kyi go 'phang*) The perfect and complete enlightenment of a Buddha that does not dwell in either samsara or nirvana. Buddhahood is an expression of the realization of perfect enlightenment that characterizes a Buddha. According to the teachings of the Buddha every sentient being's essence is the Buddha nature, primordial perfection, and therefore Buddhahood rather than being something we "attain" is the continuous, spontaneous experience of our essence.

Buddha-nature (Buddha-essence). (Skt. *tathagatagarba* Tib. *de shin sheg bä nying po / de bzhin gshegs pa'i snying po*) The essential nature of all sentient beings; one's limitless potential. In Mahayana literature it is the inherent potential for enlightenment in all beings. In Mahamudra, rather than being a potential that needs to be developed in order to attain enlightenment, it is one's intrinsic nature that upon being realized is enlightenment.

Buddhapalita. (Tib. *Legdenje / Legs ldan 'byed*) Circa 4th century. An Indian master and proponent of the Prasangika-Madhyamaka (Middle-way) approach.

Chakravartin. (Tib. *korlo jur wa / 'khor lo sgyur ba*) Literally "the turner of the wheel" this refers to a universal monarch, a king who propagates the dharma and starts a new era.

Chakra. (Tib. *tsa kor / rtsa 'khor*) Literally meaning "circular channel" this word refers to the circular nature of some parts of the complex systematic description of physical and psychological energy channels.

Chakrasamvara. (Tib. *korlo dompa / 'khor lo sdom pa*) A meditational deity which belongs to the Anuttarayoga tantra set of teachings. A main yidam or tantric deity of the New Schools.

Chandrakirti. (Tib. *Dawa Drakpa / zla ba grags pa*) A seventh century Indian Buddhist scholar of the Madhyamaka School who is best known as the instigator of the Prasangika (consequence) approach of logical reasoning in his two treatises on emptiness.

Commentary. (Skt. *shastra*, Tib. *tan chö / bstan bchos*) The Buddhist teachings are divided into the words of the Buddha and the commentaries others made to his works (*shastras*).

Completion stage. (Tib. *dzog rim / rdzogs rim*) In the Vajrayana there are two stages of meditation: the creation/development stage and the completion stage. The completion stage also has two stages: the completion stage with marks is the six doctrines and the completion stage without marks is the practice of essence Mahamudra, resting in the un-fabricated nature of mind.

Consciousnesses, eight. (Skt. *vijñana*, Tib. *nam she tsog je / rnam shes tshogs brgas*) The first five of these are the five sensory consciousnesses of sight, hearing, smell, taste, touch and bodily sensation. The sixth is the mental consciousness, the seventh is the afflicted consciousness, and the eighth is the ground consciousness.

Consciousnesses, six. The five sensory consciousnesses and the mental consciousness.

Consequence or Prasangika School. (Tib. *tan jur / thal 'gyur*) The Rangtong Middle-way or Madhyamaka School has two main sub-schools, the Svatantrika and the Prasangika. The Prasangika tradition comes from Buddhapalita's commentaries on Nagarjuna's works that were further elaborated on by Chandrakirti. In this tradition nothing about the nature of genuine reality is asserted, because reality is said to be beyond conceptual fabrication. Instead the faults in the arguments of others are pointed out by showing the "consequences" of these arguments.

Creation stage. (Skt. *utpattikrama*, Tib. *che rim / bskyed rim*) In the Vajrayana there are two stages of meditation: the development and completion stages. The method of the creation stage is meditations involving the visualization and contemplation of deities for the purpose of purifying habitual tendencies and realizing the purity of all phenomena. In this stage visualization of the deity is established and maintained.

Dark age. (Skt. *kaliyuga* Tib. *tsöden ji du / rstod ldan gyi dus*) A dark age is either a time when no Buddha has come or a time when the five degenerations are present. The five degenerations are: 1) The degeneration of time, meaning outer events such as wars and social unrest are *becoming* worse; 2) The degeneration of beings, meaning that beings mind-streams are becoming coarser; 3) The degeneration, or shortening, of life spans; 4) The degeneration into delusions or an increase in beings' disturbing emotions that causes mental instability; 5) And the degeneration of view, meaning people's understanding of reality is growing further from the truth. Based on these five degenerations we are now living in a dark age.

Definitive meaning. (Skt. *nitartha* Tib. *nge don / nges don*) The Buddha's teachings that state the direct meaning of dharma. They are not changed or *simplified* for the capacity of the listener, in contrast to the teachings of provisional meaning.

Desire realm. (Tib. *dö kam / 'dod khams*) Comprises the six realms of gods, demi-gods, humans, animals, hungry spirits and hell-beings. Not all the gods are included within this realm, however, as some gods abide in the form and formless realms.

Dharani. A particular type of mantra, usually quite long.

Dharma. (Tib. *chö / chos*) This has two main meanings: first, any truth, such as "the sky is blue"; and secondly the teachings of the Buddha (also called the "Buddha-dharma").

Dharma protector. (Skt. *dharmapala*, Tib. *cho chong / chos skyong*) A Buddha, bodhisattva or powerful but ordinary being whose job it is to remove all interferences and bestow all necessary conditions for the practice of pure dharma.

Dharmadhatu. (Tib. *chö ying / chos dbyings*) The Sanskrit term *dharma* means "truth" or "phenomena" and *dhatu* means essence. Therefore it means the "essence of phenomena." In the Tibetan term *ying* means "sphere without center" and *chö* means dharma. Therefore the Tibetan term means "expanse of phenomena." This term is usually used to refer to the emptiness that is the essence of phenomena and this essence is the all-encompassing expanse that has no origin, or beginning and out of which all phenomena arise. The dharmadhatu and dharmakaya are essentially the same; they are two indivisible aspects of the same thing. The term dharmakaya emphasizes its wisdom aspect while the term dharmadhatu emphasizes its emptiness aspect.

Dharmakaya. (Tib. *chö ku / chos sku*) One of the three bodies of Buddhahood, it is enlightenment itself. That is to say wisdom beyond any point of reference. (see *kayas, three*)

Dharmakirti. (Tib. *chö drak / chos grags*) Famous Buddhist master of the seventh century who specialized in logic.

Dharmata. (Tib. *chö nyi / chos nyid*) Dharmata is often translated as "suchness," "the true nature of things" or "things as they are." It is phenomena as they really are or as seen by a completely enlightened being without any distortion or obscuration, so one can say it is "reality," the nature of phenomena and mind.

Disturbing emotions. (Skt. *klesha*, Tib. *nyön mong / nyon mong*) Also translated as "afflictive emotions," or "poisons." They are any disturbance or distortion of consciousness. The main kleshas are desire, anger and ignorance.

Dzogchen. (Skt. *mahasandhi*) Literally "the great perfection," these are the teachings beyond the vehicles of causation, first taught in the human world by the great Vidyadhara Garab Dorje.

Egolessness. (Skt. *anatman* Tib. *dag me / bdag med*) Also called selflessness. There are two kinds of egolessness: the egolessness of other – the emptiness of external phenomena – and the egolessness of self – the emptiness of a personal self.

Egolessness or selflessness of person. (Skt. *pudgalanairatmya* Tib. *kang sag dag me / gang zag bdag med*) This doctrine asserts that when one examines or looks for a personal self, there is none. The person does not possess an independent or substantial self (Skt. *atman*, Tib. *bdag-nyid*). This position is held by most Buddhist schools.

Egolessness or selflessness of phenomena. (Skt. *dharma-nairatmya* Tib. *chö dag me / chos bdag med*) This doctrine asserts that not only is there no self of person, but when one examines outer phenomena they also find this to be empty or lacking an independent, substantial nature. This position is not held by the Hinayana schools but is put forth by all Mahayana schools.

Eight-fold noble path. Right view, right thought, right speech, right action, right livelihood, right effort, right mindfulness and right concentration.

Eight lineages. The practice of these Eight Chariots of the Practice Lineages of Tibetan Buddhism are as follows: 1) **The Nyingma Lineage.** The main doctrinal lineage of Kama, the transmission lineage of tantra, from the first transmission of Buddhism to Tibet. (Key scriptural sources include: *Scripture of the Great Assemblage, Guhyagarbha Tantra.* In addition, the *Eight Sadhanas Sections,* and the core of Dzogchen, *The Heart Essence.*) 2) **The Kadampa Lineage.** The Old Kadampa School is the lineage of Atisha. (Key scriptural sources include: *The Graded Path for the Three Types of Individuals: Lamp of the Path of Enlightenment, Key Instructions of the Practices of Sixteen Spheres* and similar texts.) This lineage became the New Kadampa School after the time of Tsongkhapa. Since then it has emphasized philosophical doctrines. 3) **The Sakya Lineage.** The lineage of the glorious Sakyapa. (Key scriptural sources include: *The Instruction on the Nine-fold Path and Result.*) 4) **The Marpa Kagyü Lineage.** This lineage is composed of the Four Major and Eight Minor Schools of the Marpa Kagyü Tradition. (Key scriptural sources include: *The Four Transmitted Precepts Consolidated in One, The Path of Skillful Means, The Six Dharmas of Naropa,* and *The Path of Liberation Mahamudra.*) 5) **The Shangpa Kagyü Lineage.** (Key scriptural sources include: *The Lineage of Yogi Khyungpo Naljor,* and *The Teachings of the Five-fold Ultimate Reality.*). 6) **The Zhije and Chö Lineages.** This is the lineage of the "Pacification of Suffering" and the "Genuine Dharma of Severance" founded by Phadampa Sangye and Machik Lapdron. (Key scriptural sources include: *Pacification of Suffering* and its branch teaching *The Genuine Dharma of Severance* and related texts.) 7) **The Jor-truk Lineage.** The lineage of the "Six Applications" of Vajra Yoga Instruction, it is also known as the Jonangpa Lineage. (Key scriptural sources include: *The Intention of the Root Tantras, The Essence of All Completion Stage Practice, The Six Applications of Kalachakra.*) 8) **The Nyen-drub Lineage.** The "Four Branches of Approach and Accomplishment" is the Great Yogi Orgyenpa Rinchenpal's Lineage. (Key scriptural sources include: *The Three Vajra Instructions of Body, Speech, and Mind.*)

Eight mental constructs or complexities are mental formulations that phenomena have such attributes as arising and ceasing, being singular or plural, coming and going, and being the same or being different.

Eight worldly concerns. (Tib. *jik ten chö je / 'jig rten chos brgyad*) These keep one from the path; they are attachment to gain, attachment to pleasure, attachment to praise, attachment to fame, aversion to loss, aversion to pain, aversion to blame and aversion to a bad reputation.

Emptiness. (Skt. *shunyata* Tib. *tong pa nyi /stong pa nyid*) A central theme in Buddhism. It should not be mistaken for nihilism for it merely indicates the lack of a truly existing independent nature of phenomena. Positively stated, phenomena do exist but as mere appearances or interdependent manifestations of a limitless mind that is also free of true existence. Viewing all phenomena, including the mind, this way frees one from solipsism. The basic view of emptiness is interpreted differently by different Buddhist schools.

Empowerment. (Skt. *abhisheka* Tib. *wang / dbang*) The conferring of power or authorization to practice the Vajrayana teachings, the indispensable entrance door to tantric practice. To do a Vajrayana practice one must receive its empowerment from a qualified lama. One should also receive the practice instruction (Tib. *tri / khrid*) and the textual reading (Tib. *lung / lung*).

Enlightenment. (Tib. *jang chub / byang chub*) Its definition varies according to the different Buddhist traditions but it is usually considered to be the same as Buddhahood. The Hinayana tradition defines it as liberation from birth in samsara, with a mind free of ignorance and emotional conflict. The Mahayana tradition holds that enlightenment is not complete without the development of compassion and a commitment to use skilful means to liberate all sentient beings. In the Vajrayana teachings, the foregoing stages of enlightenment are necessary, but ultimate enlightenment manifests through the purification of ego grasping and concepts. The final fruition of complete enlightenment transcends all duality and conceptualization.

Eternalism. (Tib. *tag ta / rtag lta*) The belief that one's identity or consciousness has a concrete essence which is independent, everlasting and singular.

Experience and realization. (Tib. *nyam tog / nyams rtogs*) An expression used to describe insight and progression. "Experience" refers to temporary meditation experiences and "realization" to unchanging understandings of phenomena's nature.

Father tantra. (Tib. *pa ju / pha gyu*) There are three kinds of *Anuttarayoga* tantras. The *father tantra* is concerned with transforming aggression, the *mother tantra* with transforming passion and the *non-dual tantra* with transforming ignorance.

Five actions of immediate consequence. These lead one to a lower realm in the next life, without delay. They are: 1) killing one's father, 2) killing one's mother, 3) killing an arhat, 4) intentionally wounding a Buddha and causing them to bleed, and 5) creating a schism in the sangha.

Five Buddha families. (Tib. *rig nga / rigs lnga*) These are the Buddha, Vajra, Ratna, Padma and Karma families.

Five paths. (Tib. *lam nga / lam lnga*) According to the sutras there are five paths or stages we progress through to becoming Buddhas: the path of accumulation, the path of application, the path of seeing/insight (attainment of the first bodhisattva level), the path of meditation and the path of no more learning (Buddhahood). The five paths cover the entire process from beginning dharma practice to complete enlightenment.

Five poisons. (Tib. *dug nga / dug lnga*) These are five temporary mental states that inhibit understanding: ignorance, pride, anger, desire and jealousy. The three root poisons are ignorance, desire and anger.

Five wisdoms. (Tib. *yeshe nga / ye shes lnga*) The dharmadhatu wisdom, mirror-like wisdom, wisdom of equality, discriminating wisdom and all-accomplishing wisdom. They should not be understood as separate entities but rather as different functions of one's enlightened essence.

Fixation. (Tib. *dzin pa / 'dzin pa*) The mental act of holding on to a material object, experience, concept or set of philosophical ideas.

Form realm. (Tib. *zug kham / gzugs kham*) God realms of subtle form.

Formless realm. (Tib. *zug me chi kham / gzugs med kyi kham*) The god realm of unenlightened beings who have practiced the four absorptions: infinite space, infinite consciousness, nothing whatsoever and neither presence nor absence (of conception).

Four empowerments. (Tib. *wang zhi / dbang bzhi*) The empowerments of the vase, secret, wisdom-knowledge and precious word.

Four extremes. (Tib. *tha zhi / mtha' bzhi*) Existence, non-existence, both and neither.

Four immeasurables. (Tib. *tha zhi / mtha' bzhi*) Immeasurable love, compassion, emphatic joy and impartiality.

Four kayas. (Tib. *ku zhi / sku bzhi*) Nirmanakaya, sambhogakaya, dharmakaya, and svabhavakakaya.

Four Noble Truths. (Tib. *pak pay den pa shi / 'phags pa'i bden pa bzhi*) The Buddha began teaching with a talk in India at Sarnath on the Four

Noble Truths. These are the truth of suffering, the truth of the cause of suffering, the cessation of suffering and the path that leads to the freedom from suffering. These truths are the foundation of Buddhism.

Four preliminaries. (Tib. *ngön dro zhi / sngon 'gro bzhi*) Refers to the four general preliminaries, which are the four thoughts that turn the mind (precious human birth, impermanence, karma cause and effect and the shortcomings of samsara) and the four special preliminaries, which are the four practices of prostrations, Vajrasattva recitation, mandala offering and guru yoga.

Four seals. (Tib. *tawa kar tag kyi chag gya zhi / lta bkar btags kyi phyag rgya bzhi*) The four main principles of Buddhism: all compounded phenomena are impermanent, everything defiled (with ego-clinging) is suffering, all phenomena are empty and devoid of a self-entity, and nirvana is perfect peace.

Gampopa. (1079-1153 C.E.) One of the main lineage holders of the Kagyu lineage in Tibet. A student of Milarepa, he established the first Kagyu monastery and is also known for his text the *Jewel Ornament of Liberation.*

Ghanachakra. (Tib. *tsog chi kor lo / tshogs kyi 'khor lo*) This is a ritual feast offering which is part of a spiritual practice.

Graded path. (Tib. *lam rim*) The process by which a being is guided along the path to enlightenment through three principle paths of 1) renunciation, 2) the enlightened motive of bodhichitta and 3) a correct understanding of emptiness (wisdom).

Guru. (Tib. *lama / bla ma*) In the Tibetan tradition this refers to a realized teacher

Habitual patterns. (Skt. *vasana.* Tib. *bakchak / bag chags*) These are patterns of conditional response that exist as traces or tendencies and are stored in the alaya-vijnana, the eighth consciousness sometimes called the storehouse or all-base consciousness. This consciousness is so called because it is a repository of all karmically conditioned patterns. All dualistic or ego-oriented experiences leave a residue that is stored in the alaya-vijnana until a later time when some conscious occurrence activates the habitual pattern. Stimulated by this experience a response in the form of a perception or an action is generated. This response leaves its own karmic residue, stored again in the unconscious repository, and the cycle continues. The explanation of this system is a central teaching of the Chittamatrin tradition of Mahayana Buddhism.

Heart Sutra. (Skt. *Mahaprajnaparamita-hridaya-sutra* Tib.*sherab nyingpo /*

shes rab snying po) One of the shorter sutras on emptiness.

Hevajra. (Tib. *kye dorje / kye rdo rje*) This is a "mother tantra" of the Anuttarayoga class, which is the highest of the four yogas. "He" is said to be an exclamation of joy. Hevajra transforms sense pleasures into joy through the realization of the unity of form and emptiness. He is depicted in two, four, six, twelve, and sixteen-armed forms, dancing in union with his consort who is usually Nairatmya.

Higher realms. The three higher realms are birth as a human, demi-god and god.

Hinayana. (Tib. *tek men / theg dman*) Literally, the "lesser vehicle" this is the first of the three *yanas*, or vehicles. This vehicle includes the first teachings of the Buddha that emphasized the careful examination of mind and its confusion. It is the foundation of Buddha's teachings and mainly focuses on the four truths and the twelve interdependent links. Its result is individual liberation.

Interdependent origination. (Tib. *ten drel / rten 'brel*) The twelve links of causal connections that bind beings to samsaric existence and thus perpetuate suffering: ignorance, karmic formation, consciousness, name and form, the six sense bases, contact, sensation, craving, grasping, becoming, birth, old age and death. These twelve links are like an uninterrupted vicious circle, a wheel that spins all sentient beings around and around through the realms of samsara.

Jamgon Kongtrul Lodrö Thaye. A great non-sectarian master of the nineteenth century and author of more than one hundred volumes.

Jnana. (Tib. *yeshe / ye shes*) Enlightened wisdom that is beyond dualistic thought.

Kadampa. (Tib. *bka' gdams*) A major Tibetan Buddhist school founded by Atisha (993-1054 C.E.).

Kanjur. (Tib. *bka' gyur*) The Tibetan translations of the direct teaching of the Buddha.

Kagyu. (Tib. *bka' rgyud*) *Ka* means oral and *gyu* means lineage; the lineage of oral transmission. One of the four major schools of Buddhism in Tibet (The other three are the Nyingma, the Sakya and the Gelugpa schools). The Kagyu was founded in Tibet by Marpa and is headed by His Holiness Karmapa.

Kalachakra. (Tib. *du kor / dus 'khor*) A tantra and a Vajrayana system taught by Buddha Shakyamuni.

Kamalashila. An eighth-century Indian scholar who was a student of Shantarakshita and is best known for winning the debate with the

Chinese scholar Hashang Mahayana at Samye monastery. He also wrote the famous text the *Stages of Meditation*.

Karma. (Tib. *le / las*) Literally meaning "action" this term often refers to the unerring law of cause and effect; that positive actions bring happiness and negative actions bring suffering. The actions of each sentient being are the causes that create the conditions for both their next birth and the circumstances they will encounter in that lifetime.

Karma Kagyu. (Tib. *karma bka' rgyud*) One of the eight schools of the Kagyu lineage of Tibetan Buddhism which is headed by His Holiness Karmapa.

Karmapa. The name means Buddha activities. The Karmapas are the head of the Kagyu school of Buddhism and were the first to implement the tradition of incarnate lamas. The Karmapas are thought to be emanations of the bodhisattva Avalokiteshvara.

Kayas, three. (Tib. *ku sum / sku gsum*) There are three bodies of the Buddha: the nirmanakaya, sambhogakaya and dharmakaya. The dharmakaya, also called the "truth body," is the complete enlightenment or the complete wisdom of the Buddha – unoriginated wisdom beyond form. This body manifests as the sambhogakaya and the nirmanakaya. The sambhogakaya, also called the "enjoyment body," manifests only to bodhisattvas. The nirmanakaya, also called the "emanation body," manifests in the world as, for example, Shakyamuni Buddha. Sometimes a fourth kaya is also referred to, the svabhavakakaya, which is the "essence body," the unity of the other three.

Key instructions – A key instruction establishes a line of reasoning in a teaching. Seeing this line of reasoning we can then distinguish between the form and the content of the teaching. If acted upon this understanding generates a liberating personality transformation that is then repeated at each level of the teachings. Key instructions awaken those who receive them to the nature of the experience the teachings are pointing to.

King Indrabodhi. An Indian king during the time of the Buddha who become an accomplished master. He symbolizes the person of the highest caliber who can use sense pleasures as the path of practice.

King Trisong Detsen. He was the Tibetan dharma king (790 - 858 CE) who invited Guru Rinpoche and Shantarakshita to Tibet to establish the dharma there.

Kriya tantra. (Tib. *ja ju / bya rgyud*) One of the four classes of tantras that emphasizes personal purity.

Lama. (Skt. *guru* Tib. *bla ma*) This is either the Tibetan word for *guru* or a title given to some practitioners who have completed extended training. There are many different explanations of the etymology of this word but one way to think of it is that *la* means "high" – in that nobody has higher spiritual realizations than the guru – and that the *ma* means "mother" – in that they express the compassion of a mother. In this way this word indicates the union of wisdom and compassion, the feminine and masculine qualities.

Lineage gurus. (Tib. *ju lama / rgyud blama*) The lineage gurus or lamas are the beings who have transmitted our practices and studies. We can trace this lineage back, from today's gurus to their gurus and so on, all the way to the Buddha himself.

Lojong. (Tib. *blo sbyong*) Mind Training. The Mahayana meditation system of the early Kadampa School, brought to Tibet by Atisha.

Lotsawa. Sanskrit for "translator."

Lower realm. The three lower realms are the states hell beings, hungry ghosts and animals are born into.

Luminous. (Tib. *selwa / gsal ba*) In the third turning of the wheel of dharma, the Buddha taught that although everything is void this voidness is not completely empty because it is also luminous. This luminous or clear characteristic enables all phenomena to appear and is inseparable from emptiness or, in Sanskrit, *shunyata*.

Luminosity. (Skt. *prabhasvara* Tib. *osel*) Literally "free from the darkness of unknowing and endowed with the ability to cognize." This term has two aspects: "empty luminosity," like a clear open sky, and "manifest luminosity," such as colored light images, and so forth. Luminosity is the uncompounded nature present throughout all of samsara and nirvana.

Madhyamaka. (Tib. *u ma / dbu ma*) This most influential of the four schools of Indian Buddhism was founded by Nagarjuna in the second century C.E. The name comes from the Sanskrit word meaning "the Middle-way," the middle way between eternalism and nihilism. The main postulate of this school is that all phenomena – both internal mental events and external physical objects – are empty of any true nature. The school uses extensive rational reasoning to establish this emptiness. It does, however, hold that phenomena exist on the conventional or relative level.

Mahakala. A dharmapala or protector of the dharma and dharma practitioners.

Mahamudra. (Tib. *cha ja chen po / phyag rgya chen po*) This term literally means "great seal" or "great symbol" and refers to the way all phenomena are sealed by the primordially perfect nature. It is a form of meditation that can be traced back to Saraha (tenth century) and was passed down in the Kagyu School through Marpa. This meditation emphasizes the direct perception of the mind rather than rational analysis. The term "Mahamudra" can also used to describe the meditational experience of the union of emptiness and luminosity, the non-duality of the phenomenal world and emptiness, or as a name for the Kagyupa lineage.

Mahapandita. (Tib. *pan di ta chen po*) *Maha* means great and *pandita* Buddhist scholar.

Mahasiddha. (Tib. *drup thop chen po / sgrub thob chen po*) A much realized practitioner. *Maha* means great and *siddha* means accomplished. In particular this term refers to the Vajrayana practitioners who lived in India between the eight and twelfth centuries. The biographies of some of the most famous are found in the text *The Eighty-four Mahasiddhas*.

Mahayana. (Tib. *tek pa chen po / theg pa chen po*) Literally the "Great Vehicle." These are the teachings that can be traced back to the second turning of the wheel of dharma, a teaching that the Buddha gave at Vulture Peak Mountain, Rajgir. Mahayana philosophical schools appeared several hundred years after this but are based on this teaching. From the perspective of the Mahayana the purpose of enlightenment is to liberate all sentient beings, as well as oneself, from suffering and because of this they emphasize shunyata (see *shunyata*), compassion and universal Buddha nature.

Maitreya. The Loving One. The bodhisattva regent of Buddha Shakyamuni, presently residing in the Tushita heaven he will be the fifth Buddha of this kalpa.

Mala. (Tib. *trengwa / phreng ba*) A rosary that usually has 108 beads.

Mandala. (Tib. *chil kor / dkyil 'khor*) This Sanskrit word means either a "ring" or a "totality." It is translated into Tibetan as "chil kor," which literally means "center and surrounding" but is used in different ways. Often it refers to a diagram used in various Vajrayana practices that usually have a central deity and four surrounding directions.

Manjushri. (Tib. *jam bel / 'jam dpal*) One of the eight bodhisattvas. He is the personification of transcendent knowledge.

Mantra. (Tib. *ngag / sngags*) 1) A synonym for the Vajrayana. 2) A particular combination of sounds symbolizing the nature of a deity, for example OM MANI PEME HUNG. These are invocations to various meditation deities which are recited in Sanskrit. These Sanskrit syllables, representing various energies, are repeated in different Vajrayana practices.

Mantra vehicle. (Tib. *ngag chi tegpa / sngags kyi theg pa*) Another term for the Vajrayana.

Mara. (Tib. *du / bdud*) Difficulties encountered by practitioners. The Tibetan word *du* means heavy or thick. In Buddhism maras symbolize both the passions that overwhelm us as well as that which obstructs the appearance of wholesome roots and progress on the path to enlightenment. There are four kinds: *skandha-mara*, which is incorrect view of self; *klesha-mara*, which is being overpowered by negative emotions; *matyu-mara*, which is death and interrupts spiritual practice; and *devaputra-mara*, which is becoming stuck in the bliss that comes from meditation.

Marpa. (1012-1097 C.E.) Marpa was a Tibetan who made three trips to India and brought back many tantric texts, including the Six Yogas of Naropa, the Guhyasamaja, and the Chakrasamvara practices. His root teacher was Naropa, a student of Tilopa, the founder of the Kagyu lineage. Marpa founded the Kagyu lineage in Tibet.

Mental consciousness. (Tib. *yi chi namshe / yid kyi rnam shes*) The sixth consciousness is the faculty of thinking which produces thoughts based upon the experiences of the five sense-consciousnesses or its own previous content. (see *consciousnesses, eight*).

Mental factors. (Tib. *sem jung / sems hyung*) Rather than being mind itself, mental factors are more long-term propensities of mind. They include the eleven virtuous factors such as faith, detachment and equanimity; the six root defilements such as desire, anger and pride; and the twenty secondary defilements such as resentment, dishonesty and harmfulness. (See appendix)

Middle-way. (Tib. *u ma/ dbu ma*) or Madhyamaka school. A philosophical school founded by Nagarjuna and based on the Prajnaparamita sutras of emptiness. (see Madhyamaka)

Milarepa. (1040-1123 C.E.) Milarepa was a student of Marpa who attained enlightenment in one lifetime. He was named *Mila,* which literally means "what a person,"by the deities and the name *repa* means "cotton-clad one." His student Gampopa established the (*Dagpo*) Kagyu lineage in Tibet.

Mind-only School. Also called the Chittamatra School this is a major school of the Mahayana tradition founded by Asanga in the fourth century. It emphasizes that every thing is a mental event.

Mother tantra. (Tib. *ma ju / ma rgyud*) There are three kinds of tantras: *the father tantra*, which is concerned with transforming aggression; the *mother tantra*, which is concerned with transforming passion; and the non-dual tantra, which is concerned with transforming ignorance.

Mudra. (Tib. *chak gya / phyag rgya*) In this book this term refers to a "hand seal" or gesture that is performed in specific tantric rituals to symbolize certain aspects of a practice. It can also mean a spiritual consort, or the "bodily form" of a deity.

Nagarjuna. (Tib. *ludrup / klu sgrub*) An Indian master of philosophy, founder of the Middle-way or Madhyamaka School, author of the *Mula-prajna* (the Roots of Wisdom) and other important works. (2nd – 3rd century)

Naropa. (956-1040 C.E.) An Indian master best known for transmitting many Vajrayana teachings to Marpa who took these back to Tibet before the Muslim invasion of India.

Ngöndro. (*sngon 'gro*) Tibetan for preliminary practice. One usually begins the Vajrayana path by doing the four extraordinary preliminary practices: 111 000 refuge prayers and prostrations, 111 000 Vajrasattva mantras, 111 000 mandala offerings, and 111 000 guru yoga practices.

Nihilism. (Tib. *che ta / chad lta*) Literally "the view of discontinuance" this is the extreme view of nothingness: no future births or karmic effects, and the non-existence of the mind after death.

Nirmanakaya. (Tib. *tulku /sprul sku*) There are three bodies of the Buddha; the nirmanakaya or "emanation body" is the one that manifests in the world. An example of such an emanation is the Shakyamuni Buddha. (see *kayas, three.*)

Nirvana. (Tib. *nya ngen le de ba / mya ngan las 'das pa*) The Sanskrit word *nirvana* literally means "extinguished," as in the extinguishing of suffering. The Tibetan translation of this word means "to abide beyond sorrow." Through spiritual practice individuals in samsara can attain a state of enlightenment in which all false ideas and conflicting emotions have been extinguished. This is called nirvana. The nirvana of a Hinayana practitioner is arhathood, freedom from cyclic existence. This is the nirvana of extinction. The nirvana of a Mahayana practitioner is Buddhahood, freedom from the extremes of dwelling in either samsara or the perfect peace of an arhat. In the Vajrayana tradition there is also natural or innate nirvana, referring to the naturally abiding uncorrupted state of the mind.

Nyingma. (Tib. *snying ma*) The oldest school of Tibetan Buddhism that is based on the teachings of Padmasambhava and other masters of the eighth and ninth centuries.

Obscurations, two.(Tib. *drib nyi / sgrib gnyis*) There are two categories of obscurations or defilements that cover one's Buddha nature: the defilement of disturbing emotions (see *disturbing emotions, five poisons*); and the defilement of latent tendencies, the obscuration of dualistic perception or the intellectual/cognitive obscurations. The first category prevents sentient beings from freeing themselves from samsara and the second prevents them from gaining accurate knowledge and realizing truth.

Oral instructions. (Tib. *men ngag, dams ngag / man ngag, gdams ngag*) As opposed to the scholastic traditions, the oral instructions of the Practice lineages are concise and pithy so they can always be kept in mind. Practical and to the point, they are effective in dealing directly with problems in practice.

Pandita. (Skt.) A great scholar.

Paramita. (Tib. *par chin / phar phyin*) "Transcendental" or "Perfect"action. These are pure actions free from dualistic concepts that liberate sentient beings from samsara. The six paramitas are: generosity, moral ethics, patience, diligence, meditative-concentration, and wisdom-awareness. The ten paramitas are the above six and skillful means, aspiration, strength, and primordial wisdom.

Paranirvana. The passing of a Buddha from this realm. Buddhas are not said to die, since they have reached the stage of deathlessness, or deathless awareness.

Particularist or Vaibhashika school. (Tib. *chedrag mawa / bye brag smar ba*) One of the four major schools of Indian Buddhist philosophy studied in Tibet. Its tenets are Hinayana. Sometimes translated as the Particularist school, it defines relative truth as whatever can be broken down into parts and ultimate truth as that which cannot be broken down, indivisible atoms and moments of consciousness for example.

Prajna. (Tib. *she rab / shes rab*) In Sanskrit it means "perfect knowledge" and can mean wisdom, understanding or discrimination. Usually it means the wisdom of seeing things from a high (i.e., non-dualistic) point of view.

Prajnaparamita. (Tib. *she rab chi parol tu chinpa / shes rab kyi phar rol tu phyin pa*) Transcendent perfect knowledge. The Tibetan literally means, "gone to the other side" or "gone beyond" as expressed in the Prajnaparamita mantra, OM GATE GATE PARAGATE PARASAMGATE BODHI SVAHA. This realization of emptiness is expressed in the *Prajnaparamita Hridaya* or *Heart Sutra* and many other sutras.

Prajnaparamita sutras. Used to refer to a collection of about forty Mahayana sutras that all deal with the realization of prajna.

Pratyekabuddha. (Tib. *rang jel / rang rgyal*) "Solitary Awakened One." One who has attained awakening for himself, on his own, with no teacher in that life. Their realization is generally placed above that of a hearer arhat and below that of a fully realized Buddha. It is the fruition of the second level of the Hinayana path and comes about through contemplation on the twelve interdependent links in reverse order. They are disciples of the Buddha's body.

Provisional meaning. (Tib. *drang don*) The teachings of the Buddha that have been simplified or modified to suit the capabilities of the audience. This contrasts with the definitive meaning.

Pure realm. (Tib. *dag zhing*) Realms manifested by Buddhas that are totally free from suffering and in which the dharma can be received directly. These realms are presided over by various Buddhas such as Amitabha, Avalokiteshvara, and Maitreya who presides over Tushita.

Rangjung Dorje. (1284-1339 C.E.) The Third Karmapa, especially well known for writing a series of texts widely used in the Kagyu school.

Rangtong School. (Tib. *rang stong*) The Madhyamaka or Middle-way is divided into two major schools; Rangtong (empty of self) and Shentong (empty of other). The Rangtong approach comes from the second turning of the wheel of dharma and teaches that reality is empty of self and beyond concepts.

Relative truth. (Tib. *kunzop chi denpa / kun rdzob kyi bden pa*) Also translated as "seeming reality". There are two truths: relative and absolute or ultimate truth. Relative truth is the perception of an ordinary (unenlightened) being who sees the world with all his or her projections based on the false belief in "I" and "other."

Rinpoche. Literally "very precious" this is a term of respect used for gurus in Tibetan Buddhism.

Sacred outlook. (Tib. *dag nang / dag snang*) Awareness and compassion lead the practitioner to experience emptiness (*shunyata*). From this realization luminosity manifests as the purity and sacredness of the phenomenal world. Since this sacredness comes out of the experience of emptiness, the absence of preconceptions, it is neither a religious nor a secular vision. It is not conferred by any god, seen clearly the world itself is sacred because of its own nature. In fact, it could be described as a meeting of the spiritual and secular visions.

Sadhana. (Tib. *drup tap / sgrub thabs*) Tantric liturgy and procedure for practice, usually emphasizing the generation stage.

Samadhi. (Tib. *ting nge dzin*) "Adhering to even-ness." A state of meditative concentration.

Samantabhadra. (Tib. *kun zang / kun bzang*) *Samanta* means "all" and *bhadra* means "excellent," therefore this word literally means "he who is all-pervadingly good" or "he whose beneficence is everywhere." There are two Samantabhadras, one is synonymous with the dharmakaya and the other is one of the eight main bodhisattvas. As one of the eight main bodhisattvas Samantabhadra is an embodiment of all the Buddhas' aspirations. In the Vajrayana tradition Samantabhadra is the primordial Buddha and representative of the experiential content of the dharmakaya.

Samaya. (Tib. *dam tsig*) In the Vajrayana this refers to the vows or commitments made to a teacher or practice. There can be many details to this commitment but essentially it consists of outwardly maintaining a harmonious relationship with the vajra master and one's dharma friends and inwardly not straying from the continuity of the practice.

Sambhogakaya. (Tib. *long chö dzok ku / long spyod rdzogs pa'i sku*) There are three bodies of the Buddha, the sambhogakaya, also called the "enjoyment body," is a realm of the dharmakaya that only manifests to bodhisattvas (see *kayas, three*).

Samsara. (Tib. *kor wa / 'khor ba*) "Cyclic existence." The conditioned existence of ordinary life, in contrast to nirvana, where suffering occurs because one still possesses attachment, aggression and ignorance. Through the force of karma motivated by ignorance, desire and anger one is forced to take on the impure aggregates and circle the wheel of existence until liberation.

Sangha. (Tib. *gen dun / dge 'dun*) "Virtuous Ones." The Sanskrit word *sangha* refers to a "group" and in the Tibetan translation of this word *gendun*, *dun* means intention or motivation and *ge(n)* means virtuous – "one with a virtuous motivation." The *sangha* is also one of the three jewels. In general it refers to the followers of Buddhism, and more specifically to the community of monks and nuns. The exalted sangha are those who have attained a certain level of realization of the Buddha's teachings.

Shantarakshita. An Indian master who was an abbot of Nalanda University. He was invited to Tibet by King Trisong Detsen in the eighth century and thus helped establish Buddhism there.

Seven branch prayer. (Tib. *yen lag dun / yen lag bdun*) A common prayer that consists of the following seven parts or "branches." 1. Prostrating to all lamas of the lineage, the Buddhas and bodhisattvas. 2. Making offerings. 3. Confessing negative actions. 4. Rejoicing in the merit of others. 5. Requesting the lamas, Buddhas and bodhisattvas to remain in cyclic existence and teach the dharma. 6. Beseeching them not to pass away. 7. And dedicating the merit that has arisen through our practice to the enlightenment of all sentient beings. Paying homage counteracts pride; presenting offerings counteracts greed; acknowledging and confessing evil acts counteracts aggression; rejoicing in the good that others do counteracts jealousy; requesting spiritual teachings counteracts stupidity; asking the Buddhas and teachers to remain present in the world counteracts the view of permanence; and dedicating virtue to the welfare of others leads to the attainment of full awakening.

Seven limbs of awakening. The virtues of faith, insight, samadhi, joy, diligence, mindfulness and equanimity. Externally they are represented by the seven articles of royalty.

Shamatha. (Tib. *shinay / zhi gnas*) See tranquility meditation.

Shamatha with support. (Tib. *shinay ten ce / zhi gnas rten bcas*) The practice of calming the mind while using an object of concentration, material or mental, or simply the breath.

Shamatha without support. (Tib. *shinay ten me / zhi gnas rten med*) The act of calming the mind without any particular object. Resting undistractedly. This practice serves as a prelude for Mahamudra and should not be mistaken for the ultimate result.

Shantideva. A great bodhisattva of classical India, author of the *Bodhisattvacharyavatara: the Guide to the Bodhisattva's Way of Life.* (late seventh century – mid eighth century CE.)

Shastra. (Tib. *tan chö /bstan bcos*) The Buddhist teachings are divided into two categories: the words of the Buddha and the commentaries of others on his works, the *shastras*.

Shentong school. (Tib. *gzhan stong*) The Madhyamaka or Middle-way is divided into two major schools, Rangtong (empty of self) and Shentong (empty of other). The Shentong view comes from the third turning of the wheel of dharma and explains that ultimate reality is the inseparability of emptiness and luminosity.

Shravaka. (Tib. *Nyen tö / nyan thos*) A "Hearer" is one who seeks, or has attained arhathood, liberation for themselves through listening to the Buddha's teaching and gaining insight into selflessness and the four truths. They are disciples of the Buddha's speech.

Shunyata. See *emptiness*.

Siddha. (Tib. *drup top/ sgrub thob*) An accomplished Buddhist practitioner.

Siddhi. (Tib. *ngödrup / dngos grub*) Literally "direct accomplishment" this refers to the spiritual accomplishments of practitioners. The "supreme siddhi" is complete enlightenment and there are "common siddhis" like the eight mundane accomplishments.

Six realms. (Tib. *rikdruk / rigs drug*) These are the six realms that beings in samsara can be born into: the god realm in which beings have great pride; the jealous god, or titan, realm in which there is much intrigue and fighting; the human realm, which is the considered the best realm to be born into because here one has the best possibility for achieving enlightenment; the animal realm, which is characterized by stupidity; the hungry ghost realm, which is characterized by great craving; and the hell realm, which is characterized by aggression.

Six Yogas of Naropa. (Tib. *naro chödruk / na ro chos drug*) These six special yogic practices were transmitted from Naropa to Marpa and consist of the subtle heat practice, the illusory body practice, the dream yoga practice, the luminosity practice, the ejection of consciousness practice and the bardo practice.

Skandha. (Tib. *pung pa /phung pa*) Literally meaning "heap" this term refers to the five groups of physical and mental constituents that make up a sentient being: physical form, sensations, conceptions, formations and consciousness. These can also be seen from the perspective of the five basic transformations that occur when an object is perceived. The first, physical form, includes all sounds, smells, etc., everything that is not thought. The second and third are sensations (pleasant and unpleasant, etc.) and their identification. The fourth are mental events, which can actually include the second and third aggregates. The fifth is ordinary consciousness, such as the sensory and mental consciousnesses.

Skilful means. (Skt. *upaya,* Tib. *tab / thabs*) At the Mahayana level, this is one of the ten paramitas and refers to dedicating the merits of all one's deeds to the benefit of all sentient beings. At the Vajrayana level, it refers to the practices of the internal yogas that manipulate the subtle body's energies and channels.

Sugata. An epithet for the Buddha.

Sugatagarbha. Another term for the Buddha nature.

Sukhavati. (Tib. *Dewachen / bde ba chen*) The pure realm of Buddha Amitabha, "The Land of Great Bliss."

Supreme siddhi. (Tib. *ngödrub chog / dngos grub mchog*) Another word for enlightenment.

Sutra. (Tib. *do / mdo*) Sometimes the term "sutra" is used to cover all of the teachings given by the Buddha himself. At other times it is used to mean the Buddha's non-tantric teachings and at yet other times it is used more precisely to mean one of the three sections of the dharma called the Tripitaka or Three Baskets. In the Tripitaka there are the Sutras, the Vinaya and the Abhidharma. The sutras are mainly concerned with mind training, meditation or samadhi; the Abhidharma is mainly concerned with the development of wisdom and understanding; and the Vinaya is mainly concerned with discipline and the rules of morality and conduct. In its narrowest sense the sutras are one of these three sections of the Buddha's teachings, and in its broadest sense it means all of the teachings given by the Buddha.

Sutra Mahamudra. (Tib.*do chag chen / mdo'i phyag chen*) The Mahamudra system based on the Prajnaparamita scriptures and emphasizing Shamatha, Vipashyana and the progressive journey through the five paths and ten bhumis.

Sutra or Sautrantika School. (Tib.*do depa / mdo sde pa*) One of the four major schools of Indian Buddhist philosophy studied in Tibet. Its tenets are Hinayana. This school has further sub-schools but basically its view is that relative truth is that which is generally characterized and ultimate truth is that which is specifically characterized and can perform a function. An example of a generally characterized object would be thinking of fire, this appears as a concept to our mind but not the five senses. An example of a specifically characterized phenomenon would be fire itself, which appears to the senses and can actually burn. According to the Sautrantika School our perceptions are generally a mix of these two.

Sutrayana. (Tib.*dö tegpa / mdo'i theg pa*) The sutra approach to achieving enlightenment, which includes the Hinayana and the non-tantra Mahayana.

Svabhavakakaya. (Tib. *ngowo nyi chi ku / ngo bo nyid kyi sku*) The "essence body." Sometimes counted as the fourth kaya it is the unity of the first three.

Tantra. (Tib. *ju / rgyud*) Literally, tantra means "continuity" or "thread." In Buddhism it refers to two specific things: the texts (resultant texts, or those that take the result as the path) that describe the practices leading from ignorance to enlightenment, including commentaries by tantric masters; and the way to enlightenment itself, encompassing the ground, path and fruition. One can divide Buddhism into the sutra and tantra traditions. The sutra tradition primarily involves the academic study of the Mahayana sutras and the practice of the six perfections. The tantric path primarily involves the Vajrayana practices, whose texts are the tantras themselves.

Tantra Mahamudra. (Tib. *ngag chi chag chen / sngags kyi phyag chen*) Tantra, or Mantra Mahamudra is the practice connected to the Six Yogas of Naropa.

Tara. (Tib. *drol ma / sgrol ma*) An emanation of Avalokiteshvara, she is said to have arisen from one of his tears. She embodies the female aspect of compassion and is a very popular deity in Tibet. Her two common iconographic forms are white and green.

Tathagatagarbha. Another term for the Buddha-nature, the inherently present potential for enlightenment in all sentient beings.

Ten non-virtuous actions. (Tib. *mi ge chu / mi dge bcu*) Killing, stealing, sexual misconduct, lying, slander, abusive words, idle gossip, covetousness, ill-will and wrong views. Acts are non-virtuous or unwholesome when they result in undesirable karmic effects. Thus, this list of ten unwholesome acts is usually discussed in relation to karma. The first three are actions of body, the next four are actions of speech, and the last three are mental activity. The ten virtuous actions are the opposite of these.

Tenjur. (Tib. *bstan 'gyur*) The Tibetan translations of the *shastras*, which are themselves mainly commentaries to the teachings contained within the Kanjur. This collection also includes meditation tantras, and healing, scientific and technical instructions, etc.

Theravada. (Pali. Skt. *theravadin* Tib. *neten päde / gnas brtan pa'i sde*) Literally "the vehicle of the elders" this term refers to one of the four basic schools of the Shravakas in ancient India or the Buddhist tradition that descended from it and still exists today in Sri Lanka, Thailand and other countries.

Three Jewels. (Tib. *kön chok sum / dkon mchog gsum*) Literally "the three precious ones," the three jewels are the essential components of Buddhism: the Buddha, dharma and sangha. The Buddha is the Awakened One, the dharma is the truth he expounded, and the followers living in accordance with this truth are the sangha. Firm faith in the three precious ones makes one a "stream enterer." The three precious ones are objects of veneration and are considered "places of refuge." Buddhists take refuge by pronouncing the threefold refuge formula and thus acknowledge formally that they are Buddhists.

Three natures or three aspects of experience are: the imaginary nature (Skt. *parikalita*, Tib. *kun tag / kun rtag*), the dependent nature (Skt. *paratantra*, Tib. *zhen wang / gzhan dbang*) and the truly existent nature (Skt. *parinispanna*, Tib. *yong drub / yongs grub*).

Three realms. These are the three categories of samsara. The desire realm includes existences where beings are reborn with coarse bodies due to their karma, ranging from the deva paradises to the hell realms. The form realm is where beings are born due to the power of meditation, and their bodies are of subtle form. These are the meditation paradises. The formless realm is where beings are born after achieving very refined meditative states (samadhi) in their previous life. Being born into the formless realm means their processes of thought and perception cease.

Three roots. (Tib. *tsawa sum / rtsa ba gsum*)The guru, yidam and dakini. The guru is the root of blessings, the yidam is the root of accomplishment and the dakini is the root of activity.

Three sufferings. (Tib. *dug ngel sum / sdug bsngal gsum*) These are the suffering of suffering, the suffering of change, and pervasive suffering (meaning the suffering inherent in all samsara).

Three vehicles. (Tib. *thekpa sum / theg pa gsum*) Hinayana, Mahayana and Vajrayana.

Tilopa. (928-1009 C.E.) One of the eighty-four mahasiddhas who became the guru of Naropa who transmitted his teachings to the Kagyu lineage in Tibet through his student Marpa.

Tonglen. (Tib. *gtong len*) Giving and taking. A bodhichitta practice of giving one's virtue and happiness to others and taking their suffering and misdeeds upon oneself.

Torma. (Tib. *torma*) Literally meaning "that which diffuses," these are sculptures made out of tsampa and molded butter that are used as offerings or as representations of deities. There are many different types of tormas and many traditional designs for each type.

Tranquility meditation. (Skt. *Shamatha* Tib. *Shinay / zhi bnas*) Along with *Vipashyana* or insight this is one of two main types of meditation. Also translated as "calm abiding" this term refers to the meditative practice of calming the mind in order to rest free from the disturbances of mental activity.

Tripitaka. (Tib. *de nö sum / sde snod gsum*) The three collections of teachings: the Vinaya, Sutra and Abhidharma.

Tushita paradise. (Tib. *gan dan / dga' ldan*) This is one of the pure realms of the Buddha. Tushita is in the sambhogakaya and therefore is not located in any place or time.

Two accumulations. (Tib. *tsog nyi / tshogs nyis*) The accumulation of merit with concepts and the accumulation of wisdom that is beyond concepts.

Two truths. Relative and ultimate truth. Relative truth describes the superficial and apparent mode of all things. Ultimate truth describes the true and unmistaken mode of all things. These two are described differently in the different schools: progressing up from the Hinayana schools towards the Shentong Middle-way School the descriptions become deeper and closer to the way things actually are.

Ultimate truth. (Tib. *dondam denpa / don dam bden pa*) There are two truths or views of reality: relative truth, which is seeing things as ordinary beings do with the dualism of "I" and "other"; and ultimate truth, which transcends duality and sees things as they are.

Uncommon preliminaries. (Tib. *Tun mong ma yin bä ngöndro / thun mong ma yin pa sngon 'gro*) One usually begins the Vajrayana path by doing the four preliminary practices which involve 111,000 refuge prayers and prostrations, 111,000 Vajrasattva mantras, 111,000 mandala offerings, and 111,000 guru yoga practices.

Vairochana. (Tib. *nam par nang dze / rnam par snang mdzad*) The sambhogakaya Buddha of the Buddha family.

Vajra. (Tib. *dorje / rdo rje*) Usually translated as "diamond like" or "adamantine" this word may refer to either an implement held in the hand during certain Vajrayana ceremonies, or to a quality that is diamond like because of its purity and ability to endure.

Vajra posture. (Tib. *dorje chi trung / rdo rje dkyil dkrungs*) This refers to the full-lotus posture in which the legs are interlocked. When one leg is placed before the other, as many Westerners sit, it is called the half-lotus posture.

Vajradhara. (Tib. *Dorje Chang / rdo rje 'chang*) "Holder of the vajra." *Vajra* means indestructible and *dhara* means holding, embracing or inseparable. As the central figure in the Kagyu refuge tree, Vajradhara indicates the transmission of the close lineage of the Mahamudra teachings to Tilopa. Vajradhara symbolizes the primordial wisdom of the dharmakaya and wears the ornaments of the sambhogakaya Buddha, which symbolize its richness.

Vajrasattva. (Tib. *Dorje Sempa / rdo rje sems dpa*) The sambhogakaya Buddha of purification who embodies all five Buddha families. Vajrasattva practice is part of the four preliminary practices and is usually associated with purification.

Vajravarahi. (Tib. *Dorje Phagmo / rdo rje phag mo*) A dakini who is the consort of Chakrasamvara. She is the main yidam of the Kagyu lineage and the embodiment of wisdom.

Vajrayogini. (Tib. *Dorje Nanjor* or *palmo / rdo rje rnal 'byor ma* or *dpal mo*) A semi-wrathful female yidam.

Vajrayana. (Tib. *dorje tek pa / rdo rje thegs pa*) Literally, "diamond-like vehicle" or "the vehicle of indestructible capacity." *Vajra* here refers to method, so this term refers to the method yana. There are three major traditions of Buddhism (Hinayana, Mahayana, Vajrayana). The Vajrayana is based on the tantras and emphasizes the clarity aspect of phenomena. Practitioners of this vehicle take the result as the path.

Vasubandhu. (4th Century C.E.) A great fourth-century Indian scholar who was the brother of Asanga and wrote the Hinayana work the *Abhidharmakosha* explaining the Abhidharma.

Vidyadhara. Holder of knowledge or insight: the energy of discovery and communication. An accomplished master of the Vajrayana teachings.

View, meditation and action. (Tib. *tawa gompa chöpa / lta ba sgom pa spyod pa*) The philosophical orientation; the act of growing accustomed to that – usually in sitting practice –; and the implementation of that insight during the activities of daily life. Each of the three vehicles has its particular definition of view, meditation and action.

Vinaya. (Tib. *dul wa / 'dul ba*) One of the three major sections of the Buddha's teachings that describes ethics or what to avoid and what to adopt. The other two sections are the Sutras and the Abhidharma.

Vipashyana. (Tib. *lhaktong / lhag mthong*) Sanskrit for "insight meditation." This meditation develops insight into the nature of reality (Skt. *dharmata*). One of the two main aspects of meditation practice, the other being Shamatha. Vipashyana has a different focus according to the different vehicle.

Wheel of dharma. (Skt. *dharmachakra* Tib. *chökor / chos 'khor*) The Buddha's teachings correspond to three "turnings of the wheel" of dharma or three levels: the first turning was the teachings on the Four Noble Truths and the selflessness of person; the second turning was the teachings on the emptiness of person and phenomena; the third turning was the teachings on luminosity and Buddha nature.

Yana. Means "vehicle" or "journey." There are three yanas: the narrow (Hinayana), great (Mahayana) and indestructible (Vajrayana).

Yidam. (Tib. *yid dam*) *Yi* means mind and *dam* means pure or "inseparably tied to." This term is also often translated as "tutelary deity." The yidam represents the practitioner's awakened nature or pure appearance and embodies the qualities of Buddhahood. Yidam practices are part of the Vajrayana.

Yidam meditation. (Tib. *yidam gom / yid dam sgom*) Yidam meditation is the Vajrayana practice in which one visualizes the yidam.

Yogatantra. (Tib. *naljor ji ju / rnal 'byor gyi rgyud*) Literally "union tantra" this refers to a tantra that places emphasis on internal meditations.

Yogi. (Tib *nal yor wa / rnal 'byor ba*) Tantric practitioner.

Yogini. (Tib *nal yor ma/ rnal 'byor ma*) Female tantric practitioner.

Index

A
Abhidharma 18, 41, 42, 46, 50, 90, 91, 94, 98, 103, 106, 216-218, 223, 226, 288
Abhisamayalankara 68, 69, 70
Abhisheka 59
Accumulate of merit 59, 151, 175, 226, 255
Accumulation of wisdom 59
Amitabha 20, 127, 128, 133, 141, 297
Anuttarayoga Tantra 19, 49, 50, 61, 125, 260, 295
Arhathood 94, 237, 238
Aryadeva 51, 90, 91, 95
Asanga 51, 69, 90, 91
Atiyoga 19, 295
Autonomist school 92, 93, 94, 95, 97, 98, 255
  Svatantrika 92, 282

B
Bodhgaya 193, 275
Bodhichitta
  Actual bodhichitta 148
  Aspiring bodhichitta 148, 149
  Relative bodhichitta 146, 157-160, 167, 171, 172, 177, 250, 251
  Ultimate bodhichitta 146, 157, 158, 160, 164-169, 172, 173, 178, 181, 182, 246, 250, 251
Bodhisattva level 80, 225, 254, 285, 286, 307, 317
Bodhisattva vows 46, 58, 148, 149, 184, 250
Bodhisattvacharyavatara 148, 192, 195
Buddha-essence 28, 34, 69, 70, 298
Buddha-nature 28, 34, 69, 81, 82, 105, 141, 228, 248, 251, 275
Buddhahood 28, 31, 44, 46, 47, 63, 70, 97, 110, 111, 115, 116, 123-126, 129, 141, 142, 148-150, 162, 164, 167, 169, 170, 175, 176, 178, 184, 188, 191, 193, 209, 220, 224, 225, 240, 242, 250, 263, 266, 278, 279, 285, 293, 296, 307

C
Chakrasamvara 47, 59, 60, 65
Chakravartin 124, 312
Charya Tantra 19, 49, 50, 61, 295
Chenrezig 20, 58, 64, 100, 123, 124, 126, 128, 129, 131, 135-137, 139, 199
  Avalokiteshvara 64, 100, 116, 123-132, 134-141, 160, 220,

242, 276
Cognition
  Valid cognition 90, 91, 94, 109-111
  Direct valid cognition 109, 110
  Inferential valid cognition 109, 110
Consciousness
  Eight consciousness 229, 230
  Six consciousnesses 228
Consequence school 92, 93, 97, 98, 282
  Consequentialist 255
  Prasangika school 92, 282

D

Definitive meaning 232, 234, 236, 237, 239, 240, 242
Desire realm 209, 222, 223, 225, 301
Dharmachakra 163, 293
Dharmakaya 16, 18, 19, 31, 32, 34, 37, 57, 71, 81, 121, 258, 261, 280, 287, 293
Dharmakirti 51, 90, 91
Dignaga 51, 90, 91
Dzogchen 61, 200, 256, 295

E

Eight lineages 54, 296
Eight-fold path 251, 293
Enlightenment 17, 31, 39, 42, 47, 63, 78, 80, 83, 93, 111, 115, 117, 123, 125, 126, 141, 161-163, 166, 188, 193, 224, 231, 257, 258, 278, 285,
Eternalism 266

F

Five Buddha families 62, 128, 297
Five strengths 178, 179, 182
Form realm 222, 223, 225, 301
Formless realm 209, 213, 224, 225, 301
Four contemplations 58, 149
Four foundations 59

G

Gampopa 54, 56, 136, 295, 308
Ganachakra 47
Gelugpa lineage 53, 54, 110, 175, 295
Guhyasamaja 48, 50, 256
Gunaprabha 51, 90, 91
Guru Rinpoche 52, 72

H

Heart Sutra 68, 69, 75, 245
Hevajra 49, 50, 64, 258, 309
Hinayana 200, 298

J

Jamgon Kongtrul 30, 37, 54, 146, 298, 306

K

Kadampa lineage 53, 146, 175
Kagyu lineage 53, 54, 56, 113, 295, 296
  Karma Kagyu 54, 56, 113, 296
  Marpa Kagyu 53-56
  Shangpa Kagyu 53-56
Kalachakra 48, 50, 54, 256, 259, 276
Kamalishila 92
Kanjur 51, 52, 297

Index

Karmapa 50, 54, 72, 84, 117, 269, 279, 293, 295
Kriya Tantra 19, 49, 50, 58, 61, 260, 295

L

Limitless potential 70, 74, 75, 76, 82, 83, 85, 86, 104, 152, 162, 208, 252
Lojong 145-147, 156, 158, 165, 179, 182, 184-188, 321
Lower realm 51, 134, 135, 284

M

Madhyamaka 90-98, 103, 104, 106, 108, 109, 255, 282, 298
Maha Ati 256
Mahakala 59, 60, 177
Mahakali 59, 60
Mahamudra 56-58, 61, 141, 200, 243, 250, 256, 262-269, 271, 273-275, 279, 281, 282, 293, 294, 296, 305-308
Mahasiddha 51, 53, 64, 108
Mahayana 18-20, 27, 28, 45, 51, 69, 108, 156, 165, 175, 179, 189, 191, 195, 202, 232, 246-248, 251, 253, 255-258, 298, 307,
Mahayoga 19, 295
Maitreya 51, 52, 68, 69
Mandala 42, 48, 59, 84, 139, 175, 222, 259, 275, 276, 295
Manjushri 116, 160, 242, 276
Mantra 59, 60, 62, 64, 130, 134, 135, 138, 139, 141, 196, 197, 256, 294, 302
Meditation
 Analytical meditation 248
 Creation stage 295
 Completion stage 258, 295
 Placement meditation 248
Post-meditation 157, 160, 169, 187, 254, 255, 256, 306
Middle-way 90, 92-94, 104, 255, 282, 298
Milarepa 54, 55, 63, 205, 210, 226, 248, 273, 295, 308
Mind-only school 92, 93, 95-97, 108, 109, 282, 298, 299
 Chittamatra 92, 282, 298

N

Nagarjuna 51, 65, 90, 91, 92, 93, 95, 108
Naropa 48, 53, 258, 294, 296
Nature of the mind 59, 200, 296, 299
Ngondro 59, 296
Nihilism 104, 266
Nirmanakaya 31, 42, 43, 84, 116, 164, 257, 259, 275, 276, 287, 294
Nirvana 41, 126, 164, 242, 294, 306
Non-dualistic 16, 18, 70, 71, 81, 82, 105, 111, 137, 160, 165, 166, 220, 234, 239, 242
Nyingma lineage 53, 54, 61, 64, 295, 297
Nyungne 59, 138, 296

P

Particularist school 94, 95, 108, 109, 282, 298, 300, 301
Physical posture 117, 209, 213
Potala 131, 133, 134
Prajnaparamita 40, 53, 67-78, 83, 90, 103, 106, 211, 254, 293

Daughter Sutra 67, 71
Mother Sutra 71
Pramana 90, 91, 94, 95, 98, 99, 103, 105, 106, 107, 109, 110, 112
Primordial wisdom 15, 17, 21, 22, 73-76, 81, 85, 87, 89, 100, 101, 109, 116, 121, 141, 180, 242, 272, 297
Prince Siddhartha 28, 30, 42, 43, 162, 163, 193, 247, 263, 273, 276, 294
Purification 43, 59, 62, 146, 158, 209, 211, 231, 302

R

Rajgir 40, 78, 83
Rangtong 80-83, 92, 93, 105, 282, 298, 312, 326, 328
Relative emptiness 250
Relative truth 75, 76, 112, 252, 266, 298

S

Sakya 53, 54, 295
Samaya 21, 62, 68, 69, 70, 184
Sambhogakaya 31, 42, 43, 59, 84, 116, 129, 257, 259, 275, 276, 287, 294
Seven branch prayer 161, 164
Shakyamuni Buddha 15, 17, 39, 42, 65, 133, 138, 139, 180-182, 214, 233, 234, 246, 271, 294, 308
Shakyaprabha 51, 90, 91
Shamatha 156-158, 161, 200-205, 208, 209, 211, 213, 222-225, 230, 231, 241-243, 245, 246, 248-251, 254, 258, 259, 296, 305-307
   Calm abiding 167, 168, 170, 201, 202, 209, 211, 245, 249, 305

Shantarakshita 52, 92, 93
Shantideva 148, 192, 195, 242
Shastra 51, 69, 91
Shentong 80-83, 92, 93, 104, 105, 255, 256, 282, 298-300
Shunyata 53, 78, 171
Six ornaments 51, 90
Six perfections 125
Six realms 130, 134, 235, 284, 301
Six Yogas 59
Sutra 18, 20, 41, 42, 45, 46, 50, 63, 64, 67-69, 71, 75, 76, 92, 94-96, 98, 108, 109, 228, 245, 256, 282, 298, 300, 301

T

Tantra 18, 37, 41-43, 45-50, 53, 54, 65, 83, 94, 141, 228, 256-260
Tara 124, 125, 159, 242
Tathagatagarbha 34, 141
Ten paramitas 251, 297
Tenjur 51, 52, 108
Terma 257
Theravada 19, 108, 230, 243, 246, 250, 256
Three natures
   Dependent nature 96, 97, 299, 300
   Imaginary nature 96, 97, 299
   Perfectly existent nature 96, 97, 299, 300
Three yanas 200, 256
Tilopa 48, 257, 294
Tonglen 158, 159, 174, 251
Tripitaka 94
Trisong Detsen 52
Tsema 90, 91, 109-112
Turning of the wheel of dharma 18, 40, 41, 78, 117

Index 341

First turning 117, 293
Second turning 18, 78, 293
Third turning 18, 41, 293
Tushita 69, 223
Twelve links 211, 247, 303, 304

U
Ultimate emptiness 166, 250, 251
Ultimate meaning 18, 228
Ultimate teaching 16, 18, 19
Ultimate truth 76-78, 109, 111, 112, 240, 271,
Upasaka 47, 48, 56, 58
Uttaratantra 51, 295

V
Vairochana 209, 297
Vajradhara 31, 45, 294
Vajrakilaya 64, 65
Vajrasattva 59, 62, 302

Vajravarahi 47, 48, 59, 60, 65, 140, 260
Vajrayana 19, 20, 26, 37, 46, 47, 50, 56, 65, 101, 119, 126, 156, 175, 187, 200, 230, 243, 245, 246, 250, 256-258, 294, 309
Vajrayogini 47, 186, 260
Varanasi 17, 40, 83, 163, 231
Vasubhandu 51, 90, 91
Vinaya 41, 42, 45-47, 50, 90, 91, 94, 103, 106, 293
Vipashyana 200-202, 213, 230, 241, 243, 245-251, 253-259, 261, 296, 307
    Temporary Vipashyana 249, 254

Y
Yidam 59, 129, 294
Yoga 19, 49, 59, 61, 260, 295

SHERAB LING

His Eminence Tai Situpa is the founder and Spiritual Head of Sherab Ling, a monastic community based in the Himalayan foothills of Northern India dedicated to preserving the ancient teachings and traditions of Buddhism. It serves an ever-increasing community from across India, the kingdoms of Nepal and Bhutan, and of course Tibet. It also attracts pilgrims, tourists and visitors from all over the world, and offers complete facilities for practitioners – including Shedra and three-year retreat – who wish to study and practice in the traditional manner.

Built on 2½ acres of land 30 metres in front of the Sherab Ling Institute – the original monastery, is Palpung Monastery, named after the Tai Situpa's original monastery, which was once the principle Kagyu monastery in Kham, Eastern Tibet. It had over 1000 monks, housed the leading monastic college of the area and was renowned for it's extensive library and art collection. Palpung led the way in painting skills and was the source of the Karma Gadri style of painting. "Palpung," more thoroughly interpreted means: "The Glorious Accumulation where Talented People are Cultivated." The new building was designed by Tai Situpa, and is built of modern materials but finished in traditional Tibetan architectural fashion. The concept of the design follows the ancient science of geomancy. It has monks quarters, three shrine halls, six shrine rooms, and all the traditional and modern monastic features. The main shrine halls overlook a large sandstone courtyard which will host bi-annual ritual Lama-dance.

Institute of Buddhist Studies
"Sherab Ling"
P.O. Upper Bhattu, Baijnath, Kangra District
Himachal Pradesh, 176-125, INDIA
Ph: (01894) 63013/63757 Email: office@sherabling.org

Care of Dharma Books

Dharma books contain the teachings of the Buddha. They have the power to protect against lower rebirth and to point the way to liberation. Therefore, they should be treated with respect.

These considerations may be also kept in mind for Dharma artwork, as well as the written teachings and artwork of other religions.